Real Estate Market Research and Analysis

Real Estate Market Research and Analysis

Chris Leishman

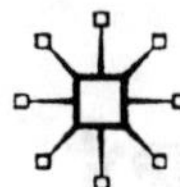

First published 2003 by
PALGRAVE MACMILLAN
Houndmills, Basingstoke, Hampshire RG21 6XS and
175 Fifth Avenue, New York, N.Y. 10010
Companies and representatives throughout the world

PALGRAVE MACMILLAN is the global academic imprint of the Palgrave Macmillan division of St. Martin's Press, LLC and of Palgrave Macmillan Ltd. Macmillan® is a registered trademark in the United States, United Kingdom and other countries. Palgrave is a registered trademark in the European Union and other countries.

ISBN 0–333–98086–7

This book is printed on paper suitable for recycling and made from fully managed and sustained forest sources.

A catalogue record for this book is available from the British Library.

A catalog record for this book is available from the Library of Congress.

10 9 8 7 6 5 4 3 2 1
12 11 10 09 08 07 06 05 04 03

Printed and bound in Great Britain by
Creative Print & Design (Wales), Ebbw Vale

Contents

List of Figures

List of Tables

Foreword

Although property market analysis can be traced back to the work of the prominent institutional economist, Richard T. Ely, at the end of the nineteenth century, it is only recently that academic and professional research activity has matured. While early research effort emerged from a range of diverse property-related disciplines, including economics, law, human geography, urban planning and construction, more recently methodological developments worldwide have begun to mirror trends in the USA by encompassing advancements in business studies and finance. In fact, even a cursory glance at the major property research journals will reveal that the vast majority of research papers published deploy quantitative techniques.

With this in mind it is disappointing to find that property educators are still reliant on generic business studies and social science texts to support courses in applied statistics, research methods and market analysis.

Chris Leishman has written to fill this gap and is to be congratulated for doing so. Although his book rightly focuses on quantitative analysis of property data, it also provides a useful introduction to the broader developments in property market analysis. The real strength of the book is that it draws together, in a single source, problems from basic property economics and an introduction to the statistical and econometric methods that can help analyse these. Importantly, the book improves on existing texts on statistics for business or social science research methods by developing applied property market examples and by locating these examples in the context of key developments in the maturing property research literature.

For these reasons the text will justifiably become essential reading for those studying property economics, statistics for property and applied market analysis.

University of Aberdeen CRAIG WATKINS

Acknowledgements

A number of friends and colleagues have been of great assistance to me during the inception and production of this book. I am thankful to Dr Craig Watkins, senior lecturer at the University of Aberdeen, and Dr Will Fraser for many useful and insightful discussions and suggestions. Fran Warren, research associate at Heriot-Watt University, provided me with much valuable assistance reviewing the literature, obtaining references, proof-reading and giving constructive informal feedback. I am also very grateful to Alison and Peter for putting up with my lengthy and frequent absences. I am particularly indebted to the undergraduate and postgraduate students in the School of the Built Environment, Heriot-Watt University. Over the past few years, answering their many difficult questions has required frequent recourse to a disparate collection of books. Those efforts have directly led to my production of this volume.

Heriot-Watt University CHRIS LEISHMAN

1

Introduction

INTRODUCTION

It is logical to suppose that an accepted way of conducting research is more likely to exist in a well-developed discipline that is described by an extensive and long-lived literature consisting of theoretical and empirical analyses. If the discipline of economics is to be regarded as one still in its infancy, real estate economics is, by comparison, little more than embryonic. Published economic analyses do not date much farther back than the nineteenth century and there were few empirical economic analyses before the middle of the twentieth century. One of the consequences of this is that real estate market analysis can be both difficult and challenging since our understanding of real estate market processes is still developing fairly rapidly.

Real estate market research and analysis often draws on theory and techniques borrowed from other disciplines, particularly economics, finance and geography. However, there are few texts aimed specifically at students and practitioners with an interest in real estate economics research. The objectives of this book are to provide a general overview of research philosophy and research practice in the real estate economics discipline. The book reviews a range of applied quantitative empirical methods in common usage in both academic and applied (practical) real estate market research and analysis and provides a detailed examination of selected research-based studies to demonstrate the application of quantitative methods in real estate research and analysis. Other objectives of the book include the framing of real estate economics research theory and practice in the context of recent trends and developments in the evolving real estate economics research agenda and the provision of insights into the use of qualitative and behavioural research in the real estate economics discipline.

The book does not consider every possible aspect of real estate research. Instead, it focuses primarily on the use of quantitative methods in real estate research and market analysis although the book also contains some coverage of behavioural and quantitative research methods, primarily as a complement to applied quantitative methods. Furthermore, the book focuses on research and analysis based on real estate markets and market dynamics including local market analysis and prediction/forecasting. Research issues concerned with real estate investment analysis or valuation practice and methods are not covered in this book except in passing. Finally, the book assumes that the reader will have at least an elementary background in statistics and some background in real estate economics. The relationship between this book and real estate economics, statistics and investment analysis texts is discussed in more detail in Chapter 12.

The book is organised as a set of ordered chapters. Chapters 1 and 2 are concerned with philosophical, conceptual and methodological issues in real estate research and analysis. In particular, Chapter 2 provides a discussion of research methods with a specific real estate economics context. The chapter covers aspects such as the characteristics of real estate and broad types of applied and academic real estate research and analysis. Chapters 1 and 2 are intended to be of particular value to undergraduate and post-graduate students of real estate economics university courses although the chapters also contain material that will be of interest to practising real estate researchers.

Chapters 3 and 4 provide a general overview of descriptive and inferential statistics, sampling theory, hypothesis testing and the use of regression models. Although these chapters contain real estate specific examples in places, most of the material is quite general and may be familiar to readers with some experience of other research and quantitative methods texts in the social sciences.

Chapters 5 to 11, inclusive, set out a detailed series of applied empirical research methods and techniques specifically orientated towards research and analysis in the real estate economics discipline. Chapters 5 and 6 are concerned with quantitative methods designed to facilitate the explanation, prediction and forecasting of commercial real estate rents, rent indices and rental growth. The material in these chapters will be of value to practising real estate researchers and students alike. Chapter 5 is focused on single equation rent determination theory and provides a review of a number of published single equation rent models. Theoretical and practical considerations in the construction and estimation of such a model are considered. Chapter 6 is concerned with multi-equation rent models and more advanced theoretical and practical modelling issues including aspects such as data limitations, data smoothing and an overview of some more advanced econometric modelling methods.

Quantitative methods of housing market research and analysis are the subject of Chapter 7. The chapter provides an overview of housing market specific research and practical issues before examining several micro and macro quantitative analysis techniques. Although the chapter is focused on housing, it also provides a detailed review of hedonic regression models. These are a specialised form of multiple regression models and are appropriate for usage in most sectors of real estate market research and analysis. While the content of the chapter will be of particular value to researchers with an interest in the economics and dynamics of private (owner occupied) housing markets, the chapter will also be of value to those with an interest in modelling real estate values and market dynamics in other use sectors.

Chapter 8 is focused on the analysis of real estate markets at the local level with particular emphasis on the analysis of office market prices and dynamics. The chapter also contains further information and reviews of published hedonic regression models and may be seen as complementary to some of the material in Chapter 7. Chapter 9 considers retail real estate market research with a particular emphasis on gravity and spatial interaction models, while Chapter 10 provides an overview of real options, option pricing theory and several real estate research applications of option pricing models. Finally, Chapter 11 sets out a discussion of behavioural real estate research and an overview of the evolving real estate economics research agenda. The chapter introduces the idea that qualitative research methods may be used as a complement to quantitative methods and several qualitative data collection methods, in common usage in social science research, are set out. Chapter 12 provides conclusions and guidance on further reading.

The remainder of this chapter is concerned with the theoretical, empirical and practical issues that face real estate market researchers. The chapter also provides a general overview of the scientific research process. It includes an examination of good research practice as well as definitions of a number of key terms such as explanation, prediction, science, concepts, theories and models. The chapter is particularly relevant to undergraduate students of degree subjects in real estate and related disciplines.

BACKGROUND TO REAL ESTATE MARKET ANALYSIS: WHAT IS A MARKET?

An appropriate way in which to begin to understand some of the problems to be faced when undertaking real estate market analysis is to examine the very concept of 'a market'. Many simple neoclassical analyses begin with the well-rehearsed theory of Perfect Competition (see Sloman, 2000, or, for the real estate market context, Ball *et al.*, 1998). The perfect competition theory is based upon the idea that firms are price-takers. Individual firms cannot influence the price at which their goods, or the goods of their rivals, are sold to consumers. Explicit in the theory is the assumption that the industry comprises an enormous number of competing firms each with a tiny share of the market. The market share of individual firms is so small that the firm cannot influence the market price by either increasing or decreasing production. The firms are homogeneous (identical) in every sense and they each produce and sell a homogeneous good. So there is nothing to distinguish one firm from another or the product of one firm from that of another firm.

Similarly, the individuality of consumers is assumed away in the Perfect Competition theory. Indeed, consideration of consumers is limited to an assumption that firms simply respond to a given market-wide level of demand by producing their homogeneous good and selling it at the uniform market price. Since all firms produce a homogeneous good, any firm that attempts to increase its price above the market price will observe demand for its good vanishing completely.

The homogeneous firms collectively form what is described as 'the industry'. There are no barriers to firms entering or leaving the industry. This simply means that there are no onerous start-up costs to be faced by new firms considering entering the industry and there are no legal or other regulatory barriers to entry. Similarly, firms are not dissuaded from leaving the industry by financial or contractual barriers. The freedom of entry and exit assumption is important because the logical follow-on is that the firms in the industry all make normal profits. The term 'normal profits' has a special meaning in economics and describes a profit level that is just sufficient, and no more, to make it worthwhile for a firm to stay in the industry. Any level of profits that is lower than normal profits causes the firm to leave the industry. The assumption here is that a firm cannot stay in business if it is generating less than normal profits. If firms in the industry are deriving any level of profits in excess of normal profits then new firms are attracted into the industry. The consequent increase in supply of the homogeneous good causes the market price to drop so that firms in the industry may only make normal profits.

In the Perfect Competition theory firms are assumed to maximise their profits to the point of normal profits. Since the market price for the homogeneous good cannot be influenced by the firm, each firm achieves profit maximisation by choosing the level of production at which marginal revenue is equal to marginal cost (MR = MC). Firms are assumed to face a U-shaped average cost curve which simply means that the production cost per unit of output is very high at both low and high levels of output. A firm will be able to compete in the industry and make normal profits if its average cost curve has a minimum point which is equal to the market price of the homogeneous good. The firm's demand curve is also equivalent to its average revenue and marginal revenue curves. This is because the firm is a price-taker and its chosen level of output has no bearing on the market price of the good. The market price is dictated by the interaction of industry-wide supply with market-wide demand.

The final assumption that underpins the theory of perfect competition is that all producers and consumers have perfect or total information. This is an extremely important assumption since, for example, consumers always know the market price of the homogeneous good and will not purchase from a firm that attempts to increase its price. Similarly, firms know the profit level of all other firms and so the entry of additional firms to the industry becomes automatic as soon as supernormal profits are made.

Imperfect Competition

The Perfect Competition theory of market structure is to be regarded as an idealistic theory upon which to base comparisons of less than 'perfectly competitive' forms of market structure. In practice it is unlikely that any market or industry could be found that conforms to the rigid assumptions of the perfect competition theory. Microeconomic theory provides additional theories of market structure and firm pricing/output behaviour. These are regarded under the general heading of 'imperfect competition' since they are essentially formed by relaxing one or more of the assumptions of the Perfect Competition theory. The theory of 'Monopolistic Competition' is perhaps the best known of these.

The Monopolistic Competition theory of market structure is closely related to that of perfect competition. It is assumed that the market or industry is made up of a large number of identical firms which have freedom of entry and exit to and from the market. The main differences between the monopolistic and the perfect competition theories are that a monopolistically competitive market is assumed to have fewer competing firms than a perfectly competitive one and firms in a monopolistically competitive market do not produce a homogeneous good. Instead, firms are assumed to produce and supply differentiated but highly substitutable goods.

The different firms in the industry produce goods that are very similar in nature but have slight differences. These differences enable individual firms to market their goods as, in some respects, unique products. In some cases, firms may produce goods that are all but identical but which are differentiated by 'branding'. In other cases, products may be homogeneous but individual firms are the sole suppliers within particular local spatial market areas. In this case, although firms are producing and marketing identical goods, their unique position in a local market would allow them to operate a limited form of monopoly. Where a firm supplies an homogeneous good in a monopolised local market, consumers may travel elsewhere to purchase the good but must bear higher transport costs as a consequence. Thus the firm with the local monopoly may charge more for the good than the closest competitor yet still capture demand from local consumers. This is subject to the proviso that the local price does not exceed that charged by the nearest competitor plus consumers' travelling costs (including the cost of travelling time) to the nearest competitor's outlet.

The smaller number of firms operating in a monopolistically competitive market, as compared with a perfectly competitive one, together with the fact that firms supply physically or spatially differentiated goods mean that firms do not face a perfectly elastic demand curve for their product. Instead, firms face highly elastic but downward-sloping demand curves. This means that firms are not strictly price-takers and can increase the price at which they sell their own good. To do so will lead to a reduction in the quantity of their good demanded by consumers. Conversely, firms can lower the price of their good in order to increase the quantity of their good demanded. As with firms in the Perfect Competition theory, firms in a monopolistically competitive industry may be able to make supernormal profits in the short run if average costs can be reduced below the level of average revenue for a given level of output. As with the Perfect Competition theory, firms are assumed to maximise their own profits and they set their output level such that marginal revenue equals marginal cost (MR = MC). At this level of output, the firm may be able to make supernormal profits in the short run provided that the firm's average revenues exceed its average costs.

In the long run, as with the Perfect Competition theory, firms cannot make supernormal profits because new firms have freedom of entry to the market. If established firms are making supernormal profits then new firms will join the industry and increase the market supply of goods until average revenues have fallen and eliminated the opportunity for firms to make supernormal profits. When this occurs, new firms no longer have an incentive to join the industry and average revenues stabilise at the level of firms' average costs. Assuming that supernormal profits are made in the short run, new firms enter the industry in the long run. The new firms begin supplying their own differentiated products that are close substitutes for the goods supplied by existing firms. As this occurs, market supply increases and the demand (average revenue) curve shifts to the left from the point of view of each individual firm in the industry. As the average revenue curve shifts, the profit level diminishes. When firms are making normal profits again new firms no longer enter the industry.

THE REAL ESTATE MARKET CONTEXT

The Perfect Competition and Monopolistic Competition theories are reviewed in order to provide a simple framework for the analysis of market behaviour. It should be noted in particular that there are probably no examples of perfectly competitive markets. Furthermore, there may be many shades of imperfect competition, ranging from industries with many producers to those with a small number of producers. In the case of the former, firms are likely to behave similarly to those in conditions of perfect competition, that is, have very little control over the price at which they sell their output. At the other extreme, firms in an oligopoly (a special case of monopolistic competition) are likely to be in a position that entails considerable discretion in terms of their pricing and output behaviour. Furthermore, the decisions of firms in this case are likely to be interrelated. The factors that are likely to influence the degree of competition and interaction between firms include:

- the number of firms in the industry
- the homogeneity of firms
- the homogeneity of the product (substitutability)
- the complexity of the product
- the completeness of information available to consumers
- the homogeneity of consumers
- the role and importance of space in forming the 'market'

The simple general models examined so far can be important in real estate analysis since they are often used, explicitly or implicitly, in the development of more complex models. There are several competing research paradigms in real estate economics (the following section examines paradigms in more detail) but the dominant paradigm is sometimes referred to as New Urban Economics or simply Urban Economics and is sometimes dubbed 'neoclassical' analysis. According to this paradigm, reasoning follows a logical process in which real estate markets are initially assumed to be efficient, well-functioning and equilibrating entities much like the hypothetical market depicted in the perfect competition model. Empirical models developed from such lines of reasoning may be improved by relaxing some of the rigid underlying assumptions concerning information efficiency and competition but the fundamental hypothesis that markets are essentially efficient remains. Similarly, firms (real estate occupiers, investors and developers) are assumed to be rational, well-informed profit maximisers.

There are, as noted above, competing paradigms. The most important of these are:

- the institutional economics paradigm
- the structure and agency paradigm
- the behavioural paradigm

The emphasis of this book is on the Urban Economics or neoclassical paradigm and this is largely because research in this paradigm is strongly associated with model building, prediction, forecasting and other forms of applied analysis that are heavily based on empirical research. Although the neoclassical paradigm is dominant in real estate economics research, alternative paradigms often provide preferable explanations to those obtained using reasoning according to the neoclassical paradigm. Furthermore, disappointing and unexpected empirical results obtained from applied neoclassical analyses can often be explained with reference to an alternative paradigm. Consequently, theoretical perspectives other than those with a neoclassical origin are often referred to throughout the book. In particular, the prominence of institutional economics and behavioural research in real estate economics is growing over time. This is discussed in more detail later in the book, particularly in Chapter 11 which is focused on behavioural research and the use of qualitative research methods as a complement to quantitative methods. However, before advancing on to these issues it is worth examining the nature of the scientific research process and, in particular, the interactions between knowledge, scientific understanding and empirical research processes. The remainder of this chapter considers these processes in some detail.

REAL ESTATE RESEARCH AND RESEARCH PARADIGMS

What Is Research and What Is Science?

Research can be defined as any methodologically sound process that adds to the existing body of knowledge of a subject. The accumulation of knowledge is the essential goal of research. Knowledge collectively allows the explanation and prediction of empirical phenomena. Research need not directly seek explanations or attempt predictions of empirical phenomena: investigative studies also qualify as research provided they are conducted scientifically and add knowledge to a field, discipline or subject/area of interest within a field or discipline. Where investigative or exploratory research is undertaken, the eventual purpose is to facilitate further research that does seek to explain and/or predict some empirical phenomenon or phenomena.

Science, and hence scientific research, can be viewed as either normal or revolutionary (Kuhn, 1970). As the name clearly suggests, revolutionary science or research involves the sudden or rapid establishment of a new paradigm (school of thought). The new paradigm is, at first, resisted by the scientific community. By contrast, normal science encompasses the verification and justification of the current paradigm. In other words, normal science is all about testing and improving existing theories and concepts that have been established by past research. An important part of research in the tradition of normal science is replication. This is a process in which original theoretical and/or empirical analyses are repeated using new data, different case studies or different assumptions. The purpose of replication is to test the limits of accepted theory.

As a rule almost all practising and academic researchers in a given discipline are active in normal, rather than revolutionary, science (research). Their concern is with the testing and improvement of existing theory and knowledge rather than challenging it. Kuhn (1970) argued that research designed to test and/or verify an existing theory creates the conditions necessary to give rise to revolutionary research. The scientific community will tend to resist participation in, and acceptance of, revolutionary research. This is primarily because practitioners and academic researchers are taught their subject by working closely with their peers and revolutionary research tends to require scientists to challenge fundamental ideas and beliefs in their field.

Revolutionary research normally occurs after a prolonged period of growing disillusionment with an accepted theory or paradigm. As researchers carry out empirical analyses of the accepted theory their intention is to test and verify the theory. In some cases researchers report problems with the way in which the theory works. For some theories a growing body of literature cataloguing the failings of the theory may develop over a long period of time. This literature provides the catalyst for revolutionary research.

Over time, research in a given field or discipline is likely to follow lengthy periods in which most works and studies may be described as 'normal'. These will be interspersed with brief periods of 'revolutionary' research. However, the scientific community tends not to accept new theories and/or paradigms immediately. Even during the period in which empirical evidence of the existing theory's failings is building up, researchers tend to continue to accept the dominant paradigm. After a new revolutionary theory or paradigm is constructed, there is a split in the scientific community. Ultimately, the revolutionary theory or paradigm may be universally adopted. When this happens, all research based on it is no longer revolutionary but, instead, is normal since it is concerned with testing and improving the accepted theory or paradigm.

This book is wholly concerned with research in the Kuhnian realm of normal science. The research and analysis methods reviewed in this book are all about constructing models and analyses based on the current accepted view of real estate market theory. In some cases research may lead to an adaptation or refinement of existing theory but the research methods examined in this book are not concerned with revolutionary science.

Explanations, Concepts, Theories and Models

There are two main categories or types of scientific explanation: deductive and inductive. The latter is also referred to as probabilistic. Deductive explanations are normally associated with the physical sciences since they are based on some fact or 'law'. Since the law is known to hold, a logical and accurate extension of it will also hold. For example, if we were seeking to explain some phenomenon such as friction then we might use the law of gravity as part of the foundations for the explanation. Since the law of gravity is known to be valid, an explanation scientifically developed from accurate reasoning based on it will also be valid.

Inductive or probabilistic explanations are common in the social sciences. Here, explanations are often derived from observation, hence inductive explanations are often drawn from empirical, rather than theoretical, analysis. An example of an inductive explanation can be found in Keynes's analysis of the consumption function. Keynes hypothesised that consumption is a function of disposable income. However, he specified the consumption function, a linear equation including a constant and a slope coefficient on disposable income (marginal propensity to consume), by carrying out analysis of observed data. This is a fairly typical, though simple, example of inductive reasoning in economics. Real estate market research is best viewed as a specialised branch of applied economics.

If a phenomenon can be explained satisfactorily then the phenomenon can also be predicted. For example, if we estimated the specification and form of the consumption function in the UK using past consumption and income data then we also have the ability to predict consumption in the present, and possibly the future, given recent or forecast levels of disposable income. Such a prediction would be based on an inductive explanation.

When we are seeking an explanation for a phenomenon, it is common to conceptualise and generalise in order to simplify the problem. The purpose of generalising is to reduce the number of objects so that a concept can be constructed. As a rule, it is necessary to first generalise in order to conceptualise. In the earlier exposition of the perfect competition model, two of the concepts developed were that of the price-taking firm and the rational consumer. The concepts were constructed by first generalising about firms, consumers and firms' products. In the perfect competition model the degree of generalisation is pronounced: we assumed that all firms, consumers and products are completely identical. There is an obvious link between the degree of generalisation undertaken and the extent to which a theory can adequately reflect reality. It is commonplace in economics to first construct theories based on pronounced generalisation. Subsequent development of the simple theories are carried out incrementally by reducing the generalisation progressively. A good example of this is provided by the exposition of the imperfect competition (monopolistic competition) model earlier in this chapter. This model is essentially a development of the perfect competition model since it involves a reduction in the generalisation about firms' products (the assumption about product homogeneity).

The construction of concepts is as important to the construction of theories as generalisation is to the construction of concepts. The simplest way to think of a theory is as a collection of related concepts. All theories are constructed using more than one concept. We can refer to the perfect competition model again in order to see how a theory can be constructed from

Table 1.1 Concepts and generalisations in the perfect competition model

Concept	*Generalisation*
The firm	Firms are homogeneous with perfect information and have the same profit motives and production functions (cost structures).
The product	Homogeneous.
The consumer	All consumers are rational and have perfect information.
Market demand	The demand curves of individual consumers can be aggregated to a market demand curve for the homogeneous good.
Price	There is a single market-determined price for the homogeneous good.
Profits	The equilibrium state is found at the point of normal profits.

several concepts. The concepts, and generalisation behind them, are defined in Table 1.1.

As discussed earlier, these generalised concepts can be formed together in order to derive theoretical predictions about market behaviour. The interrelated set of concepts represents a theory.

Up to this point we have examined the meaning of concepts and theories but have made only occasional mention of models. A model is some abstraction from, or simplistic representation of, reality. Models may be either physical, visual or symbolic. In social science research models are often symbolic. Interrelated sets of concepts that constitute a theory are shown in a model as sets of equations or as different variables in an equation.

The underlying purpose of constructing a model is to improve understanding of how concepts relate to each other or how a theory works. The examples given so far in this chapter are simple and there is no real need to construct models to demonstrate how the concepts relate to each other. However, many theories are sufficiently complex that constructing a model is sensible. Throughout the remainder of this book numerous examples of real estate market models are reviewed and their underlying concepts and theories are discussed.

Further uses of models include the simulation of reality in cases where data cannot be collected – or not without great cost – and the empirical testing of a theory. Empirically testing theories is an important element of research and, as later chapters demonstrate, it is common practice in social science research to collect data for the purpose of testing a model that represents a theory. This is a pragmatic approach because most theories cannot be tested directly. Instead, it is common to test a model that represents the theory.

The Scientific Research Process

Following a well-thought-out, methodologically sound process is central to scientific research. Note that the subject-matter of the research and the facilities used to conduct it are not direct determinants of whether the research is scientific. The research process and methods determine whether the research is scientific or not. It is needless to say that research involving laboratories, white-coated technicians and high-precision equipment is not necessarily scientific. Meanwhile, research involving manipulation of numerical data or qualitative techniques (interviewing and surveying) is not necessarily unscientific. Research that is badly planned, which seeks to answer poorly defined research questions or which uses questionable methods is not scientific and is therefore of little value. Research based on well-defined and logically constructed research questions using appropriate methods of investigation is scientific and potentially has value. We will take a look at assessing the potential value of research outcomes later in this section.

There is a strong relationship between theory and research and, as a general rule, research is justified by the need to establish, improve or test one or more theories or concepts. As noted earlier, concepts can be regarded as the building blocks from which theories are constructed. Models, which often consist of one or more equations, can be constructed as a simplification of reality and a representation of a theory and can be tested empirically. The feedback relationship between theory and empirical research is well-rehearsed. Howard and Sharp (1996), for example, identify seven stages to the scientific research process:

(1) Identify a broad area of study
(2) Select the research topic
(3) Decide the approach
(4) Formulate the plan
(5) Collect the data or information
(6) Analyse and interpret the data
(7) Present the findings

Although this chapter has already defined and discussed concepts, theories and models, it should be noted that consideration of these does not come at the beginning but well into the research process. Howard and Sharp's (1996) research process is best viewed from the perspective of an undergraduate student and implicitly assumes that the prospective researcher faces a situation in which a research project must be undertaken and the initial problem is in finding or selecting a suitable research area. The first stage to their research process therefore involves identifying a broad area to study. The technique to be employed is to start with a broad idea and then progressively narrow it down. For example, we might start with an expression of interest in the economics of the office market. In order to narrow this down, we might elect to examine only the economics of the user market. To further narrow it down, we might focus on an investigation into the short and long-run determination of rental values.

Naturally, many real estate market researchers are not undergraduate students at all but are qualified professional or academic researchers. In these cases, 'finding' a suitable research area is unlikely to be a problem and the research process is likely to begin at stage two of the process shown above. The 'research problem' is the reason or justification for carrying out the proposed research and is identified through a review of the literature. Since scientific research is concerned with the accumulation of knowledge the first real step should always be a thorough and detailed literature review. The purposes of a literature review can be summarised as follows:

(1) to find out everything that is known about a phenomenon
(2) to determine what is not known about the phenomenon
(3) to consider what research would add to an understanding of the phenomenon

A literature review is an exploratory piece of work that determines what is, and is not, known about an area of interest. By definition, it also provides the justification for carrying out further research. The obvious places to search for previous research include academic/learned journals, books, dissertations and theses, trade and practical journals, printed media, discussion/occasional papers/research reports and government publications. After the research problem is identified, a research proposition or hypothesis should be constructed. This involves crystallising the research problem further and adapting it into a clearly defined and empirically testable proposition. Strictly speaking, this is an important part of the scientific research process. However, the construction of formal hypotheses is likely to be undertaken by academic, rather than practising, researchers. A hypothesis is a theorised answer to a research problem and normally takes the form of a statement of cause and effect. A research problem may give rise to only one hypothesis or may be divided into several hypotheses. The critical points about hypotheses are that they must be specific, unambiguous and empirically testable. Research that is practically orientated, or applied research, is likely to be concerned primarily with replicating previous analyses in order to adapt them to new cases, different spatial areas or more up-to-date time frames. The limited scope for developing and adapting theory often means that formal hypotheses are not required but the research objectives still need to be clearly defined.

Stage three of Howard and Sharp's (1996) research process involves deciding on the empirical approach to adopt in order to test the hypotheses or accomplish the research objectives. The methods of analysis that may be appropriate for use in real estate market analysis form the main subject-matter of this book. For the moment, it is sufficient to note that in selecting an appropriate empirical method or methods we must also define the overall study approach, the level of aggregation of the analysis (national, regional, local, etc.) and the data required for testing the hypothesis or accomplishing the research objectives. These study parameters may be referred to as the 'research plan' while stages five and six involve the data collection and analysis. Again, these issues are the subject of considerable discussion throughout the remainder of this book and are therefore not examined in detail in this chapter.

CONCLUSIONS

This chapter has briefly introduced some of the problems that face real estate researchers by beginning with a review of the simple neoclassical microeconomic models of perfect and monopolistic competition. Many of the applied research methods examined in this book, together with some accepted theories, implicitly assume that real estate markets possess characteristics not far removed from those of these simple neoclassical models. In fact, real estate markets tend to be informationally inefficient, complex entities in which a relatively small number of 'producers' and 'consumers' interact. Furthermore, real estate is highly heterogeneous and, more important, possesses a unique spatial dimension since no two properties may share the same identical location. These facts greatly complicate real estate market analysis. Furthermore, analyses based on the assumption that real estate markets are efficient may produce misleading or surprising results. These considerations are examined in greater detail throughout the course of the book. For more detail regarding the peculiarities and inefficiencies of real estate markets see Harvey (2000), Balchin *et al.* (1995) and Ball *et al.* (1998).

REFERENCES

Balchin, P., Bull, G. and Kieve, J. (1995) *Urban Land Economics and Public Policy*, 5th edition (Basingstoke: Macmillan).

Ball, M., Lizieri, C. and MacGregor, B.D. (1998) *The Economics of Commercial Property Markets* (London: Routledge).

Harvey, J. (2000) *Urban Land Economics*, 5th edition (Basingstoke: Macmillan).
Howard, K. and Sharp, J.A. (1996) *The Management of a Student Research Project*, 2nd edition (London: Gower).
Kuhn, T.S. (1970) *The Structure of Scientific Revolutions*, 2nd edition (University of Chicago Press).
Sloman, J. (2000) *Economics*, 4th edition (Harlow: Pearson Education).

2

Research Practice and Real Estate Market Analysis

INTRODUCTION

This chapter continues the development of a background in real estate economics research by considering the characteristics of real estate and real estate markets and by briefly examining different types of real estate research. The emphasis of the chaper is on academic studies although brief consideration is also given to commissioned and contract research projects. The chapter is likely to be of particular interest to undergraduate real estate economics students and may lend some assistance in the selection and management of a final year dissertation project.

THE CHARACTERISTICS OF REAL ESTATE

Some of the difficulties encountered by real estate market analysts can be understood simply by examining the characteristics of real estate markets. The first important difference between real estate markets and the perfect competition theory examined above is that the real estate market can be divided into a number of sectors (see Fraser, 1993; Ball *et al.*, 1998; Brown and Matysiak, 2000 for a thorough discussion). The property market consists of the retail, office, industrial and residential sectors. The retail sector has two sub-sectors (city centre/'High Street' and out-of-town). To a lesser extent this also applies to the office sector. In the case of housing there are several sub-sectors defined by tenure rights (private owner occupied, private rented and social rented).

The fact that real estate markets consist of a number of different sectors is important in the sense that we are not considering a well-defined and self-contained market but a series of quite different, yet potentially interlinked, market sectors. Furthermore, even within one of these sectors, individual properties are likely to exhibit a degree of heterogeneity. This is the second important difference between real estate markets and the perfect competition theory. If we take rental office property as an example, it should be apparent that most office markets contain a wide array of property/ construction types, stock conditions, space specification, sizes, and so on, at any one time. Even two properties of an identical design, age and condition are not completely identical since there are always locational differences, however minor, between different properties. These physical and locational differences may be of importance in determining demand at the individual property level. It is obvious, for example, that differences in location even within a street can be of importance in the retail real estate sector. In general we can say that heterogeneity is defined by:

- physical differences (age, construction type, condition, specification, and so on)
- locational differences (position within a city, neighbourhood or street)
- legal/regulatory differences (tenure, lease conditions, and so on)

Legal or regulatory differences between otherwise identical properties may be of importance. In the rental user market we should expect differences in the demand and market price (rent) for space depending on investors' required lease length and other lease terms such as repairing obligations, rent review frequency and break (termination) options. This leads us to the third important difference between the real estate market and the perfect competition theory. The role of property law and regulation is not simply of importance in adding to the heterogeneity of real estate – it also acts to split real estate markets into distinct institutional sectors. This stems partly from the fact that real estate is a durable good. Real estate yields a flow of services (for example, to occupiers) over a long period of time. This means that individual properties may be occupied by a series of different occupiers during their life span. Equally, firms or occupiers may change their premises from time to time as their space requirements, business practices and the physical condition of the property change. Meanwhile, durability together with the existence of a letting market mean that real estate can act as an investment medium. Although this will vary from country to country to a certain extent, we can generally say that real estate markets are divided into use, investment and development sectors, and Ball *et al.* (1998) refer to these, together with the land market, as a set of four interlinked submarkets. We will examine the economics within and between these sectors in some detail later in the book. For the moment, it is sufficient to simply acknowledge that there are several sectors to the real estate market (within a given use sector). The dynamics and behaviour of the user market (the market for supplying and securing space for occupation) is often quite distinct from the investment market. The latter is clearly linked to markets for other forms of investment such as gilt and equity markets. The speculative-trader side of the development sector clearly links the user and investment sectors since agents in this sector are concerned with the production and letting of space in the user market. Typically, finished and let developments are sold on by developers to investors.

The interaction between different sectors of the real estate market, and between other markets and the real estate market, highlights the fourth difference between real estate markets and the perfect competition theory. The real estate market is not independent of other markets. For example, we would expect significant changes in equity market conditions to have an impact on the investment sector of the real estate market.

There are a number of other ways in which the real estate market differs markedly from the perfect competition theory. The market is characterised by a relatively low volume of irregular transactions. This tends to exacerbate the fact that neither consumers nor producers have access to perfect information. Information on transaction prices is not publicly available in all countries, but, even if it were, the highly heterogeneous nature of real estate renders it difficult to compare the transaction price (or rent) of one property with another. Furthermore, information on letting, occupation or investment opportunities may be difficult and costly to collect. The result is that occupiers in particular, and sometimes investors and developers, are not well informed. This situation is radically different from the hypothetical case set out in the exposition of the perfect competition theory earlier.

It may be worth adding to this already fairly extensive list the issue of rationality. In the perfect competition theory both producers and consumers are assumed to be rational. In other words, producers attempt to maximise their profits and consumers will not purchase a homogeneous good from a firm if the price it charges is higher than the market price for that good. This is a logical assumption to make, particularly given the assumptions about perfect information and an enormous number of producers and consumers. Of course, it is not beyond the scope of our imagination to suppose that an irrational producer or consumer will appear in an industry now and then but in the perfect competition theory it is implicit that such occurrences have no impact on market prices or market behaviour overall. When we examine the real estate market the supposition that producers and consumers are rational is less defensible. We know, for example, that the market comprises a relatively small number of producers and consumers and that the market is characterised by poor informational flows. Producers and consumers are also highly hetergeneous and may differ in terms of their main line of business, firm size, revenue and profit objectives, management style and so on. These facts allow us to construct a plausible hypothesis that the behaviour of firms is an important factor in real estate market pricing and dynamics. In fact, this hypothesis is the foundation for an entire branch of relatively recent literature that will be examined later in the book.

In summary, the real estate market differs from the simply perfect competition theory in the following ways:

(1) Markets consist of a number of distinct but interlinked sectors
(2) Properties are heterogeneous
(3) The market is split into use, investment and development sectors
(4) The market is not independent of other markets
(5) Low and irregular transactions volume
(6) Poor information flows
(7) Rational consumers and producers?

These basic differences between real estate markets and sectors and the idealistic cases of perfect and monopolistic competition provide a wealth of research questions. A great many published real estate market analyses are motivated by explicitly acknowledging one or more of the facts referred to above in order to investigate and/or predict the consequences for market outcomes. The following section examines different types of real estate market analyses and research projects in more detail.

BROAD TYPES OF REAL ESTATE MARKET RESEARCH

For most real estate and construction professionals the undergraduate dissertation will be their first real estate research experience. Most undergraduate degree programmes have a course structure that includes assessment of a substantial and semi-independent piece of research. Normally this piece of work is undertaken in the final year of study and contributes towards final honours degree classification. The importance of the undergraduate research dissertation cannot, therefore, be understated in an academic context.

Regrettably, the undergraduate dissertation is the last, as well as the first, research experience for many real estate and construction professionals. In some cases graduates will extend their academic credentials by continuing on to study for a postgraduate degree, often a Masters degree. Almost all Masters degree course structures contain a research dissertation as part of the final assessment. Clearly, the requirements of a Masters dissertation exceed those of an undergraduate one. Normally the word-limit is around double that of an undergraduate dissertation while there is also an expectation among examiners that Masters dissertations should be more theoretically/conceptually advanced and/or contain more ingenious, complex or advanced empirical analysis.

For the small minority that decide to proceed still further down the academic route, the M.Phil. and Ph.D. theses are, in comparison with undergraduate and postgraduate dissertations, very lengthy and typically very 'academic' pieces of work. Most M.Phil. theses run to around 40,000 words in length. The requirements of a doctoral thesis vary from institution to institution. Some universities stipulate a maximum word-limit of around 80,000 words while others stipulate a maximum number of pages together with limitations on font size and style. The requirements are also likely to vary depending on the faculty within which the thesis is submitted. In the UK, real estate departments can belong to economics, geography or engineering faculties, depending on institution. In the US, real estate departments tend to belong to either economics or finance faculties.

As noted above, most graduates do not progress much further down the 'academic' route. It is important to note that not all doctoral graduates seek employment in academia. Some go on to become 'policy makers' in public sector employment while others go on to take specialised positions in the private sector. In the economics and finance sectors there is an established market for researchers qualified to doctoral level, and during the past twenty years or so a similar market has begun to develop in the real estate and construction sectors. There is now a small, but important and gradually expanding, market for applied research skills in the private sector.

One of the purposes of this chapter is to contextualise the content of the book by considering what real estate research is and, more important, why it is carried out. The chapter considers the requirements of a good piece of real estate or construction research. This is carried out sequentially for undergraduate and postgraduate dissertations. The chapter then moves on to examine applied research in the private sector. Given the complexity and diversity of M.Phil. and Ph.D. research, no real consideration is given to this type of research project. For those considering a move in this direction, suitable advice would be to identify a practising academic with similar research interests in order to discuss the matter with them!

SEVERAL RESEARCH 'DOMAINS'

The foci of research projects are wide and varied but some generalisation is possible. Most projects fall somewhere in a spectrum ranging from highly academic, theoretical or conceptual projects through to concise, highly defined applied projects. Clearly, academics and postgraduate students are more likely to run a project the focus of which is close to the 'academic' end of the spectrum. Meanwhile practitioners and public sector organisations are more likely to run a project the focus of which is closer to the 'applied' end of the spectrum. Undergraduates, in practice, normally carry out final year research projects with a focus that is somewhere between the academic and applied ends of the spectrum. A brief and simple categorisation of five broad research project types is given in Table 2.1.

Table 2.1 A brief categorisation of research projects

Project	*Objectives*	*Researchers*	*Methods*
The classic academic project.	Accumulation of knowledge; incremental development of theory.	Academics, postgraduates.	A combination of theoretical and empirical analysis.
The policy-orientated academic project.	Assessment of disparity between predicted and actual effects of policies; theorised design of new policies; assessment of the implications of policy on theoretical understanding of market issues and phenomena.	Academics, public sector organisations, undergraduates, postgraduates, practitioners.	Largely tried and tested quantitative and qualitative applied research methods and techniques possibly with occasional experimental or ingenious adaptation of existing techniques for a defined purpose.
The practice-orientated academic project.	Assessment of the influence of practice on changing predicted outcomes and implications for theoretical understanding of market issues and phenomena (behavioural research).	Academics, public sector organisations, undergraduates, postgraduates, practitioners.	As above.
The consultancy project.	To obtain answers to specific research questions or to produce a defined output such as an operational model meeting given performance criteria.	Practitioners, commissioned research contractors, consultants (sometimes academics acting as consultants).	Well-rehearsed, tried and tested applied research methods and techniques, the credibility of which is beyond question.
The commissioned research project.	Provide data and/or analysis in order to permit the client or main contractor to continue analysis designed to provide answers to specific research questions or to produce defined outputs such as operational models.	Commissioned research contractors.	As above.

Table 2.1 gives a simple representation of the likely focus of several different types of research project together with the research methods that may be employed. Of course the table underplays the diversity of academic, student and applied research projects. In practice, academics often carry out practical/policy orientated and applied research while student dissertations range from highly conceptual to almost pure applied pieces of work. With that caveat in place, it is probably beyond dispute that few researchers other than academics are likely to engage in purely conceptual and theoretical work for the sole purpose of expanding knowledge and understanding about real estate market processes. Meanwhile, practitioners' research projects will almost always be geared towards producing well-defined outputs, such as operational models or forecasts. The following sections give further general guidance on undergraduate, postgraduate and applied research projects.

THE REAL ESTATE UNDERGRADUATE DISSERTATION

In general, an undergraduate dissertation is likely to take one of four basic approaches:

(1) Investigative
(2) Theoretical or conceptual
(3) Empirical
(4) Applied

A good undergraduate dissertation will contain a balance of new research with rehearsal of established theory and fact. In practice this is difficult to achieve and undergraduate dissertations in real estate and construction disciplines often suffer a diminution of marks as a consequence of missing this balance! A further complexity is the fact that the balance or threshold between new research and review of previous research is dependent on the approach taken in the dissertation. For example, an investigative research dissertation is likely to contain a greater proportion of new research than a theoretical/conceptual one.

However, students tend not to have considerable freedom of choice with respect to the best approach to take in their undergraduate research dissertation. The choice of approach very much depends on the nature of the research topic, research questions and the extent of previous research in the chosen area of interest. As a general guide, the links between research topics, research questions and appropriate dissertation approach are likely to be formed along the following lines:

Investigative Approach

The investigative dissertation tends to be one of the most common forms of dissertations submitted in the final year of undergraduate real estate and construction degree programmes. Regrettably, it is often clear to examiners that a dissertation has been constructed according to this approach simply because its author either could not decide on a better (more appropriate) approach or, more frequently still, the author did not plan out the research properly and, having run out of time just before the submission date, completed his/her write-up to discover that their work is little more than broadly investigative. There is a clear warning here. Poorly undertaken investigative undergraduate research dissertations tend not to be well received by examiners. This is not because investigative research projects do not have a place in an undergraduate real estate or construction course. Rather, such dissertations have a particular place and purpose but they are used far more frequently, and in a much greater range of circumstances, than they should be.

The classic justification for employing an investigative approach to constructing an undergraduate dissertation arises when very little is known about the research topic or research question(s). If this is the case then construction of detailed hypotheses and carefully planned-out data collection and empirical testing become inappropriate. In other words, a certain amount of existing knowledge is necessary before it becomes possible to construct hypotheses and an empirical research plan. If this existing knowledge does not exist then it becomes inappropriate to follow such an approach. In these circumstances a better approach involves collecting basic or fundamental information in a pre-planned way. The following hypothetical examples demonstrate when an investigative research approach may be appropriate. Note that the employment of any and all approaches to research need to be carefully and methodically justified.

Example 1

A student wishes to construct a quantitative rent determination model for the office market in the captial city of a small African nation state. After carrying out a preliminary literature review the student does not find any published previous research focusing on any aspect of land, property, planning or urban economics in the African state which is of interest to the student. It is clear, therefore, that the literature contains nothing to inform the student how the commercial property market works in this country; whether there is an established commercial property market at all; the role of the public sector in the provision of property in this country; whether there is an office sector if there is a commercial property market; even whether property is leased rather than owner occupied; and so on.

Since the student knows almost nothing about the background to the research question, the research question becomes inappropriate. It is based on the assumption that a commercial property market exists, that it is largely private sector driven and that there is an identifiable office sector.

A more appropriate approach in these circumstances is to carry out an investigative research project in order to yield useful information to some or all of the above-noted unanswered questions. Since answers to these questions will be useful to a subsequent round of researchers interested in conducting more detailed studies, a piece of carefully planned investigative research will be of value.

Example 2

An undergraduate student wishes to construct a quantitative rent determination model of the London office market. After carrying out a preliminary literature review the student collects some data from published office market reports, planning registers and other sources for official students. After a break of several months, the student interviews five surveyors in order to collate their views on the determinants of office rents. A few months later, while studying for examinations, the student realises that time is running out and therefore constructs a written literature review. The broad findings of the interviews are then written up and formed into a separate chapter. In order to procure some impressive numerical results the student quickly estimates a simple rent determination equation just like one shown in a 15-year-old published paper. On completion the dissertation has a strong investigative 'feel'. It is written as an investigation into the determinants of office rents. It contains a couple of narrative literature review chapters outlining what other researchers have done, some general discussion about what surveyors think about rent models and a small piece of very basic numerical work which replicates the equation that an author estimated and published quite a long time ago.

Theoretical or Conceptual Approach

Dissertations that follow this approach will tend to be the most highly prized by examiners, who are themselves, after all, academics. However, producing a good theoretical/conceptual undergraduate dissertation is, in practice, extremely difficult and this approach therefore represents something of a 'high risk/high reward' option.

Theoretical/conceptual dissertations are particularly justifiable when the chosen research topic is not well informed by accepted theory. Probably the main difficulty is that both the justification of conducting a theoretical/conceptual approach to a dissertation, and the ease of carrying it off well, are dependent on the developmental stage of the literature that informs the chosen research area. Where the relevant literature is well established and thorough it is difficult to find an appropriate gap or shortfall that requires development. Where the relevant literature is very sparse it will be difficult to achieve a sufficiently narrow focus to the analysis.

The key ingredients of a good theoretical/conceptual undergraduate dissertation include a long, thorough and well-structured literature review and an abundance of original analysis based on it. In such a dissertation, 'analysis' is likely to entail a sound examination of the accepted or indisputed state of theory, thorough discussion of other authors' reasoning, identification of linkages between the work of other authors and accepted theory and, perhaps most important, some original discussion and reasoning linked firmly to the review of accepted theory and literature review. The latter represents the author's original contribution to thinking in the chosen area, although, at undergraduate level, this element of the work need not be particularly long, deep or ground-breaking.

Empirical Approach

This approach represents something of a hybrid between the investigative and theoretical/conceptual approaches. As discussed in Chapter 1, there is (or should be) a strong two-way relationship between theory and empirical research. Replication and incremental advancement are important concepts in the context of empirical research.

Replication involves carrying out empirical research (experimentation) with an expectation that the results will tend to reinforce the accepted theory that gave rise to the empirical research design. So, for example, if an author has published a rent determination model relating to one UK urban office market, then further empirical research should be expected to yield similar results for other UK urban office markets.

The concept of incremental advancement is similar to replication but, as the name suggests, it is concerned with the gradual development or adaptation of an accepted theory through successive rounds of new empirical research. Empirical research in this tradition implicitly recognises that the accepted theory is not perfect but, at the same time, that the theory is essentially valid and indisputable. In the real estate economics literature it is not uncommon to find papers published in series or cycles. The cycle begins with a simplistic model of some real estate economics phenomenon (such as commercial rent determination), and successive papers published by the same, and other, authors gradually develop the modelling approach and performance.

As mentioned earlier, the empirical research dissertation is essentially a hybrid of investigative and theoretical/conceptual approaches. Good undergraduate dissertations constructed using this approach will have a strong foundation of theory developed and written from a thorough and detailed literature review. In this sense the empirical research dissertation is similar to one constructed using the theoretical/conceptual approach. However, an empirical research dissertation is likely to contain less analysis of the ideas, theories and concepts identified in the literature review. Instead, it is likely to contain discussion that outlines the limits of the accepted theory. For example, the theory may have been tested in relation to some urban markets but not others. Or there may be some doubt as to whether a model estimated using data up to the early 1980s will replicate if estimated using a more recent series of data. During the literature review, the empirical research dissertation will therefore appear to be building a case for carrying out a further empirical study in order to test, push or refine the known limits of the accepted theory.

The empirical research itself should be devised and planned very carefully with a strong link to the preceding theoretical discussion. The approach taken in the empirical research should be driven by the research questions, hypotheses and objectives constructed as a result of having written up the literature review.

An important element of the empirical research dissertation, and one which is frequently missed out or given very little attention, is a retrospective examination of the literature review with direct consideration of the empirical results reported in the dissertation. As outlined earlier, there should be a strong two-way relationship between theory and empirical findings. Thus, a dissertation constructed using the empirical research approach must, in essence, contain 'analysis of the analysis'. In other words, the author should comment on and discuss each of the empirical findings in order to explain whether the results are expected or unexpected; whether data or modelling limitations help explain any unexpected results and whether there is any need to reconsider parts of the accepted theory in light of the empirical results. However, it is also important to recognise that all empirical research has its limitations and these must be carefully considered when drawing conclusions about the accepted theory. Going too far when drawing conclusions is another common mistake made in empirical research dissertations at undergraduate level.

Applied Research Approach

Undergraduate dissertations are often constructed using an applied research approach. A simple definition of applied research is any research that focuses on the practical implications of previous theoretical and empirical findings together with policy-orientated research. This encompasses research projects that examine the reactions of firms and individuals to policies and policy changes, disparity between the planned and actual outcomes of policy changes, systematic error and other human behavioural research, and so on.

One of the primary justifications for carrying out applied research is to investigate disparities between predicted (theoretical) outcomes and actual outcomes. In other words, the underlying question in many pieces of applied research is 'This is how it works in theory but how does it work in practice?' An alternative way to view applied research is to recognise that the accepted theory or theories under investigation will rarely be complete or perfect explanations of the processes or phenomena being described. This means that when the theory is used to predict outcomes then there will inevitably be some error, and this gives rise to the question of whether the error is acceptable or whether it is so fundamental or significant that the theory or theories require revisiting. So, applied research can also be viewed as investigative research designed to evaluate the diparity between predicted and actual outcomes.

As with dissertations that follow the empirical research approach, applied research dissertations often fall short of 'a good piece of work' as a result of the fact that few or no links are constructed between the findings and the theory or theories that the dissertation is purporting to investigate. The structure of an applied research dissertation should be very similar to an empirical research dissertation. Applied research has a different meaning in the context of practitioner research – here the term can be taken as broadly covering any research project designed to provide answers to defined problems using methods drawn from accepted theory and practice.

Summary

The following table sets out a simplified procedure for choosing an appropriate approach for carrying out an undergraduate research project.

	Appropriate	*Inappropriate*
Investigative	• There is a justification for researching the chosen topic. That is, there is a definable and worthwhile research question. • The literature contains few or no examples of research in the chosen topic area and the formulation of hypotheses or planning or empirical research is inappropriate.	• A broad area of study has been chosen but no research questions have been formulated. • The literature contains examples of previous published research that is more advanced than the investigative work proposed.

	Appropriate	*Inappropriate*
Theoretical/ conceptual	• The chosen research area is informed by a fairly well-established literature. • There is some (possibly limited) accepted theory/theories: that is, some level of undisputed theoretical view relating to the research area. • Rehearsed theory is either incomplete or lacking or there is some evidence that it is flawed in some way.	• The chosen research area is very well informed by a voluminous literature setting out a thorough rehearsed (indisputed) theory or theories.
Empirical	• The chosen research area is informed by a well-established literature. • The literature contains at least some examples of empirical research designed to test the limits of the accepted theory. • Previous published empirical research is not complete or cannot be construed as collectively representing a complete and exhaustive test of the accepted theory and all of its limits.	• The chosen research area is not well informed by an established literature such that there is essentially no accepted theory to empirically test. • The volume of previous published empirical work is so great and comprehensive that it is not possible to identify gaps in the empirical testing necessary to fully test the theory and its limits.
Applied	• The chosen research area is informed by a well-established literature. • There is some doubt as to the relationship between predicted theoretical and actual outcomes. • There is doubt as to the likely consequences of a recent or proposed policy change.	• The literature is not sufficiently developed so as to permit outcomes to be predicted.

THE REAL ESTATE POSTGRADUATE DISSERTATION

For postgraduate dissertations most UK institutions impose a word limit roughly double that of an undergraduate dissertation. In addition, there is a normal expectation among academic institutions, and their staff, that postgraduate dissertations should contain more advanced and demanding research than an undergraduate dissertation. Postgraduate research projects are unlikely to follow purely applied or investigative approaches although some projects may have investigative elements.

The key ingredients of a good postgraduate dissertation are more difficult to identify since such dissertations tend to be more specialised, longer and more complex than undergraduate dissertations. However, some general rules apply:

- The overall standard should be closer to a good-quality piece of published academic output than a published piece of applied research (research report).
- The literature review sections are likely to be lengthy but focused, informative and very well structured. The contributions of cited authors will be analysed critically and related to other cited works in addition to simply being summarised. The literature review sections will contain a significant amount of argument and analysis inspired by the cited works but representing the student's own thoughts and work.
- Research questions and hypotheses will be very well formulated and designed. Spending considerable time on careful editing and structuring is worthwhile in order to create the impression that the research questions and hypotheses form themselves or 'grow' out of the literature review.
- The empirical research will be well designed and clearly linked to the research questions and hypotheses. Empirical research in a postgraduate dissertation is likely to be fairly extensive while drawing on a well-thought-out and rigorous quantitative, qualitative or mixed methodology.
- Conclusions will be detailed and highly analytical. Empirical findings should be clearly linked back to the earlier review of theory and previous empirical studies, with the implications of the findings clearly drawn out. Importantly, limitations to the empirical work should be carefully identified in order to place the significance of the findings in context. Writing a short section that identifies the limitations to the research often leads researchers to identify other issues that might have been researched, other forms of analysis that might have been used, other forms of testing, alternative data sources, and so on. It is worthwhile writing these up into a section specifying possible directions that future research projects in the same area might usefully take.

The highest-rated academic journals in the discipline can be used to obtain quality benchmarks. As noted earlier, a good postgraduate dissertation is likely to be close in quality and complexity terms to a piece of academic research, so the depth and rigour of the theoretical analysis and literature review together with the complexity and rigour of the empirical work in a dissertation should, to some extent, mirror the standards found in relevant published academic output. However, it is important to note that papers published in academic journals are normally considerably shorter than postgraduate dissertations. The scale and scope of the research problems under examination in many such papers are similar to the scale and scope of a research problem that might be examined by a postgraduate research project. Therefore, there should be an expectation that postgraduate dissertations will contain a little more detail, and the literature review sections are likely to be written in a more informative and discussive style. In addition, it is important to note that almost all papers published in good academic journals spend a considerable amount of time in the peer-reviewing and editorial processes. This means, inevitably, that papers are published after they have been improved in response to suggestions from anonymous reviewers, and this tends to give published papers a highly polished appearance that can be difficult to replicate in a piece of work that is not peer reviewed in the same way.

REAL ESTATE RESEARCH IN PRACTICE

As noted earlier in the chapter, applied research projects, as run by researchers other than academics and students, are likely to be highly defined pieces of work geared towards the production of either hard outputs (such as useful models or forecasts) or answers to practice and policy orientated research questions. Research projects are carried out by both public and private sectors and there are basically three types of such projects defined by the way in which the outputs are procured:

- Projects that are run in-house
- Contract research projects
- Commissioned projects

In-house projects are carried out by the research departments, or individuals with research skills, in public and private sector organisations with real estate market and wider interests.

Private sector organisations tend to be geared towards the production of research outputs that either form inputs to the production of saleable outputs or are themselves directly saleable outputs. For surveying firms this tends to mean that research teams focus on the production of models, forecasts, market analyses and other similar types of research output that can be sold to clients as advice or else can be assimilated in market reports and reviews either for sale or as a form of marketing. Given the information inefficiencies that dominate commercial and industrial real estate markets there is a strong argument that firms that offer market advice can enhance their reputation by running a prominent research function.

The objectives of public sector organisations are remarkably similar to private sector organisations. They tend to be motivated to undertake research in order to gather information on the performance and effectiveness of policy, to design new policies and to maintain up-to-date information to permit them to respond to requests from policy-makers, politicians and the public. In other words, public sector research departments are also interested in 'what is going on' rather than 'how markets work'.

Contract research projects are broadly designed by an organisation's in-house research team, and suitable contractors are normally asked to respond (tender) to a project brief written by the in-house team. The relatively narrow focus of research departments in public and private sector organisations means that the necessary breadth of skill, and sometimes the resources, are not available to permit projects to be carried out by the in-house research team. Many of the public sector organisations with an interest in real estate and housing markets and policy maintain a research programme in order to allow numerous projects to be designed and contracted out on an ongoing basis. Programmes are evaluated and updated, normally at least once a year.

There may be interaction between in-house and contract research projects in the sense that private sector organisations with research departments often tender for work contracted out by public sector organisations. It is also not uncommon for public sector clients to join together in order to contract out a research project. This may happen, for example, where two government departments or other public sector organisations share a common interest in a particular piece of policy, proposed policy change or topical market phenomenon.

Commissioned projects tend to be relatively small-scale and, above all, very highly defined pieces of work. Typical examples might include a specific household or consumer survey designed to procure data to be analysed as part of a wider project or procurement/enhancement of a specific dataset (economic data, house prices, rental value data, and so on). Small commissioned projects are often let to market research firms or data providers. The range and quality of service provided by market research firms is quite variable, with some specialising in the provision of high-quality advice on choosing sampling frames, questionnaire design and analysis of the results, and others specialising in the provision of lower-cost 'no frills' data collection.

Requirements of Project Briefs

Contract research projects and small commissioned projects are normally let to contractors following a tendering process in which prospective contractors respond to a project brief. The project brief should describe:

- The background to the project including a very brief review of circumstances that have led to the need for a research project.
- The research questions and hypotheses (if appropriate).
- Suggested methodology (possibly in outline).
- Specific required outputs.
- Key dates including the closing date for submission of tenders, the date on which the contract will be let and when each of the outputs is required by the client.
- The required elements of prospective contractors' tenders.

Generally, research contracts are more successful when the client has a good awareness of the background to the research problems, the issues to be addressed by the contractor and, above all, a well-defined notion of the outputs required from the main contractor. In their tenders, prospective contractors will provide their own review of background issues, background literature search results and interpretation of the need for further research. Tenders will contain detailed proposals on carrying out the research together with proposed methodology and anticipated outputs. Clearly, contractors' proposals are more likely to accord with clients' requirements when the project brief is detailed and specific rather than undetailed or vague.

Financial arrangements usually take one of two main forms. Some project briefs give an outline budget while others make no mention of a budget. For project briefs with an outline budget contractors ultimately compete on the quality and amount of work proposed since all bidders will have very similar tender amounts. In these circumstances the reputation (track record) of the contractor together with the number and profile of researchers in the proposed research team become more significant. Other important factors can include the extent of contractors' other committments, value for money as demonstrated by the number of days' input to the project from the various proposed team members and their respective day rates and the amount and nature of other research work that contractors have ongoing. Contractors that are carrying out similar or related projects may be able to demonstrate that their selection will bring added value to the project. Public sector research contracts let as part of established research programmes are often of the 'outline budget' type.

The one-off (bespoke) research projects that are let by public sector clients from time to time, and almost all private sector research contracts, tend to follow the other model. Prospective contractors prepare a tender document as above but, since they have no indication of outline budget, the financial considerations are more important, in theory at least. In practice, the detail and clarity offered by project briefs does not tend to vary considerably between the 'outline budget' and 'no budget' models with the result that contractors may still seek to add value to the project brief by attempting to open up important issues that have been missed in the brief. Ultimately, however, contractors will seek to minimise their tender amount while offering a thorough research project that fully addresses the requirements of the project brief.

CONCLUSIONS

This chapter has continued the development of general research issues and those specific to real estate research by reviewing different types of real estate market analysis and research projects. The remainder of the book is concerned with research techniques and methods. The next two chapters provide simple background on sampling theory, hypothesis testing and regression analysis, since a background in these subjects is frequently assumed in the remainder of the book.

REFERENCES

Ball, M., Lizieri, C. and MacGregor, B.D. (1998) *The Economics of Commercial Property Markets* (London: Routledge).

Brown, G.R. and Matysiak, G.A. (2000) *Real Estate Investment: A Capital Market Approach* (London: Financial Times).

Fraser, W.D. (1993) *Principles of Property Investment and Pricing*, 2nd edition (Basingstoke: Macmillan).

3

Sampling Theory and Hypothesis Testing

INTRODUCTION

As we noted in the previous chapter, explanations in the social sciences (including real estate economics) are almost always derived from inductive (probabilistic) logic. In this chapter we turn to examine some fundamental principles of empirical research. Here, the focus is mainly on the business of testing hypotheses (theorised statements of cause and effect) and this is typically done with reference to the laws of probability. The chapter is a discussion of descriptive and inferential statistics that are useful in real estate market analysis but the emphasis of the chapter is on inferential, rather than descriptive, statistics. Inferential statistics are useful when testing ideas, hypotheses and other forms of analysis related to the concept of 'cause and effect'. Descriptive statistics are concerned with basic analysis of datasets and are often used in preliminary analysis. Throughout the chapter a basic background in statistics is assumed. Readers unfamiliar with basic descriptive statistics such as measures of central tendency and measures of dispersion are advised to refer to an introductory statistics text before reading further in this chapter.

There are two underlying objectives to the chapter. First, the statistics and statistical testing procedures outlined in the chapter are of direct relevance to quantitative research in the social sciences and may be used in their own right as forms of analysis designed to empirically test hypotheses. Perhaps more importantly, the chapter provides a background knowledge and understanding of descriptive and inferential statistics that is essential to gaining an understanding of the more complex analytical methods covered in later chapters.

WHY DO WE NEED INFERENTIAL STATISTICS?

Empirical analysis is central to the researcher's aim of constructing and testing probabilistic explanations for observed phenomena in social science research. Arguably, the role of empirical research in the social sciences is more important than in the physical sciences. As noted in the last chapter, in the social sciences explanations are often constructed based on observed phenomena (inductive logic) while in the physical sciences explanations are more likely to be developed from existing theories or laws that are known to be valid (deductive logic). In practice, this often means that real estate researchers are not entirely free to construct perfect (laboratory conditions) experiments in order to test the validity of their explanations. In part, this is because explanations, concepts and theories are likely to involve large groups of people or firms (and their behaviour) and expensive physical property. Real estate researchers will rarely be able to construct laboratory conditions in order to observe the behaviour of people, occupiers or firms, and empirical research is therefore often concerned with the analysis of secondary datasets. Preliminary analyses drawing on descriptive statistics are a useful step in conducting more detailed empirical work. For example, when investigating whether variable Y is influenced or determined by variable X then as part of an empirical investigation using sample data it will be useful to know the minimum, maximum, median and mean values of these variables. It will also be of value to know the variance contained within the two samples of data, or the standard deviation of the two samples, while calculating a correlation coefficient will indicate whether or not an increase in one variable is associated with an increase (or decrease) in the other.

However, the main limitation of these statistical measures is that they cannot address questions of cause and effect. Measures of central tendency, dispersion and association are merely descriptive. To see why it is necessary to draw on statistics (specifically probability) in order to test hypotheses, consider the following simple example.

Example 1

A researcher wishes to test the hypothesis that the houses in High Street are more valuable than the houses in Main Street. Each street has 10 houses which are identical in every sense other than the fact that High Street benefits from views over a large, well-kept public park. The two streets are in close proximity in the same neighbourhood. The researcher obtains data on recent purchase prices for the 20 houses. Luckily, all 20 were placed on the market last year with the same estate agent and were all quickly sold to different buyers. The researcher's data are as shown in Table 3.1.

The data in the table clearly show that the houses in High Street achieved higher sale prices than those in Main Street. Now suppose that our hypothesis was that houses with amenity views are more valuable than those without such views. Could we still test the hypothesis with the data available? Could we still arrive at a meaningful conclusion? Example 1 may seem a little pointless

Table 3.1 Observed house purchase prices

Case	*High Street*	*Case*	*Main Street*
1	75,100	1	72,600
2	75,700	2	72,800
3	74,200	3	73,900
4	75,000	4	72,200
5	75,200	5	73,600
6	74,100	6	73,300
7	75,900	7	73,200
8	75,800	8	72,100
9	74,500	9	73,200
10	74,900	10	72,300
Average	75,040	Average	72,920

but it provides a benchmark against which to compare a more realistic example. Consider example 2:

Example 2

A researcher invents and patents a new battery-cell design. His firm wishes to know if the new-design battery cell really does last longer than the similarly priced older-generation products. The researcher purchases 10 old-design cells and compares their life against 10 of the new-design cells. The results are shown in Table 3.2.

We can see from the figures that, on the whole, the new-design cells tend to have a longer life. But can we categorically conclude that this is the case? Remember that we are dealing with samples and not populations in this example. In our sample the measured life of the new-design cells exceeds the average life of the old-design cells in 7 out of 10 cases. Unfortunately, we are not interested in knowing whether our sample of new-design cells performs better than our sample of old-design cells. We are really interested in knowing whether the population of new-design cells performs better than the population of old-design cells. The analysis of sample data is simply a tool to permit an informed judgement to be made about the populations.

At this point we need to recognise that there is really very little we can do to address the hypothesis based on the data and statistics available to us. We can conclude that the 'new design' sample mean is greater than the 'old design' sample mean. We also know that the measured life of the 'new design' cells in our sample is greater than the mean life of the 'old design'

Table 3.2 Measured cell life (in hours)

Case	*'Old design' cells*	*Case*	*'New design' cells*
1	19.02	1	19.21
2	18.76	2	19.38
3	18.90	3	19.99
4	18.72	4	19.99
5	18.61	5	19.27
6	18.76	6	18.40
7	19.07	7	18.66
8	19.28	8	18.42
9	18.54	9	19.30
10	18.69	10	19.72
Average	18.84	Average	19.23

cells in our sample seven times out of ten. However, as a consequence of 'chance variation' these facts do not permit us to draw conclusions about the populations from which the samples are drawn. In other words, we cannot rule out the possibility that different results would be obtained if we drew a new pair of samples. We can see from Table 3.2 that there is some natural or random variation in the measured life of the battery cells in both samples. This means, in essence, that a new pair of samples might demonstrate that the 'new design' cells out-perform the 'old design' cells three times out of ten or nine times out of ten. We cannot be sure that this will not be the case. As a consequence, we cannot draw conclusions about the population, or, to put this another way, we cannot say that the expected life of 'new design' battery cells is greater than that of 'old design' cells.

POPULATIONS AND SAMPLES

In the previous section we considered our ability to test hypotheses using datasets in two hypothetical examples. In the first example we were able to devise a conclusive test since the available data completely represented the population. The hypothesis concerned the price of houses in one street relative to another and we had data on the prices of all houses in both streets. The datasets were not samples and completely represented the populations. In the second example the datasets were samples and did not completely represent the populations. This fact, together with the idea of 'chance variation' prevented us from devising a conclusive test of the hypothesis. In this section we carry out a more detailed examination of populations, samples and their properties.

In almost all empirical research statistics drawn from a sample are used in order to make inferences about a population. The logic of this is that it is almost impossible, or at least impractical, to collect data for a complete population. Furthermore, as we shall see later, collecting data for a population is often inefficient and needless because inferences about populations can be made using statistical tests based on sample data.

What defines a population depends on the research question at hand but, broadly, it is the total set of observations for which a hypothesis is conjectured to hold. In example one, the hypothesis was conjectured to hold for the price of houses in one street relative to another. The population was therefore very easy to define and collect data for. In example two, the hypothesis was conjectured to hold for the life of all battery cells manufactured according to the new design relative to the life of all battery cells manufactured according to the old design. As with example one, there are two populations in this case (new-design battery cells and old-design battery cells). Unlike example one, the populations are difficult to identify and practically impossible to collect a complete dataset for – no matter how many millions of battery cells are manufactured it will presumably always be possible for firms to manufacture some more.

A sample is a relatively small set of data drawn from a population. The objective of calculating statistics for a sample is to draw inferences about the population, so it is crucial that a sample is representative of the population from which it is drawn. Provided this representativeness is achieved we may be able to test a hypothesis about a population using sample data drawn from the population. The representativeness of a sample is essentially determined by the methods used to collect it.

Random Sampling

One of the most important steps in a sampling procedure is deciding how to choose which cases from the population should be observed (sampled). Arguably, the best way to do this or the method least likely to introduce bias or unrepresentativeness, is to choose cases on a purely random basis. If the sample includes a relatively large number of observations and those cases had no more chance of being sampled than any other, then the sample itself is likely to be representative of the population.

However, randomly selecting cases from a population may be impractical except when the population itself is quite small. Furthermore, actual 'randomness' is notoriously difficult to achieve because cases must be collected using some collection method or procedure. Clearly, this is paradoxical in the sense that a procedure is a systematic process and there is therefore nothing inherently random about a procedure. Instead, a procedure must be designed to simulate the random sampling of a population.

To illustrate the difficulties, suppose that we constructed a hypothesis about households' preferences for a certain consumer good. In order to collect data a telephone survey might be undertaken by a team of market researchers using a computer that dials telephone numbers at random. This sampling method would be very close to being random, but since only households with a telephone stand a chance of being surveyed the method is not entirely random. There is an additional issue here since computers are, in fact, incapable of generating purely random numbers. By following a series of computational steps, computers are able to generate pseudo random numbers (PRNs) from a 'seed' or starting number but there are numerous studies (that are not reviewed here) that collectively demonstrate the difficulty in devising a method of generating sufficiently random PRNs.

Now suppose that the market researchers stopped people 'at random' in a busy shopping street in order to ask their questions. Although the people being surveyed are seemingly stopped at random, the sampling method itself is far from random because only people who happen to visit that shopping street on the day and time of the survey stand a chance of being surveyed. If the sample contains a disproportionate number of people with any of the characteristics that are useful in predicting preferences or product choice then the sample is not random. Such characteristics might include demographic or socio-economic profile, working hours or even preference for High Street over telephone or internet shopping.

There is a further element to the potential non-randomness of this sampling method: interviewees are chosen 'randomly' by market researchers but market researchers are people and may themselves be influenced by their own views and preferences. Is it safe to assume that the market researchers truly stop people at random? This sampling method has the potential for the introduction of bias, even if unintentionally, by the data collectors. Of course, there are safeguards against such sample selection bias and the effects can be minimised by collecting data on the demographic and socio-economic profile of respondents. The data and analyses can then be segmented into a number of groups defined by these demographic/socio-economic profiles. The objective of these simple examples is to demonstrate the ease with which bias may be introduced to sampling methods.

Stratified Random Sampling

If the population is not strictly homogeneous then we might consider using a stratified random sampling method. This is sometimes known as a quota

Table 3.3 Age profile of the population of consumers of an existing product

Consumer age group	*Number of consumers*	*Proportion of population*
20–29	112,000	24.8
30–39	143,000	31.7
40–49	136,000	30.2
50–54	43,000	9.5
54+	17,000	3.8
Total	451,000	100.0

sampling method since it may be used to ensure that a sample has a similar profile to the target population. We assume that the population is not homogeneous but contains a number of similar groups or categories. For example, a survey of consumers might take into account a number of groups defined by age, sex, marital status or occupation. The underlying assumption is that cases, observations or respondents are homogeneous within groups but that there may be differences between groups.

Suppose that we wished to collect a sample of attitudinal data from the consumers of a certain product. This might be done, for example, in order to predict consumers' response to a new product or a development from an existing product. Suppose that background research reveals that the population of existing consumers has the profile shown in Table 3.3.

If we have reasons to suppose that consumers' preferences are likely to depend partly on age then it makes sense to collect a sample within which 24.8 per cent of respondents are aged 20–29, 31.7 per cent are aged 30–39, and so on. Within the groups, respondents are selected at random. This approach will minimise the risk of bias since the sample will be representative of the population.

The need for adopting a stratified random sampling approach becomes stronger if the data collection methods are arm's-length (a questionnaire survey, for example). We may have reason to suppose that some respondents are more likely to respond (select themselves for inclusion in the sample) than others. Younger consumers may be less likely to respond than older consumers, for example. Even where more direct forms of data collection are used, such as using market researchers to approach potential consumers in a shopping street, adopting a pure random sampling method is unlikely to yield a sample that shares the same proportion of observations in each category as the underlying population.

In some circumstances the intended sample size will be known at the outset of a research project, before the data are actually collected. This is likely to be the case when, for example, a market research company is used to collect the data, since a price for the work will be negotiated at the outset and a sample size agreed. When data is collected this way the stratified random sampling method might best be described as a quota sampling method. To minimise data wastage the market research company will collect data on an agreed number of respondents in each category and are therefore working to a quota for each defined category.

One drawback to the stratified sampling method is that its use requires that we know, at the outset, the parameters that define segmentation. Sometimes this is not the case and we cannot therefore use quotas in the data collection phase of the research project. In these circumstances it is prudent to collect information on a range of parameters such as age, sex, marital status, and so on. We can test for variation in responses with respect to these parameters statistically. Such tests are examined later in this chapter.

Other Sampling Methods

The most obvious way to collect a sample is to employ a form of convenience sampling. As the name suggests, this is a method of collecting data that minimises time and effort rather than potential sources of bias. In practice, convenience sampling is quite common but the method should never be an excuse for poor data collection. Before using this method it is necessary to justify it. Justification might be on the basis that there are no grounds for believing that segmentation can be defined by a known parameter. So, if consumers' views do not appear to vary with respect to age, sex, marital status, occupation or any other logical factor, then a convenience sampling method might be justifiable.

Similarly, if we could find no reason to support the idea that office rent determinants and dynamics differed between several streets in an office district then we might be tempted to collect data from a single street. This would avoid the more difficult and expensive alternatives of collecting a sample with property proportions from each street that replicate the contribution of each street to the total stock of offices (quota sample) or a random sample with additional information on within-neighbourhood location (stratified random sample).

Sample sizes

There are no firm rules regarding the necessary size of a sample relative to the population but there are definable guidelines. These are examined later in the chapter following an examination of sampling theory, statistics and hypothesis testing.

SAMPLING THEORY

Earlier in the chapter we examined a simple example (battery cell life) in which it was not possible to categorically conclude that new-design battery cells have a longer life than old-design battery cells. In this section we examine sampling theory in order to provide a set of tools, based on principles of probability, that can be used to provide satisfactory answers to such questions. We start by looking at the Normal distribution.

The Normal Distribution

When we are testing hypotheses we generally assume that the variables we are examining are Normally distributed or that their distributions approximate to the Normal distribution. A distribution is the arrangement of the values of a variable in relation to the mean of that variable. In a standard Normal distribution, the mean is equal to zero and individual observations drawn from the mean are equally likely to be positive as to be negative. A distribution that approximates to the Normal distribution is one that possesses the same properties except that the mean is not equal to zero. Such distributions are usually referred to simply as Normal (rather than standard Normal) distributions. The standard Normal distribution is essentially a special case in which the mean of the distribution is equal to zero. All Normal distributions have a mean that is equal to the median and the mode (the average value of the variable is also the middle of the distribution of the variable). In other words, the distribution is exactly symmetrical about its mean. Normal distributions are sometimes referred to as Gaussian distributions.

A distribution can be described by a curve or by a probability density function (pdf). The cumulative probability density function for the Normal distribution takes the form shown in Figure 3.1.

To interpret the diagram assume that we are concerned with a continuous random variable x which is known to be Normally distributed. Although Figure 3.1 cannot show it, the line $f(x)$ extends from $-\infty$ to $+\infty$. However, it is also apparent that the area under the curve is practically zero when the standard deviation $= -3$ and practically 1 when the standard deviation $= +3$. When the standard deviation equals zero then the area under the curve is equal to 0.5. What does this mean? There is a 50 per cent probability that a randomly drawn value of x will lie within the range $-\infty$ to 0 standard deviations removed from zero. Equally, there is a 50 per cent probability that the value will lie within the range 0 to ∞ standard deviations removed from zero (the mean of the distribution of x).

The shape and position of the Normal distribution are determined by two parameters – μ and σ (or σ^2), i.e. the mean and the standard deviation

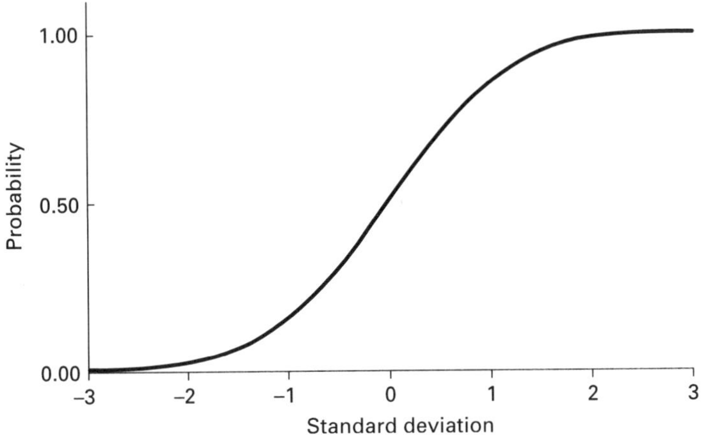

Figure 3.1 *Cumulative probability function for the Normal distribution*

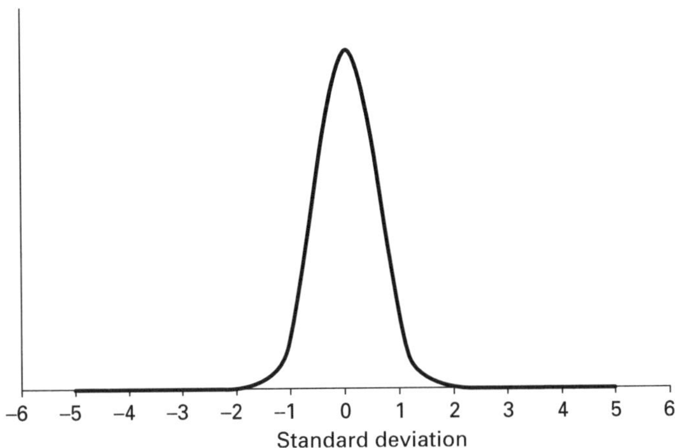

Figure 3.2 *Normal distribution with a standard deviation of 0.50*

(or variance). For the moment let us assume that we are concerned with the standard Normal distribution. Hence, the mean is equal to zero. The shape of the distribution is therefore determined by its spread or the standard deviation. When the standard deviation is small (say 0.5) then the distribution will have a small spread as shown in Figure 3.2.

When the standard deviation is larger (say 1.00) then the spread will obviously be greater (Figure 3.3).

When the standard deviation is larger still (say 2.00) then the normal distribution appears as in Figure 3.4.

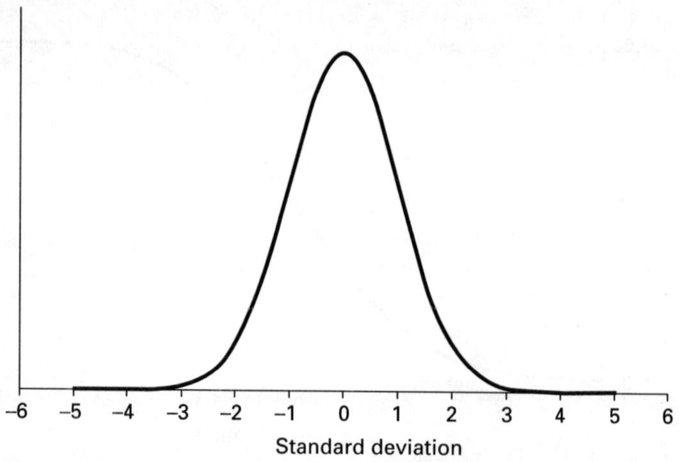

Figure 3.3 Normal distribution with a standard deviation of 1.00

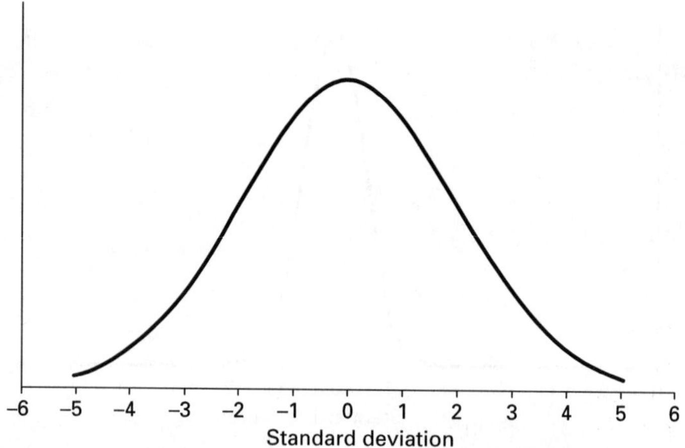

Figure 3.4 Normal distribution with a standard deviation of 2.00

No matter how small or large the standard deviation of the distribution, it is a fact that the area under the curve between −1.96 and +1.96 standard deviations of the mean is equal to 0.95. This means, in essence, that if we were to randomly draw a value of x then there is a 95 per cent probability that its value will be between −1.96 and 1.96 (assuming we are dealing with a standard Normal distribution with a standard deviation equal to 1). If the standard deviation were 2.00 rather than 1.00 then there would be a 95 per cent probability that a randomly drawn value of x would be between −3.92 and 3.92 (2×1.96).

The value of the Normal distribution for the purpose of hypothesis testing is clear. Suppose we have a continuous random variable x that is known to follow a Normal distribution with a mean of zero and a standard deviation equal to 1.00. Now suppose that we are presented with a single value of an unknown variable. How likely is it that the unknown variable is in fact x? If the value of the unknown variable were 2.00 then we could conclude that there is less than a 5 per cent chance that this value belongs to the distribution of x. This is because 95 per cent of the values of x are expected to lie within minus and plus 1.96 standard deviations of the mean (which is zero in this case). Thus, there is a 5 per cent probability that a randomly drawn value of x will be further from the mean than plus or minus 1.96 standard deviations. Strictly speaking, in fact, there is less than a $2\frac{1}{2}$ per cent probability that the variable we are presented with belongs to the distribution of x. This is because $2\frac{1}{2}$ per cent of the values of x will lie to the left of -1.96 standard deviations of the mean and a further $2\frac{1}{2}$ per cent will lie to the right of $+1.96$ standard deviations of it.

Statistical Tests Based on the Normal Distribution – The Z Test

The simple example shown above is, in fact, the first statistical test of significance that we will examine in this chapter. It is known as the Z test. The Z test is the simplest statistical test of significance. It works by calculating the number of standard deviations removed that an observed value is from its 'expected' value.

Earlier it was noted that 95 per cent of the values of a Normally distributed continuous random variable will lie within plus and minus 1.96 standard deviations of the mean of the distribution. It is also the case that 90 per cent of values lie within plus and minus 1.65 standard deviations of the mean and 99 per cent lie within plus and minus 2.58 standard deviations. This information can be used to construct the Z test.

Example

Suppose that we wish to test the hypothesis that open market rents for office space in a local market average to £200 per square metre. The hypothesis can be tested formally by collecting a sample of rents and performing a Z test.

Let us say that information on the rent of 50 offices is collected randomly from the population (all offices in the local market). We find that the mean rent is £215 per square metre and the standard deviation is equal to £50 per square metre.

We can see that the mean of the sample is not equal to £200 per square metre. However, we are interested in the mean of the population, that is the mean rent for all offices in the local market – not just that of the random sample.

If we collected a different sample we might find that the mean is different from £215 per square metre. If we repeatedly carried out random sampling and collected 50 office rents each time then we might easily find that the mean is slightly different each time.

Returning to our current example, how can we tell whether the sample mean of £215 per square metre really is representative of the population? It might be the result of 'chance variation'. To determine whether the difference is 'real' (i.e. likely to be the same in the population as it is in the sample) rather than 'chance', we carry out a hypothesis test.

The Z test works best when we have a large sample because when the Z test is used we are assuming that the distribution of the sample data approximates to the Normal distribution. As a general rule, when n (the number of observations) is at least equal to 30 then we can assume that the distribution of the sampling means approximates to the Normal distribution provided that the distribution is not obviously skewed (assymetrical). The equation for the Z statistic is as follows:

$$z = \frac{\overline{x} - u}{s/\sqrt{n}} \tag{3.1}$$

where

z = Z statistic
$\overline{x}$ = the observed sample mean
u = the hypothesised population mean
n = the total number of observations in the sample
s = estimated standard deviation of the population

We can state the hypothesis formally as follows:

H_0: The sample mean does not differ from the conjectured population mean
H_a: The sample mean differs from the conjectured population mean

Note that the hypothesis is really stated as two mutually exclusive hypotheses. By convention we rarely carry out a direct test on the alternative hypothesis (H_a). Instead, we construct a null hypothesis (the exact opposite of the alternative hypothesis) and test it. If we reject the null hypothesis, then, by definition, we fail to reject the alternative hypothesis. Note also that it is conventional not to accept an alternative hypothesis but to fail to reject it. This may seem like a convoluted process but it is important to remain conscious that hypothesis testing cannot provide definitive answers but only probabilistic answers based on the sample of data to hand. These conventions allow us to bear this fact in mind when undertaking empirical analyses.

For our current example we can calculate the z statistic as follows:

$$z = \frac{215 - 200}{50 \div \sqrt{50}} = 2.121$$

As we noted earlier, the critical value for the Normal distribution at the 5 per cent level of significance is 1.96. In other words, 95 per cent of values in the Normal distribution lie within a range plus and minus 1.96 standard deviations removed from the mean. Our test statistic is greater than 1.96 so the mean office rent from the sample is more than 2.1 standard deviations removed from the hypothesised population mean. Hence, we can reject the null hypothesis that the difference between the observed £215 and the hypothesised £200 per square metre is a consequence of chance variation. We have 95 per cent confidence in this result.

Since the null hypothesis is rejected at the 5 per cent level of significance we know automatically that it would also be rejected at the 10 per cent level of significance. However, what about the 1 per cent level of significance (99 per cent confidence)? Earlier we noted that the critical value for the Normal distribution at the 1 per cent significance level is 2.58. This is in excess of the test statistic so we would not be able to reject the null hypothesis at the 1 per cent level of significance. In other words, we cannot be 99 per cent confident that the population mean is not £200 per square metre since £215 falls into the range plus and minus 2.58 standard deviations removed from this hypothesised mean.

The *t* Distribution

Having briefly examined one of the simplest and most commonly used distributions – the Normal distribution – we turn now to consider the *t* distribution.

The simplest way to conceptualise the *t* distribution is to consider it as a Normal distribution which has been adjusted to take account of the inaccuracies that can arise when dealing with small samples. Earlier we noted that statistical tests based on the Normal distribution tend to work best when a large sample is used and that a sample containing 30 observations is the smallest sample for which the Normal distribution can be used. The problem is that statistical tests based on the Normal distribution are not particularly robust with respect to sample size. In many cases, the *t* distribution provides a more robust alternative to the Normal distribution. Table 3.4 sets out a sample of critical values for the *t* and the Normal distributions. As the figures

Table 3.4 Critical values for the t and Normal distributions

d.f.	*t: 10%*	*t: 5%*	*t: 1%*	*Z: 10%*	*Z: 5%*	*Z: 1%*
1	6.314	12.706	63.656			
2	2.920	4.303	9.925			
3	2.353	3.182	5.841			
4	2.132	2.776	4.604			
5	2.015	2.571	4.032			
				1.645	1.960	2.576
10	1.812	2.228	3.169			
30	1.697	2.042	2.750			
50	1.676	2.009	2.678			
100	1.660	1.984	2.626			
1000	1.646	1.962	2.581			

show, the *t* critical values differ substantially from the Normal distribution when the number of degrees of freedom is small. The differences gradually diminish as the degrees of freedom increase. When around a thousand degrees of freedom are available the difference between *t* and Normal critical values becomes negligible. For this reason, the *t* distribution may safely be used even where a large number of degrees of freedom are available.

The *t* critical values can be used in place of the Z critical values for the purpose of testing an hypothesis concerning a single observation and a conjectured parent distribution. For the case of the previous example, the test statistic was equal to 2.121 and the 5 per cent critical value 1.96. When we use the *t* distribution the test statistic is calculated the same way and its value remains 2.121 although we now refer to it as the *t* statistic. The *t* critical value is 2.009, hence using the *t* distribution we draw the same conclusion: that the difference between £215 and the hypothesised mean of £200 is not statistically significant. Another way to put this is that we cannot rule out the hypothesis that the difference is simply a result of chance variation. Note, however, that if the test statistic were slightly smaller (less than 2.1) then we would continue to reject the null hypothesis using the Normal distribution (Z critical values) but we would fail to reject the null hypothesis using the *t* distribution.

THE CENTRAL LIMIT THEOREM

So far, this chapter has examined hypothesis tests based on the Normal and *t* distributions. As discussed above, the *t* distribution is essentially a Normal distribution that has been adapted to take up inaccuracies introduced by using small samples of data. Other than this fact, the t distribution is similar to the Normal distribution since it is symmetrical and converges with the Normal distribution when large sample sizes are used.

Unfortunately, we will often be faced with data whose distribution could not possibly be described as approximating to the Normal distribution. Skewed distributions, for example, could not be described as Normally distributed since the Normal distribution is symmetrical about its mean. Consider the following example:

Example

Data are collected on the length of time that house buyers live in their properties (in months) before selling and moving to a new property. Data on 100 households are collected and are summarised in Table 3.5. The data are organised in columns in ascending order for convenience.

If we construct a histogram (Figure 3.5) then we can easily see that the data are not Normally distributed. The distribution is skewed – it is relatively common for households to remain in occupation for around 25 to 55 months but the distribution has a long tail with a small number of households remaining in occupation for anything up to 155 months.

Given the distribution of the data to hand we cannot use the Z or t tests to carry out hypothesis testing. Fortunately, thanks to the Central Limit Theorem, it may still be possible to carry out some hypothesis tests.

Suppose that we collected 100 samples each of 100 observations. Instead of using the information on these 10,000 observations we might simply calculate the mean of each of the samples. This will give us a sample of 100 means. The Central Limit Theorem states that this sample of means will

Table 3.5 Households' length of stay before moving

4	14	21	27	33	42	46	51	74	85
4	14	21	27	34	43	46	54	74	93
5	14	23	28	34	43	47	57	75	102
7	17	24	29	34	43	48	58	79	105
7	17	24	29	36	43	48	60	79	130
10	17	25	29	37	44	48	64	80	132
10	18	25	29	37	44	48	66	81	144
11	18	25	29	38	45	49	67	82	144
11	19	26	31	39	45	49	69	83	151
12	21	27	33	42	45	49	72	84	155

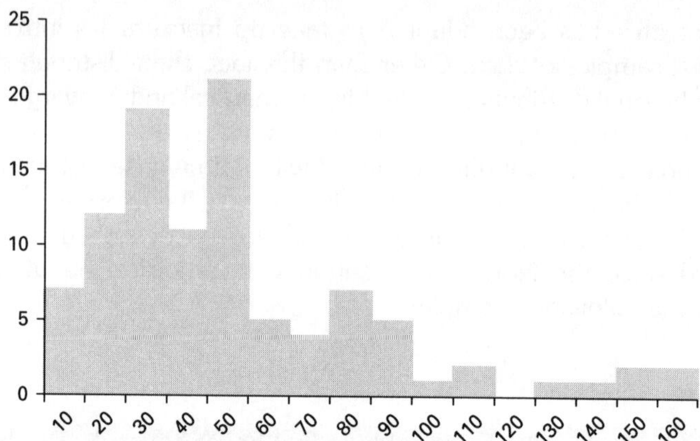

Figure 3.5 *Histogram showing the distribution of households by length of occupation*

be approximately Normally distributed even though the distributions of each of the samples is not. Another way to think of this is to imagine that we randomly select 100 observations from a sample of 10,000. Each time we do this we calculate the mean of the 100 random observations and record it as part of a new sample. If we do this a large number of times then we end up with an approximately Normally distributed sample. However, the new sample is a sample of means rather than a sample of individual observations. The Central Limit Theorem states that the convergence of the distribution of sample of means with the Normal distribution increases as sample size increases. There are two important consequences of this theorem:

(1) Even with distributions that are not Normally distributed we can construct hypothesis tests that concern the distribution's means. This is because the means are drawn from a Normal distribution (the distribution of means).
(2) Larger sample sizes give rise to distributions of means whose properties are more like the Normal distribution than smaller sample sizes. This means, in general, that larger sample sizes offer some protection against error.

COMPARING SAMPLE MEANS: THE PAIRED *t* TEST

Hypothesis tests involving distribution means often use the paired *t* test. The paired *t* test is appropriate when we are constructing a hypothesis about one sample, usually before and after some event or influence. One purpose of such a test is to find out whether the event or influence has had a significant effect. For example, we might use a paired t test to compare the best lap times of a group of athletes before and after a change to their exercise regime to test the effect of the change.

The formula for calculating the t statistic is as follows:

$$t = \frac{\bar{d} - u}{s / \sqrt{n}} \tag{3.2}$$

where

t = t statistic
$\bar{d}$ = observed mean difference, i.e. the sum of $(x_{2i} - x_{1i})$ where x_{2i} is the ith observation of the second sample and x_{1i} is the ith observation of the first sample
u = the hypothesised population mean (normally this is equal to zero)
n = the total number of observations in the sample
s = estimated standard deviation of the population

The procedure for testing a hypothesis is as follows. First, a null and an alternative hypothesis are constructed. Second, the t statistic is calculated using sample data. Third, the null hypothesis is either accepted or rejected, depending on the size of the test statistic.

If the null hypothesis is rejected then we 'fail to reject' the alternative hypothesis. Note that in statistics it is not normally possible to accept our hypothesis because it is being tested using a sample of data rather than the entire population. Instead, we look to reject the null hypothesis. As noted, the null hypothesis is the reverse of the alternative hypothesis.

Example

Suppose we measured the best lap times of professional athletes before and after a change to their exercise regime. We have two samples of data: a set of times before the change and a set of times after the change. Suppose the times, measured in minutes, are as given in Table 3.6. The means of the two samples are not shown in the table but are easily calculated. They are as follows:

$\bar{x}_1$ 1.295 minutes (77.7 seconds)
$\bar{x}_2$ 1.345 minutes (80.7 seconds)

We can see that the mean difference is 0.05 minutes (3 seconds). If we sum the last column in the table then we will arrive at the sum of the squared differences. The sum of the squared differences is equal to 0.017 minutes in this case. Dividing by the number of observations less one $(15 - 1 = 14)$ and taking the square root will yield us the standard deviation of the sample.

$$s = \sqrt{0.017 \div 14} = 0.035$$

Table 3.6 Lap times before and after a regime change

	Before	*After*	*Diff.*	$d_i - \bar{d}$	$(d_i - \bar{d})^2$
1	1.307	1.391	0.084	0.034	0.00115
2	1.302	1.314	0.012	−0.038	0.00145
3	1.274	1.384	0.110	0.060	0.00358
4	1.286	1.307	0.021	−0.029	0.00085
5	1.327	1.327	0.000	−0.050	0.00251
6	1.284	1.324	0.040	−0.010	0.00010
7	1.289	1.334	0.045	−0.005	0.00003
8	1.286	1.358	0.072	0.022	0.00048
9	1.253	1.339	0.086	0.036	0.00129
10	1.323	1.399	0.076	0.026	0.00067
11	1.279	1.305	0.026	−0.024	0.00058
12	1.350	1.387	0.037	−0.013	0.00017
13	1.288	1.365	0.077	0.027	0.00072
14	1.315	1.308	−0.007	−0.057	0.00326
15	1.263	1.336	0.073	0.023	0.00052
$\bar{d}$			0.050		
$\sum(d_i - \bar{d})^2$					0.017

Having carried out these calculations, we are in a position to calculate the t statistic. As noted earlier, the equation is:

$$t = \frac{\bar{d} - u}{s/\sqrt{n}}$$

Hence the t statistic can be calculated as follows:

$$t = \frac{0.05 - 0}{0.035 \div \sqrt{15}} = 5.53$$

As discussed earlier, we are testing the null hypothesis that the lap times before and after the change are equal. It follows that u, the hypothesised mean difference, is set equal to zero.

The next step is to find the critical value for t from a t table. This is found in Appendix 1. We can see that at the 5 per cent level with 14 degrees of freedom the critical value is 2.14. Our test statistic is 5.53. Therefore, we reject the null hypothesis. In other words, we reject the hypothesis that the lap times after the change are the same as the lap times before the change. We fail to reject the alternative hypothesis that the lap times are different.

THE χ-SQUARED DISTRIBUTION

So far this chapter has examined hypothesis tests that draw on numerical data such as commercial property rental values, incomes, house prices, runners' lap times, and so on. In this section we examine the chi-square (pronounced 'kye' square) statistic which is useful for testing hypotheses that draw on categorical data or proportions.

Example

Suppose that we wished to test the hypothesis that commercial property occupiers in the financial services sector are more likely to lease office space constructed between 1990 and 2000 than space constructed between 1980 and 1990. To test this we formally construct null and alternative hypotheses:

H_0: Financial service occupiers are no more likely to take on 1990s than 1980s space
H_a: Financial service occupiers are more likely to take on 1990s than 1980s space

We proceed to collect a sample by tracing firms in the financial service sector that have recently taken on office space. We collect 100 instances or observations and find that 40 firms located in 1980s space and the remaining 60 located in 1990s space.

We also investigate the characteristics of the available (vacant) office properties that have been on the market during the past year and find that there were 400 suitable properties of which 210 were constructed during the 1980s and 190 during the 1990s.

The basic building blocks of the chi-square test are formed by using the data to construct 'expected' and 'observed' proportions. We will examine expected proportions first. If the null hypothesis is valid (should not be rejected) then the firms we have examined should be no more likely to locate in 1980s than 1990s space and vice versa. The expected proportions are as follows:

$$\text{Expected number of firms in 1980s space: } 100 \times \frac{210}{400} = 52.5$$

$$\text{Expected number of firms in 1990s space: } 100 \times \frac{190}{400} = 47.5$$

As noted above, the observed number of firms in 1980s and 1990s space are 60 and 40 respectively. The chi-square statistic is calculated as the sum of squared residuals divided by predictions, or:

$$\chi^2 = \sum \frac{(Observed - Expected)^2}{Expected} \tag{3.3}$$

It can easily be seen from equation (3.3) that the chi-square statistic increases as the differences between observed and expected proportions increase. In other words, the statistic is a proxy for the deviation of the data from the expected state of affairs with a valid null hypothesis. In our example the chi-square statistic can be calculated as follows:

$$\chi^2 = \frac{(60.0 - 52.5)^2}{52.5} + \frac{(40.0 - 47.5)^2}{47.5}$$
$$= 2.26$$

Now that we have a test statistic, formally testing the null hypothesis is a straightforward and familiar procedure. We compare the test statistic with the chi-square critical value. As with the t critical value, we need to know the number of degrees of freedom in order to look up the correct critical value. This is slightly more complicated than calculating degrees of freedom using numerical data.

A degree of freedom can be taken to mean 'a piece of information'. When we are working with continuous numerical data then the total number of degrees of freedom is equal to the total number of observations in the sample, since each value of a continuous random variable may be different and every observation on it therefore represents a new piece of information. In the case of our current example, all of the available information in the data can be completely described simply by knowing the size of the sample and the number of firms in 1980s (or 1990s) space. Since the categories '1980s' and '1990s' are mutually exclusive, they can be described by one binary variable which takes the value 0 or 1. So we could create a variable called X which takes the value 1 for 1980s space and 0 for 1990s space. So the data only contain two genuinely unique pieces of information or degrees of freedom.

The next point to note is that we cannot look up a critical value using the total number of degrees of freedom as a guide. This is because some of the information is effectively used up by producing the test statistic. Usually one degree of freedom is used up when calculating a test statistic though this need not always be the case. When we calculated the expected number of firms in each category of office space we were required to use information on the sample size. This 'used up' one degree of freedom. So we must look up the chi-square critical value with one degree of freedom.

As before, tables of critical values may be found in the appendices. The critical value in this case is 3.84 at the 5 per cent significance level. Since the test statistic does not exceed this we cannot reject the null hypothesis. So on the basis of this dataset we conclude that firms in the financial services sector are no more likely to locate in 1990s than 1980s offices. Although there is a difference between the expected and observed numbers of firms locating in these property categories, the difference is not sufficiently large to be statistically significant.

CONCLUSIONS

The purpose of this chapter is to provide a background, or revision, to some fundamental statistical theory that will be referred to at various points in the remainder of the book. For example, the following chapter provides an introduction to simple and multiple regression models. Regression analyses are used to test hypotheses concerning cause and effect between a variable (the dependent variable) and one or more independent variables. Thus, the discussion in the next chapter assumes that the reader is familiar with basic inferential statistics and procedures for hypothesis testing. Furthermore, inferential statistics and regression models are referred to throughout Chapters 5, 6, 7 and 8 in the contexts of commercial real estate rent determination and forecasting, analysis of house prices and the analysis of real estate markets at the local level. The content of the present chapter is fairly basic although some elementary background knowledge of descriptive statistics is assumed. Although some of the hypothesis tests examined are of interest in their own right, the main value of the material in this chapter is in providing a foundation for later material. In particular, subsequent chapters on regression analysis and econometric modelling assume a thorough knowledge of sampling theory and hypothesis testing. Consequently, readers who are not comfortable with material presented in this chapter are advised to re-read it or cross-refer to an introductory statistics textbook prior to reading the following two chapters.

4

Simple and Multiple Regression Analysis

INTRODUCTION

This chapter introduces regression analysis and regression models. Regression models are also known as econometric models. In simple terms, the word 'econometric' might be taken to mean 'the application of mathematical methods to model economic phenomena'. Hence, regression methods may be used to construct a mathematical model to represent an economic theory or a set of economic concepts.

A model is, or should be, a simplification of reality that retains the important aspects of whatever aspect of reality it is that we are interested in understanding. A model has two underlying purposes. First, it should be capable of satisfactorily *explaining* how our chosen aspect of reality works. For example, if we are interested in modelling the office user market (office rents or rental growth), then our underlying interest is in understanding how supply and demand are determined and how they interact to give rise to the determination of either rental values or rental growth. Second, the model should be capable of satisfactory *prediction*. It is important to note at this point that a *prediction* should be distinguished from a *forecast*. Predictions usually refer to cases or observations within the sample used to construct a model. Forecasts usually concern cases or observations from outside the sample used to construct a model. These aspects of regression models are discussed in more detail later in the book.

CONSTRUCTING A SIMPLE MODEL – THE STRAIGHT LINE EQUATION

Consider the equation of a straight line:

$$Y = a + bX \tag{4.1}$$

The equation describes the relationship between two variables X and Y. Let us refer to the terms a and b as the parameters. Specifically, a is the intercept term or constant and b is the slope or gradient of the straight line.

The straight line equation may be used to construct a very simple rent determination model. This is illustrated by the fictitious example given in Table 4.1. Suppose that we collected data on rents and floor areas for industrial property in a local town. The data are plotted on a scatter plot. Each industrial unit has a rent and a floor area. These observations are plotted in Figure 4.1.

Table 4.1 Rent and floor area data

Area (sq. m)	*Rent (£ p.a.)*
400	9,000
450	9,750
500	10,500
550	11,250
600	12,000
650	12,750
700	13,500
750	14,250
800	15,000
850	15,750

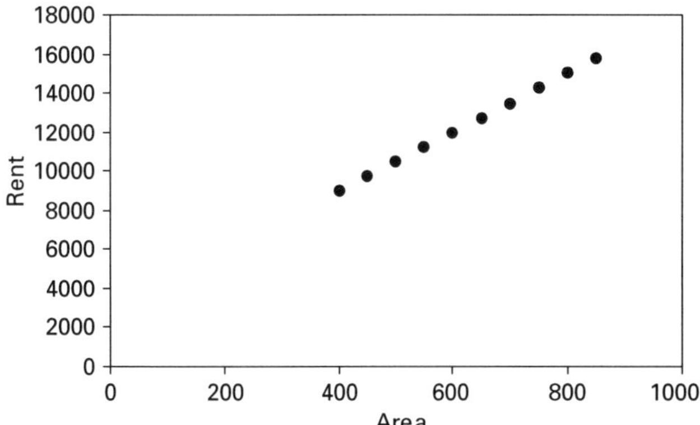

Figure 4.1 *Scatter plot of industrial unit rent and floor area*

It can easily be seen from Figure 4.1 that the relationship between rent and floor area is both linear and exact. We can calculate the parameters, a and b, of the straight line equation from the data. First, b is the slope of the line and therefore measures the change in the Y variable (Rent in this example) resulting from a unit change in the X variable (Area in this example). Since all of the data points lie on the same straight line, the value for the parameter b can be calculated using any two of the observed data points:

$$b = \frac{Y_2 - Y_1}{X_2 - X_1}$$

Using the first and last observations:

$$b = \frac{15750 - 9000}{850 - 400} = 15$$

The value for the parameter a can now be calculated using any one of the observed data points. Since a is the intercept term it is the value of the Y variable when the X variable is equal to zero. Using the first observation (Rent = £9000; Area = 400):

$$\begin{aligned} Y &= a + bX \\ 9000 &= a + 15(400) \\ a &= 9000 - 6000 = 3000 \end{aligned}$$

The results are easily interpreted. We have established that the rent for any of the industrial units examined is equal to £3000 plus a further £15 for each one square metre of floor area.

THE REGRESSION LINE

The example shown above demonstrates how a simple model might be constructed between two variables. It also provides an introduction to simple regression analysis because the essence of regression analysis is about constructing and estimating a model that takes the form of a straight line equation. Clearly, in the example shown above, all data points happen to fall exactly on the same line. We can say that the relationship between the two variables is exact. Consider a modified version of the previous example. Once again, suppose that we collected data on rents and floor areas for industrial property in a local town (Table 4.2).

As with the previous example, let us assume that we wish to construct a simple rent determination model using the floor areas of industrial units

Table 4.2 Revised rent and floor area data

Area (sq. m)	*Rent (£ p.a.)*
400	8,920
450	10,740
500	9,450
550	13,120
600	10,620
650	13,205
700	12,730
750	12,375
800	16,280
850	13,030

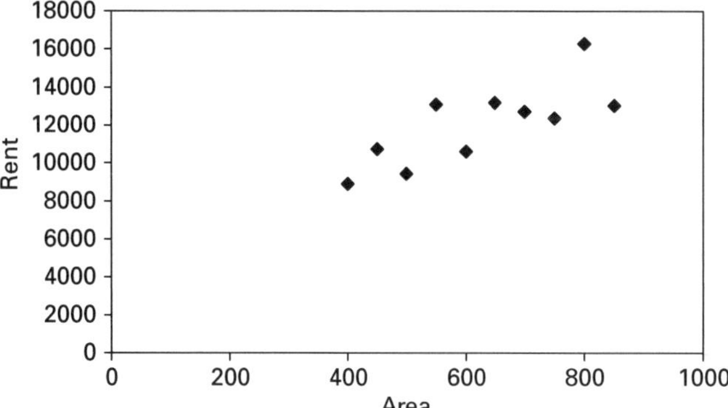

Figure 4.2 *Scatter plot of industrial unit rent and floor area (revised figures)*

to predict their rent levels. Our first step is to plot the collected data on a scatter plot (Figure 4.2).

This time we can see from Figure 4.2 that there is no exact linear relationship between area and rent. Therefore, the equation $Y = a + bX$ cannot be used to explain the level of rent using floor area as it was in the previous example. This is because there is no intercept term a or line slope b that is common to all of the data points. The problem with our model ($Y = a + bX$) is that for every given data point or observation the model is either true or not true. Since the model postulates an exact relationship between the two variables we must reject the model if we have even one data point for which the model does not hold. In the second example the rent and floor area data we collected do not conform perfectly to a straight line relationship. Yet it

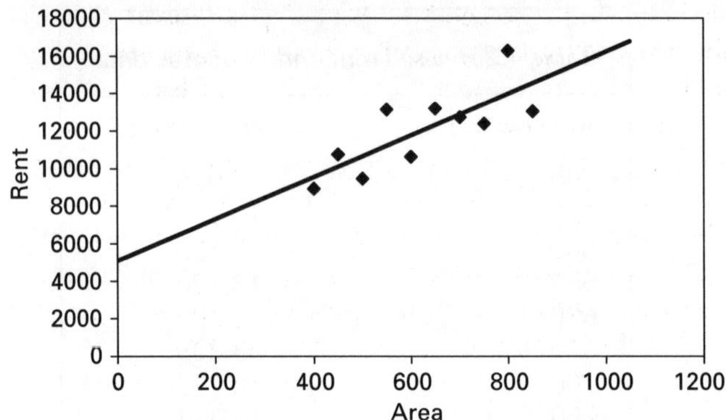

Figure 4.3 *Scatter plot and a line of best fit*

is also evident from an examination of Figure 4.2 that the points on the scatter plot do approximately form a straight line.

Let us assume, therefore, that we are no longer concerned with estimating an exact relationship between rent and floor area but may be content if we can estimate a satisfactory approximate relationship. For the time being we leave the terms 'satisfactory' and 'approximate' undefined. We will return to the issue of how to define 'satisfactory' later in this chapter.

For now, the solution is to estimate the equation of a straight line that 'best fits' the data. That is, we determine a line of best fit. This is shown in Figure 4.3.

The behaviour of the fitted line can be described by the following equation:

$$\hat{Y}_i = a + bX_i \tag{4.2a}$$

or

$$Y_i = a + bX_i + u_i \tag{4.2b}$$

where

$\hat{Y}_i$ = the estimated value of the dependent variable for the ith observation
a = constant (the same for all observations)
b = the slope or gradient of the regression line (the same for all observations)
X_i = the value of the independent variable for the ith observation
u_i = the error term or residual for the ith observation

It should be noted that the regression equation now contains a new term (u_i). This is the error term or disturbance term. Since the regression equation is a line of best fit we cannot hope that it will perfectly explain the relationship between the dependent and independent variable. Another way to think about this is to simply say that the error term is a convenience that lets us avoid the need to reject the model out of hand whenever we find a case or observation for which the equation does not exactly hold.

The regression equation shown above provides us with a predicted value of the dependent variable (Y) given a value of the independent variable (X) for each observation. However, the predicted values of Y for the i observations will not be exactly the same as the actual or observed values of Y. The difference between the estimated (predicted) and the actual (observed) value of Y for each observation is captured in the error term. Hence we can say that $\hat{Y}_i = Y_i + u_i$.

ESTIMATING THE REGRESSION LINE – LEAST SQUARES

In the previous section we noted that a regression line is a line of best fit. In this section we consider what a line of best fit actually is and how we arrive at the line of best fit using a given sample of data.

The key to determining the line of best fit lies in the error term (u_i). A line of best fit is the line that minimises the amount of unexplained variation in the dependent variable (Y). In other words, the line of best fit, or regression line, is the line that minimises the errors (u_i). In fact, the regression line is estimated by minimising the sum of the squared vertical deviations of the i predicted values of Y from the actual or observed values of Y. The sum of the squared vertical deviations is expressed as:

$$\sum_{i=1}^{n} (Y_i - \hat{Y}_i)^2 \tag{4.3}$$

If this expression were converted to words then it would be read as *the sum of i (where i ranges from 1 to n) squared deviations of the estimated value of Y from the actual value of Y*. For our current rent and floor area example, the vertical deviations of the estimated from the actual values of Y are shown in Figure 4.4.

Given that the regression line is estimated by minimising the sum of the squared deviations, expression (4.3) can be used to estimate values for the parameters (a and b) of the regression line. The formulae for a and b are as follows:

$$b = \frac{\sum X_i Y_i - \frac{\sum X_i \sum Y_i}{n}}{\sum X_i^2 - \frac{(\sum X_i)^2}{n}} \tag{4.4}$$

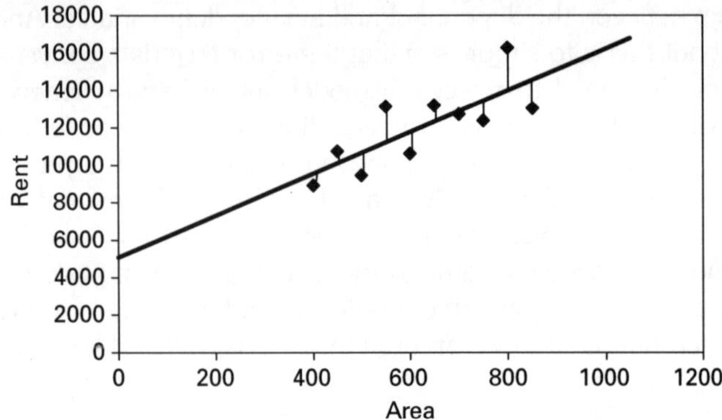

Figure 4.4 *The regression line and vertical deviations of estimated from actual values of Y*

$$a = \overline{Y} - b\overline{X} \tag{4.5}$$

where

$\overline{Y}$ = the mean value of Y
$\overline{X}$ = the mean value of X

Returning to our rent and floor area example, we can estimate the parameters a and b by using formulas (4.4) and (4.5). The process is simplified in Table 4.3.

First, we estimate the parameter b. To do this we use equation (4.4):

$$b = \frac{\sum X_i Y_i - \dfrac{\sum X_i \sum Y_i}{n}}{\sum X_i^2 - \dfrac{(\sum X_i)^2}{n}}$$

$$b = \frac{77589000 - \dfrac{752937500}{10}}{4112500 - \dfrac{6250^2}{10}}$$

$$b = \frac{2295250}{206250} = 11.128$$

In order to estimate the parameter a we use equation (4.5):

$$a = \overline{Y} - b\overline{X}$$
$$a = 12047 - (11.128 \times 625) \cong 5092$$

Table 4.3 Calculations to estimate regression equation parameters

Rent Y_i	Area X_i	X_iY_i		X_i^2
8,920	400	3,568,000		160,000
10,740	450	4,833,000		202,500
9,450	500	4,725,000		250,000
13,120	550	7,216,000		302,500
10,620	600	6,372,000		360,000
13,205	650	8,583,250		422,500
12,730	700	8,911,000		490,000
12,375	750	9,281,250		562,500
16,280	800	13,024,000		640,000
13,030	850	11,075,500		722,500
120,470	6,250	77,589,000	752,937,500	4,112,500
ΣY_i	ΣX_i	ΣX_iY_i	$\Sigma X_i \Sigma Y_i$	ΣX_i^2

In practice it is highly unlikely that any researcher would choose to compute the parameters manually as shown in the example above. The parameters or line of best fit are easily estimated using a computer package for the purpose. There are numerous software packages available and even a non-specialist package such as Microsoft Excel may be used to construct and estimate very simple ordinary least squares (OLS) regression models.

TESTING GOODNESS OF FIT

In the previous section we estimated the parameters of a regression equation designed to model the determination of industrial unit rental value. Using floor area as the sole independent or explanatory variable we estimated the following equation:

$$Y_i = 5092 + 11.128X_i + u_i$$

or

$$\hat{Y}_i = 5092 + 11.128X_i \tag{4.6}$$

In this section we are concerned with measuring the explanatory power of our model. We can see from an examination of Figures 4.3 and 4.4 that the observed rents/area plots are all close to the regression line (the line of best fit). It might be reasonable to suppose that our model is effective in explaining industrial unit rental values and effective in predicting the rental values of industrial units similar to those described in the sample data. However, we do not have a measure of just how good the model is at explaining and predicting. The drawback with including the error term in the straight line equation is that the equation will always 'fit' the data, that is, the equation or model will by construction always be true for every data point.

It is obvious that when data points lie close to the regression line then the errors or residuals will be small relative to the X variable. When the data points are widely dispersed about the regression line then the residuals will be relatively large. We can construct a suitable measure of goodness of fit, that is the model's explanatory power, by calculating what proportion of the total variation in the dependent variable is explained by the regression equation. We define the total variation in the dependent variable Y as follows:

$$\sum(Y_i - \bar{Y})^2 \tag{4.7}$$

This is known as the total sum of squares (TSS) because it measures the dispersion of the observed values for Y about the mean value of Y. We define the explained variation in the dependent variable Y as follows:

$$\sum(\hat{Y}_i - \bar{Y})^2 \tag{4.8}$$

This is known as the regression sum of squares (RSS) because it measures the dispersion of the estimated values for Y about the mean value of Y. Finally, we define the unexplained variation in the dependent variable Y as follows:

$$\sum(Y_i - \hat{Y}_i)^2 \tag{4.9}$$

This is known as the error sum of squares (ESS) because it measures the dispersion of the observed values for Y about the estimated values for Y.

Our measure of goodness of fit is known as the *coefficient of determination* and is denoted R^2. It is calculated as follows:

$$R^2 = \frac{RSS}{TSS} \tag{4.10a}$$

or

$$R^2 = 1 - \frac{ESS}{TSS} \tag{4.10b}$$

The R^2 or R square statistic measures the proportion of variation in the dependent variable that is explained by the regression equation. It can be

Table 4.4 Calculations to estimate coefficient of determination

Predicted $\hat{Y}_i$	*Mean* $\overline{Y}$	$\hat{Y}_i - \overline{Y}$	*Observed* Y_i	*Mean* $\overline{Y}$	$Y_i - \overline{Y}$
9,543	12,047	6,269,014	8,920	12,047	9,778,129
10,100	12,047	3,792,367	10,740	12,047	1,708,249
10,656	12,047	1,934,881	9,450	12,047	6,744,409
11,212	12,047	696,557	13,120	12,047	1,151,329
11,769	12,047	77,395	10,620	12,047	2,036,329
12,325	12,047	77,395	13,205	12,047	1,340,964
12,882	12,047	696,557	12,730	12,047	466,489
13,438	12,047	1,934,881	12,375	12,047	107,584
13,994	12,047	3,792,367	16,280	12,047	17,918,289
14,551	12,047	6,269,014	13,030	12,047	966,289
Totals	RSS	25,540,429	–	TSS	42,218,060

read as a percentage. Clearly, when data points lie close to the regression line then the variance explained by the line will be fairly close to the total variance in the data and the *R* square will be large. When the data are widely dispersed about the line then the *R* square will be small. By construction the *R* square statistic must range between 0 and 1.

If we return to the industrial unit rent and floor area example we can calculate R^2 (the coefficient of determination). As before we simplify this task by setting out the necessary calculations in columns. This is shown in Table 4.4.

Since R^2 (the coefficient of determination) is equal to the ratio of the explained to total variation (RSS ÷ TSS) we can easily calculate that it is equal to 0.605 in this particular case. In other words, the regression equation explains approximately 60 per cent of the variation in industrial unit rents. At this point the first weakness in the *R* square statistic becomes apparent: there is no definitive guide to interpretation. It is left to the judgement of the researcher to decide how low the *R* square must be before the model should be rejected on the grounds that it does not adequately explain the data. However, there are some general guidelines to interpretation that will be examined later.

TESTING THE SIGNIFICANCE OF PARAMETER ESTIMATES

So far we have paid relatively little attention to the disturbance term other than to say that its inclusion in the regression equation permits us to consider an approximate, rather than an exact, relationship between two variables. We also know from the last section that when the residuals are large (in relation to the X variable) then the R square statistic will be small. However, the behaviour of the residuals is very important in helping us to evaluate whether a model is valid. In simple regression analysis there are a number of assumptions about the error term. If these assumptions hold then it is possible to construct hypothesis tests on the estimated parameters. Two of these assumptions are examined in this section. Others are examined later in the chapter.

The first assumption is that the error term (u) has a zero mean. Another way to put this is that the expected value $E(u_i)$ is zero – we expect the value of the error term to be zero for each observation. While this is unlikely to occur on an observation by observation basis, the deviations of the error terms will be either positive or negative and the overall mean will be zero.

The second assumption is that the error term is Normally distributed. This means that there will be as many positive as negative values while the majority of the i residuals will be distributed closely around the mean (which is zero). To put this another way, we assume that the residuals are much more likely to be small rather than large and are equally likely to be positive or negative (see Chapter 2 for a discussion on probability and the properties of the Normal distribution).

When we put assumptions one and two together then we can say that $u \sim N(0, \sigma^2)$ or that the disturbance term is distributed Normally and has an expected value of zero and a variance equal to σ^2.

It may seem strange, at this point, to spend time devising an additional test since the regression equation contains only one independent variable (X) and we have the R square statistic which can be used to measure the proportion of variation in Y that is explained by the equation. There is a good reason why an additional test is required. The R square statistic measures the proportion of variation explained by the entire equation and not specifically by the independent (X) variable. This is of relatively minor importance at this stage but, as we shall see later in the chapter, this becomes important when we introduce additional independent variables to the equation. When we have a regression equation containing more than one such variable then it is desirable that we should have a statistic that measures the significance of each variable individually as well as the equation as a whole. Furthermore, a statistical test of the significance specifically of the parameter of the explanatory variable is desirable even when there is only one such variable, since it can be used to confirm, or otherwise, that any explanatory power that the model possesses is derived from the variable rather than the constant. Such circumstances might arise, for example, where the parameters of a model are estimated

Table 4.5 Calculations to assist in the estimation of t statistics

(1) Y_i	(2) X_i	(3) $\hat{Y}_i$	(4) e_i	(5) e_i^2	(6) X_i^2	(7) $(X_i - \bar{X})^2$
8,920	400	9,543	−623	388,378	160,000	50,625
10,740	450	10,100	640	410,112	202,500	30,625
9,450	500	10,656	−1,206	1,454,436	250,000	15,625
13,120	550	11,212	1,908	3,638,938	302,500	5,625
10,620	600	11,769	−1,149	1,319,741	360,000	625
13,205	650	12,325	880	774,048	422,500	625
12,730	700	12,882	−152	22,983	490,000	5,625
12,375	750	13,438	−1,063	1,129,969	562,500	15,625
16,280	800	13,994	2,286	5,223,967	640,000	30,625
13,030	850	14,551	−1,521	2,312,833	722,500	50,625
Totals	–	–	0	16,675,405	4,112,500	206,250

using data in which there is relatively little variation in the dependent variable.

As noted above, provided the residuals are distributed Normally and have an expected value of zero, then we can construct hypothesis tests about the parameter estimates. The test we are going to use produces a test statistic known as the *t* statistic or *t* ratio and is derived directly from the standard deviations of the parameter estimates and the residuals. To calculate these standard deviations the first step is to calculate the fitted or predicted values using equation (4.6). The difference between the observed value of Y_i and our predicted value is the error or residual. We will refer to the errors as e_i from this point on. Table 4.5 sets out the predicted values together with the residuals and squared residuals.

We are particularly interested in columns 4, 5, 6 and 7. Column (4) sets out the sum of the *n* residuals (e_i) and the sum of the squared residuals is set out in column (5). Column (6) measures the sum of the squared values of the *X* variable while column (7) measures the sum of the squared deviations between *X* and its mean. Hence, the totals in these columns are defined as follows:

Column (4) Σe_i

(5) Σe_i^2

(6) ΣX_i^2

(7) $\Sigma (X_i - \bar{X})^2$

We cannot calculate the (population) residual variance directly but it can be estimated using the sample data:

$$\sigma_u^2 = s_u^2 = \frac{\sum e_i^2}{n-k} \tag{4.11}$$

$$s_u^2 = \frac{16,675,405}{10-2} \cong 2,084,425$$

where

σ_u^2 = population variance of the disturbance term u.
s_u^2 = an estimate of the population variance of the disturbance term.
n = number of observations in the sample (10 in this example).
k = number of parameters estimated (2 in this example: a and b).

The variance of the estimate of the parameter a can be found as follows:

$$s_a^2 = \frac{s_u^2 \sum X_i^2}{n\sum(X_i - \bar{X})^2}$$

$$= \frac{2,084,425 \times 4,112,500}{10 \times 206,250} \cong 4,156,217 \tag{4.12}$$

Finally, the variance of the estimate of the parameter b can be found as follows:

$$s_b^2 = \frac{s_u^2}{\sum(X_i - \bar{X})^2}$$

$$= \frac{2,084,425}{206,250} \cong 10.1 \tag{4.13}$$

In summary,

$s_u^2 = 2,084,425$ so $s_u \cong 1,443.75$
$s_a^2 = 4,156,217$ so $s_a \cong 2,038.68$
$s_b^2 = 10.1$ so $s_b \cong 3.18$

Having obtained the standard errors of the parameter estimates the task of testing their significance is now very straightforward. We test one parameter estimate at a time and the null hypothesis is that the population or 'true' value of the parameter is equal to zero. This is tested using the t statistic as discussed earlier. For the parameter a the test statistic is:

$$t = \frac{\hat{a} - a}{s_a}$$
$$= \frac{5{,}092 - 0}{2{,}038.68} \cong 2.498$$

For the parameter b the test statistic is:

$$t = \frac{\hat{b} - b}{s_b}$$
$$= \frac{11.128 - 0}{2.498} \cong 4.455$$

Note that the null hypothesis is that the population parameters are zero. With 8 degrees of freedom the t critical value is 2.31 at the 5 per cent significance level and 3.36 at the 1 per cent significance level. We can see that both t statistics exceed the 5 per cent critical value while the test statistic for the parameter b also exceeds the 1 per cent critical value. We can conclude, therefore, that it is highly unlikely that the true values of the parameters are equal to zero. Since we reject the null hypothesis that the parameter b is equal to zero then we can also say that there is a statistically significant relationship between floor area and rent.

An alternative way to view this is to simply suppose that there are n estimates of each parameter (one for every case or observation in the sample of data used to estimate the model parameters). The overall parameter estimate is a mean of the n estimates. When we divide this mean estimate by its standard error then we obtain the t ratio. When we consider the null hypothesis that the 'true' value or population value of a given parameter is equal to zero then we can look to the t ratio to inform our judgement about how likely this hypothesis is. The t ratio essentially measures the number of standard errors that the parameter estimate is from zero. If this estimate is further from zero than (+/−) around 2 standard errors (with 30 degrees of freedom) then we can reject this null hypothesis at the 5 per cent significance level. In other words, if we repeatedly collected different samples and re-estimated the parameter then our parameter estimate would be around zero about 5 per cent of the time.

The estimated parameters of independent variables are often tested at the 5 per cent level of significance though in some cases the 1 per cent significance level may be preferable. At the 5 per cent level the critical value for the t statistic is exactly equal to 2.00 with 60 degrees of freedom and theoretically reduces to 1.96 with an infinitely large number of degrees of freedom. A common rule-of-thumb is that an independent variable is considered significant when its t statistic is equal to 2 or more. As noted, this rule cannot be used when there are fewer than 60 degrees of freedom. In order to obtain 60 degrees of freedom the regression parameters must be estimated using a sample with 60 observations plus one additional observation for each parameter to be estimated.

MULTIPLE REGRESSION ANALYSIS

Simple regression has the potential to be a useful tool in applied real estate research but it is clearly limited by the very fact that the method is geared towards deterministic relationships between two variables. The extension to simple regression, multiple regression analysis, is used more widely in property market research. It differs from simple regression analysis in that more than one explanatory or independent variable is used to explain and predict the dependent variable. The underlying assumption here is that a combination of independent variables jointly determines the dependent variable. As a consequence, multiple regression methods are an attractive research tool for those wishing to model economic phenomena, including real estate market behaviour. Capital and rental values, as well as growth, yields and development activity, are likely to be influenced by a number of different factors, and models designed to explain and predict such variables are examined in detail later in this book.

If we refer back to the very simple industrial unit rent determination example examined earlier in the chapter then it should be immediately clear that the model might be improved by the inclusion of additional independent variables in the regression equation. Although it is likely that there will be some relationship between unit size and total rent, other factors are also likely to influence rent. Expanding the specification of the model by including additional independent variables could give rise to a better model both theoretically and empirically.

In the simple industrial rent example we might consider the model better theoretically if, as a result of respecification, the equation is more plausible. In other words, a model that is good theoretically is one that accords well with the economic theory upon which it is based. If, as a result of respecification or the inclusion of additional explanatory variables, the explanatory and predictive powers of the model increase, then we may be able to say that the model has been improved empirically. Note that there is more to an empirically 'good' model than simply explanatory and predictive power. The question of what makes a model good empirically is considered in some detail in the remainder of this chapter.

THE ADJUSTED R^2 STATISTIC

As noted earlier we have focused on the R^2 statistic so far as a measure of goodness of fit. In this section we consider two additional measures of goodness of fit or the explanatory and predictive powers of a regression model whose parameters we have estimated.

In multiple regression analysis it is more usual to use the adjusted R^2 or 'R bar square' statistic rather than the R^2 statistic. The main reason for this is that using the R^2 statistic to measure the explanatory and predictive power of a multiple regression model is a flawed practice since its value cannot reduce, but may improve, with the inclusion of additional independent variables. We can see that this is the case by a cursory examination of equation (4.10b) since the calculation to obtain the statistic imposes no penalty on the number of explanatory variables included in a regression equation – it is a simple proportion of explained to total variation in the dependent variable.

The fact that the R^2 statistic cannot reduce with the inclusion of more explanatory variables does not matter in simple regression analysis in which the regression equation, by definition, contains only one independent variable. However, in multiple regression analysis it is possible to 'improve' a model (in terms of the R^2) by simply adding more explanatory variables. There are two reasons why this is undesirable.

First, seeking to improve a model's R^2 through the addition of more explanatory variables, possibly with little theoretical justification, is not in keeping with good research practice. Good research practice involves the construction and specification of a regression model by drawing on economic theory. Almost inevitably, the business of estimating a regression model is likely to involve several stages of empirical work in which the equation may be modified or respecified in each stage in an effort to improve the goodness of fit and/or reduce or eliminate empirical problems. There is a, sometimes fine, line between this normal process of model testing, improvement and respecification and an unashamedly 'data first' approach. While the former is generally thought to be acceptable, the latter is not.

The second reason why it is undesirable to use a goodness of fit statistic that does not penalise the inclusion of variables that add little or nothing to the explanatory powers of a model is more practical. We know that the significance of the individual parameter estimates can be tested using t statistics and that, consequently, the t statistics may be used as a guide to fine-tuning or re-specifying a model. It is not logical that our measure of goodness of fit should be the same no matter how many statistically insignificant explanatory variables are included in the regression equation.

Accordingly, it is usual to adopt the adjusted R^2. The main difference between the R^2 and the adjusted R^2 (R bar square) statistic is that the latter effectively imposes a penalty for the inclusion of independent variables that add little or nothing to the explanatory power of the regression equation. The R bar square statistic is calculated as follows:

$$\overline{R}^2 = 1 - (1 - R^2)\frac{N-1}{N-k} \tag{4.14}$$

where

N = number of observations
k = number of independent variables

There are no circumstances in which R bar square can exceed R square but the two statistics will be equal when k, the number of independent variables, is equal to 1. When k is greater than 1 then the R bar square will be smaller than R^2 if the additional variable(s) do not increase the ratio of the explained to total variation in the dependent variable. The main advantage of using the adjusted R^2 statistic to measure goodness of fit is that the statistic may either increase or decrease with the addition of a new explanatory variable. Like the R^2 statistic, adjusted R^2 cannot exceed 1. However, it is not restricted to a minimum of zero. Hence, it is possible to obtain a negative adjusted R^2.

THE *F* STATISTIC

The F statistic is used to test whether the overall regression equation is statistically significant. In other words, the null hypothesis is that all of the equation parameters are equal to zero. If we reject this hypothesis then we fail to reject the alternative hypothesis that the equation is of some (though possibly relatively little) use in explaining and predicting the dependent variable. The F statistic is calculated as follows:

$$F_{k-1,\,n-k} = \frac{R^2/(k-1)}{(1-R^2)/(n-k)} \tag{4.15}$$

The critical value for the test statistic is found in the F distribution with degrees of freedom equal to the number of parameters less one (numerator) and the number of observations less the number of parameters (denominator). Based on the earlier industrial unit rent example, there are 10 observations and 2 parameters so the F statistic is calculated as follows:

$$F_{k-1,\,n-k} = \frac{0.605/(2-1)}{(1-0.605)/(10-2)} \cong 12.25$$

The 1 per cent F critical value with 1 and 8 degrees of freedom is 11.26 so we can reject the null hypothesis at the 1 per cent level of significance. In other words, we fail to reject the alternative hypothesis that the equation is of some use in explaining/predicting the dependent variable.

MULTIPLE REGRESSION AND *t* STATISTICS

The use and interpretation of t statistics is more important in multiple than simple regression analysis. In simple regression analysis it is implicit that the independent variable is statistically significant if the model has a good fit (high R^2 and F statistics). In multiple regression analysis it is possible to specify and estimate a model which has a good fit but in which relatively few of the explanatory variables are significant. It is also possible to estimate a model which has a poor fit but in which several of the explanatory variables are statistically significant.

An examination of the t statistics for the estimated regression parameters permits us to determine which of the explanatory variables are significant. Variables that are not significant are normally dropped (removed from the equation) and the analysis is repeated. Removing insignificant explanatory variables is likely to improve the goodness of fit but may increase the risk of introducing bias. This is discussed in more detail later in the book.

CROSS-SECTIONAL, TIME SERIES AND PANEL MODELS

So far this chapter has examined the basic concepts of simple and multiple regression and introduced a number of the assumptions that underpin such models and some test statistics used to evaluate them empirically. At this point it should be noted that there are two broad types of regression models: cross-sectional models which are concerned with relationships at a fixed point in time and time series models which are concerned with relationships over time.

For cross-sectional models each observation may represent an individual, a household or a firm. Alternatively, an observation may represent one property or premises, a neighbourhood, a market, a local economy, a regional economy and so on. For the sake of simplicity we will assume that a cross-sectional model is concerned with a sample of data measured to a defined unit of spatial aggregation. Clearly it is improper to construct an estimate a model using a mix of spatial aggregations so a cross-sectional model may be concerned with either individual premises or individual markets but never a mix.

For time series models each observation relates to one of a series of equally spaced intervals in time: years, quarters, months and so on. Fairly recently a third broad type of regression model has enjoyed increasing usage in applied real estate research. This is the panel or pooled time series cross-sectional model. Such models share the properties of time series and cross-sectional models.

A general specification for a simple cross-sectional model is as follows:

$$Y_i = \beta_0 + \beta_1 X_{1i} + \beta_2 X_{2i} + \beta_3 X_{3i} + \cdots + \beta_k X_{ki} + u_i \quad (4.16)$$

Note that the parameters are now all denoted β by convention. This primarily reflects that fact that there is no theoretical limit to the number of explanatory variables that may be included in a regression equation (although there is an empirical limit defined by the number of observations less 1). Note also that by convention the dependent and independent variables have the subscript i and the disturbance term is denoted u. The errors or residuals are denoted e_i. There are k parameters and n observations or cases (data points). A general specification for a simple time series model is as follows:

$$Y_t = \beta_0 + \beta_1 X_{1t} + \beta_2 X_{2t} + \beta_3 X_{3t} + \cdots + \beta_k X_{kt} + \nu_t \quad (4.17)$$

This time by convention the dependent and independent variables have the subscript t and the disturbance term is denoted ν. A general specification for a simple panel model is as follows:

$$Y_{it} = \beta_0 + \beta_1 X_{1it} + \beta_2 X_{2it} + \beta_3 X_{3it} + \cdots + \beta_k X_{kit} + \nu_{it} \quad (4.18)$$

Note that this specification is essentially time series but with more than one cross-sectional or spatial dimension. In other words, the specification is basically for a time series model but the parameters are estimated using data for a number of countries, regions, cities or whatever unit of spatial aggregation defines the data.

FURTHER ASSUMPTIONS, BIAS, MISSPECIFICATION AND DIAGNOSTIC TESTING

Earlier in the chapter we examined two important assumptions about the error term or residuals of a regression equation. These were:

(1) the error has an expected value (mean) of zero; and
(2) the errors are Normally distributed.

To these assumptions we can now add:

(3) the errors have constant variance;
(4) the independent variables are not correlated with the errors; and
(5) there is no exact linear relationship between the independent variables.

When estimating and empirically evaluating a regression model it is of paramount importance that these assumptions should be satisfied. To understand why this is so, and to understand the consequences of not satisfying these assumptions, we need to return to some basic econometric theory.

When the errors are not Normally distributed

The ordinary least squares (OLS) estimators are best linear unbiased estimators (BLUE) according to the Gauss-Markov theorem where 'best' means minimum variance. This means that the fitted or predicted values of the regression parameters are unbiased estimates of the true or population parameters provided that the five assumptions are not violated. If one or more of the assumptions is violated then there are potential knock-on effects, notably affecting the standard errors. The regression errors will, by construction, have a mean equal to zero so assumption (1) will never, in practice, be violated. However, it is not uncommon to find that the errors are not Normally distributed meaning that assumption (2) has been violated. This casts doubt, in particular, on the standard errors and increases the risk of wrongly rejecting one or more null hypotheses regarding the significance of the parameter estimates. In other words, the estimated model may appear better than it really is.

When the errors do not have constant variance

Another common general problem exists where a relationship exists between one or more independent variables and the errors. If this happens it means that the errors do not have a constant variance and, hence, assumption (3) is violated. In these circumstances the errors are known as heteroscedastic and the problem is referred to as heteroscedasticity. An example is shown in Figure 4.5.

In Figure 4.5(a) the absolute value of the errors increases with X so we cannot say that the errors have a constant variance. Similarly, in Figures 4.5(b) and 4.5(c) there is evidence of heteroscedasticity.

A symptom of heteroscedasticity is incorrect estimates of the standard errors with a knock-on effect to significance tests. In other words, when we have a problem with heteroscedasticity then we can no longer rely on the goodness of fit and significance test statistics.

The examples of heteroscedasticity shown demonstrate the problem in a simple illustrative way. In practice it is not desirable to base an assessment of the behaviour of errors on a simple scatterplot and there are statistical tests for heteroscedasticity. These, together with common solutions to the problem, are examined in more detail later in the book.

(a)

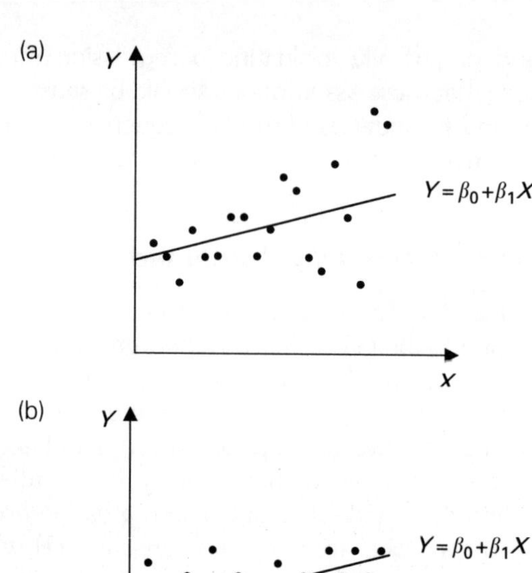

(b)

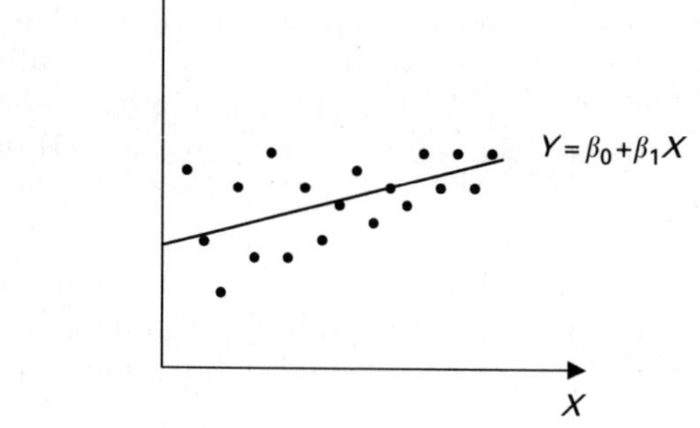

(c)

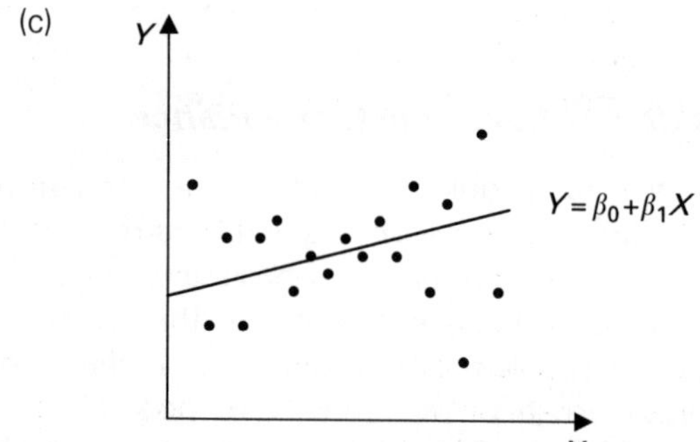

Figure 4.5 *Heteroscedastic disturbances*

When the errors are correlated with respect to time

Correlation of the errors over time is known as autocorrelation or serial correlation. This problem affects mainly time series models, primarily because there is an expectation that data will be ordered according to the value of some variable other than the dependent or independent variables (that is, time). There is no theoretical reason that serial correlation cannot affect cross-sectional models. However, in the absence of some strong reason to

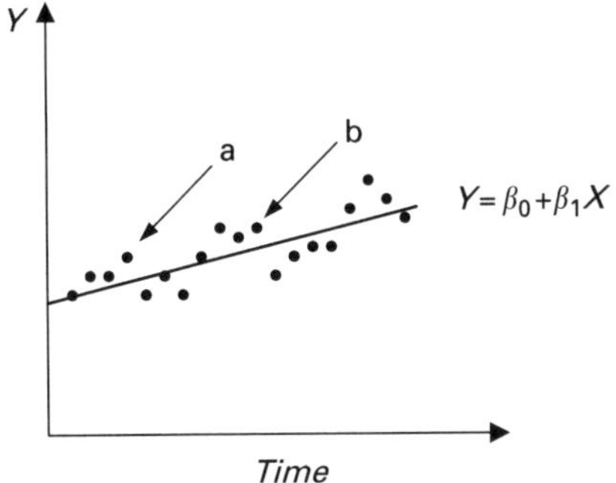

Figure 4.6 *Serial correlation*

expect that observations should be ordered in a certain way (other than with respect to the dependent or independent variables) serial correlation will not be an issue with cross-sectional models. Figure 4.6 sets out the basic concept of serial correlation.

As Figure 4.6 shows, the errors are not truly random over time but display some evidence of a relationship. If we look at observations (a) and (b) then we can easily see (without knowledge of where the data point actually is) that the observation is more likely to have been above the regression line than below it because preceding data points were above the line. So, for these cases, we could have predicted in advance that the errors were more likely to be positive than negative simply because preceding errors were also positive. This implies a certain predictability of the errors based on their observed behaviour over time. Since the errors are assumed to be Normally distributed, that is, as likely to be positive as negative for any given observation, then this is a violation of the regression assumptions.

Serial correlation is a particular problem in time series models using economic data series and this is particularly true in the case of real estate market models. Positive serial correlation is generally a more common problem than negative serial correlation. The former simply means that an error is more likely to be positive if the preceding error is positive (for the case of first order serial correlation). In the case of negative first order serial correlation an error is more likely to be positive if the preceding error is negative. Higher order serial correlation can also occur. For example, positive second order serial correlation means that an error is more likely to be positive if the error of two observations ago was positive. However, the presence of positive first order serial correlation brings the greatest cause for concern.

Serial correlation may be caused by misspecifying a regression equation, particularly by omitting one or more independent variables. Suppose that three variables combine to determine the dependent variable and a regression is estimated using only two of the independent variables. The series of errors or residuals which represents unexplained variance in the dependent variable will still contain information that could have been explained by entering the third independent variable in the regression equation. In these circumstances there may be evidence of serial correlation in the errors. In practice it is more likely that a regression equation will be specified using all known partial determinants of the dependent variable. If there is evidence of serial correlation in the errors then this could be indicative that an important, but unknown, partial determinant of the dependent variable has been omitted from the equation.

In other cases serial correlation may occur as a consequence of data measurement error. Economic data, for example, is artificially formed into series measured in terms of discrete time intervals. In reality an economic series such as gross domestic product or consumption is determined continuously. It is inevitable that when a continuous series is transformed into a discrete one then information from time period $t-1$ will be present in time period t.

Whatever the cause, serial correlation causes standard error estimates to be inefficient leading to incorrect tests of significance on parameter estimates. In other words, serial correlation does not bias the parameter estimates but in the presence of serial correlation the t statistics become unreliable as they are likely to be larger than they would otherwise be in the absence of serial correlation. Furthermore, estimates of the R^2 will be overstated.

When the independent variables are correlated

As discussed earlier, it is assumed that there is no exact linear relationship between the independent variables. An exact linear relationship between explanatory variables is referred to as perfect collinearity and its effect is to render the estimation of variable parameters impossible. This makes sense since it is clearly impossible to measure the separate effects of two independent variables on a dependent variable if both of the independent variables move together.

A potentially more serious problem may arise when there is a strong, but not perfect, linear relationship between two or more explanatory variables. If this is the case then it is theoretically possible to estimate the regression parameters using ordinary least squares but the results may be misleading. This problem is known as multicollinearity and it occurs when there is too great a linear association between variables to permit the identification of the separate influences of the explanatory variables on the dependent variable. So, while strong correlation between independent variables is not actually a violation of the regression assumptions (provided the correlation is less than perfect correlation), it is nonetheless undesirable.

Multicollinearity may be difficult to detect. One of the difficulties is that there is no real theoretical guidance to suggest how strong correlation between two independent variables must be before it can be considered unacceptable.

One of the most common sets of symptoms of multicollinearity are high R^2 and F statistics but low t statistics for some or all of the explanatory variables. It is illogical that a regression equation should have a good fit despite all explanatory variables being seemingly statistically insignificant. So a clear-cut case of multicollinearity like this is relatively easy to identify.

In some cases multicollinearity is much more difficult to detect. Suppose that we construct a regression equation that includes five independent variables and estimate the parameters. We obtain high R^2 and F statistics and three of the variables appear statistically significant from their t statistics. Now suppose that the two variables that appear not to be statistically significant happen to be highly correlated. Can we really rely on the low t statistics and fail to reject the null hypothesis that these variables' parameters are not significantly different from zero? This example is a more likely multicollinearity scenario than the first. Other than our knowledge that two independent variables are correlated there is nothing in the regression results to suggest a multicollinearity problem and, as noted earlier, there are no firm rules about what constitutes an unacceptably high level of correlation between two independent variables.

Since multicollinearity may be difficult to detect it is normal practice to produce a matrix of correlation coefficients prior to estimating the regression parameters. The correlation matrix identifies pairs of explanatory variables that are highly correlated. When high correlation is found between a pair of explanatory variables care should be taken in interpreting the regression results. It might also be prudent to enter only one of the variables into the analysis. Unfortunately, one of the simplest cures for a multicollinearity problem is to simply remove one from each pair of highly collinear variables.

Other multicollinearity solutions include using collinearity diagnostics to guide model specification and using principal components analysis in order to transform an existing set of explanatory variables into a new, uncorrelated set that retain most of the information in the orginal variables. These topics are examined later in the book.

CONCLUSIONS

This chapter is intended to provide a background in regression analysis necessary to understand the econometric methods and models reviewed at various points throughout the remainder of the book, particularly the next two chapters. The chapter is not, and is not intended to be, an exhaustive and comprehensive guide to econometric modelling. The complexity of the subject is such that entire lengthy books are devoted to the subject and the serious real estate researcher will have, or should consider purchasing, suitable econometric reference texts such as Greene (1997) or Pindyck and Rubinfeld (1997). Additional issues and methods in econometric modelling are discussed in Chapter 6 and at various other points throughout the remainder of the book. However, given the fundamental nature of the material in this chapter, readers without a good grasp of the content of this chapter are advised to re-read it before proceeding on to Chapter 5.

5

Commercial Real Estate Rent Determination Models

INTRODUCTION

Real estate modelling has expanded rapidly over recent years both in the UK and elsewhere (see Ball *et al.*, 1998; Hoesli and MacGregor, 2000, for a review). Much of the growth has been in the area of commercial real estate rent modelling although the literature also contains examples of models of yield determination and development activity. Such models, and their associated value in constructing forecasts, are likely to be of particular interest to institutional property investors such as life and pension funds. However, there is growing market awareness concerning the potential value of quantitative models of real estate market processes and dynamics. Although the construction and estimation of such models is likely to remain a relatively specialised job within the real estate profession for some time to come, there is increasingly a need for real estate professionals to have some abilities in respect of interpreting models and forecasts derived from them.

This chapter provides a brief examination of several modelling strategies. The emphasis of the chapter is on commercial real estate rent modelling. Single equation regression models are examined in detail and a number of published models are reviewed. Throughout the chapter references are made to the underlying economic theory being modelled. However, some prior knowledge is assumed and readers unfamiliar with mainstream property market economic theory are advised to refer to Ball *et al.* (1998) for a thorough treatment of the subject.

COMMERCIAL REAL ESTATE INVESTMENT AND RENT DETERMINATION

Although it may be of interest to most commercial real estate surveyors to obtain forecasts of future rental values, or rental growth, investors in commercial real estate are the primary customers of rent determination and forecasting models. Instititutional investors are interested in analysing the role that real estate investment can play in the reduction of total portfolio risk. Including commercial property in a multi-asset portfolio is likely to add to its diversification, primarily because there is some evidence that the performance of commercial property investment over the economic cycle is not mirrored by the performance of alternative investments such as gilts and equities. Gilts are normally regarded as an early performing investment in terms of the economic cycle (during and just after an economic recovery) and there is a close relationship between returns on gilts, inflation and interest rates. The early stages of an economic cycle are typically characterised by low interest rates (with the monetary policy goal of increasing money supply to stimulate economic growth) while latter stages are characterised by high levels of inflation with resultant relatively high interest rates (monetary policy deflationary measures). The interest paid on gilts is fixed throughout the life of the investment, typically, so the market price of gilts will fluctuate in response to central bank interest rates with interest rate increases leading to a fall in the market price of gilts and vice versa. Consequently, gilt prices and returns have tended to peak quite early in an economic upturn and trough in a recession. Meanwhile, share prices largely reflect expectations for corporate profits and respond to current economic activity, while anticipating the next cyclical turning point. As a result, share prices tend to peak before the top of the cycle and to bottom before the cyclical trough, lagging gilts.

In the case of commercial property investment, returns are heavily influenced by trends in rental growth (Fraser, 1986; Gardiner and Henneberry, 1988; Hoesli and MacGregor, 2000). Clearly, rental values are closely linked to economic activity since occupation demand for property is derived from the underlying profitability of the firms that occupy commercial space. If, for example, there is an increase in consumer demand for financial services then financial service firms are likely to experience an increase in profits. Assuming that growth in consumer demand is expected to continue, these firms are likely to demand more space in order to expand output. Thus, occupation demand increases and *ceterus paribus* there is an inflationary effect on commercial rents. Economic theory suggests that commercial real estate occupiers cannot, and do not, respond instantly to changes in the demand for their output. The business of taking on additional premises, or expanding, takes time. Furthermore, occupiers, faced with an upturn in the demand for their output, are likely to be cautious and may wait some time to ensure an upturn is persistent before demanding additional space. These factors suggest that upturns in occupation demand will generally lag behind upturns in corporate performance and hence equity returns.

However, the link between economic activity and commercial rental values is not so straightforward as just described, primarily because the supply side of the real estate user market cannot react instantly to changes in demand. Gardiner and Henneberry (1988) have highlighted the significance of lags between construction orders and completions as a partial determinant of short-run fluctuations in office rent levels. Following Barras (1983), they note that the construction industry cannot respond immediately to an increase in demand for floorspace, with the result that property development activity follows pronounced cycles. In the period immediately following a downturn in the economy, or recession, the property development industry is unlikely to respond immediately to an upturn in occupation demand. Growth in rental values tends to lag behind economic growth in the early stages of an economic cycle, particularly when a glut of vacant space arising during a recession 'overhangs' the letting market, effectively delaying growth even when occupation demand is increasing. Instead, there will be a period of time in which no new construction projects are started and rents rise steadily as occupation demand improves. When rents begin to reach levels that imply profitable property development conditions then new construction projects are commenced. However, a period of one to two years will elapse before this new supply of space becomes available and, during this period, rents continue to rise. Hence, the considerable time lag between planned development and the completion of finished space effectively increases the amplitude of the rent cycle: rents will rise more quickly or to higher levels when the lag is considerable.

Towards the end of an economic cycle occupation demand will be in decline but this coincides with a considerable volume of new space completions. Developers may find it impossible to abandon semi-complete construction projects, which leads to a situation in which the supply of new space may continue increasing even well after rental values have peaked and are in decline. The rapidly expanding supply of space coupled with a downturn in demand ensures that rental levels, or rental growth in a modest downturn, decline rapidly. For these reasons, the timing of commercial real estate investment performance over the economic cycle should be expected to be less consistent than gilts and equities (Key *et al.*, 1994) although there is a general tendency towards performance late in the cycle.

In this context, the significance of commercial real estate rent determination models is clear. In order to simplify matters let us assume that institutional investors construct portfolios using the three basic building blocks of gilts, equities and real estate. Since the performance of any one of these three alternative investment classes *relative to the other two* cannot be expected to remain constant over time then it follows that access to robust and reliable prediction/forecasting models will be of considerable value in constructing and managing an optimal investment portfolio in which returns are maximised and risk is minimised.

MODELLING STRATEGIES

There are numerous ways in which commercial real estate markets can be modelled. The following methods are common in real estate market research:

- Single equation regression models
- Multi-equation regression models
- Vector autoregression models (VARs)
- Error correction models (ECMs)
- Autoregressive and moving average models (AR, MA, ARMA and ARIMA)
- Autoregressive conditional heteroscedasticity models (ARCH, GARCH)

To further complicate matters, different researchers may select different modelling strategies for a mix of theoretical and pragmatic (data related) reasons. The issue of data availability, and reliability, will be examined later but at this point it is sufficient to note that the quality and reliability of available data varies from country to country and often even between regions. Aside from these issues, the choice of modelling approach is driven by a number of different factors including the spatial extent of what we have chosen to define as a market; our beliefs in how supply and demand are determined and how pricing and adjustment occur in that market; and the time period over which we believe supply, demand and pricing adjustment occur in the market.

The main focus of this chapter is on single and multi-equation rent determination models that can be used to produce forecasts of one or two years into the future. The relative complexity of time series and cointegration techniques is such that these methods are beyond the scope of this book. Furthermore, there are very few published examples of such models in real estate market research. It should also be noted that the modelling approaches examined in this chapter are firmly grounded in the underlying economic theory of commercial real estate rent determination. Earlier chapters examined the statistical requirements of a 'good' econometric model. For the purpose of this chapter, a 'good' real estate rent determination/forecasting model is defined as one that meets these statistical requirements while also according well with underlying economic theory. The logic of this is that a model can only be considered robust if it can logically be expected to replicate over time. In other words, relationships postulated and estimated using time series data should be theoretically plausible. Only if this is the case can we have any sort of reasonable expectation that the estimated relationships will continue to hold into the future.

THE UNDERLYING THEORY OF SINGLE EQUATION RENT DETERMINATION MODELS

In this section we are concerned with single equation rent determination models. Before reviewing some of the published models it is essential to consider the theoretical bases upon which such models are constructed.

Single equation models consider a single use and a single sector. For example, a great many such published models are concerned with the determination of rental values in the office market. The modelling approach requires a number of assumptions, all of which are not always made explicit by those publishing such models. The assumptions are as follows:

- The user market is independent of the investment market. Single equation rent models normally make some allowance for the development of new space though most models ignore the importance of investment market conditions to developers' decisions. Instead, the supply of new space is, implictly, seen as a function of conditions in the user market, that is, rental growth.
- In a spatial sense the market being modelled is a distinct and self-contained market which has no interaction with other local, regional or national markets. Thus, changes to supply or demand in a different market (for example another city market or a neighbouring region) are usually assumed to have no consequences for the market being modelled and the model itself is normally specified such that it cannot take account of any such interactions.
- The supply of, and demand for, office space interact, causing the market to clear and reach equilibrium. Equilibrium occurs when demand for space in a given time period is sufficient to take up the supply of space in that period and this process of market clearing is facilitated through the pricing mechanism. Hence, rents will rise in response to a *ceterus paribus* increase in demand or decrease in supply and will fall in response to a *ceterus paribus* fall in demand or increase in supply.
- The quantity of space demanded (*Qd*) in a given time period can be explained using a *structural demand equation*, and the quantity of space supplied (*Qs*) in a given time period can be explained using a *structural supply equation*.
- The individual effects on price (rent) of supply and demand can be captured in a single equation called a *reduced form equation*. The reduced form equation is the equation or model that we are interested in, since it is this equation that can be used to explain and predict the determination of rent. The reduced form equation is found by solving the structural equations.

Example 1

Suppose we have specified the following structural supply and demand equations:

$$Qd = \beta_0 - \beta_1 P + \beta_2 X_1 \qquad (5.1)$$
$$Qs = \gamma_0 + \gamma_1 P - \gamma_2 X_2$$

where

Qd	= quantity demanded
Qs	= quantity supplied
P	= price
X_1	= a variable that partially determines demand
X_2	= a variable that partially determines supply
β_0, β_1, β_2, γ_0, γ_1 and γ_2	= unknown parameters (to be estimated empirically)

For the sake of simplicity, we will ignore disturbance terms at this stage. We can see from the specification of the demand equation that demand falls when price rises. In this example it is assumed that some other variable X_1 causes demand to rise (this could be operating profits, expectations of profits or output prices for example). The structural supply equation is specified such that supply rises in response to price and shares an inverse relationship with some other variable X_2. In order to find our reduced form equation for price we simply rearrange the structural equations. We have assumed that the market will clear and reach equilibrium through the pricing mechanism. Hence we can say:

$$Qs = Qd$$

Thus:

$$\gamma_0 + \gamma_1 P - \gamma_2 X_2 = \beta_0 - \beta_1 P + \beta_2 X_1 \qquad (5.2)$$

Rearranging yields:

$$\gamma_1 P + \beta_1 P = \beta_0 - \gamma_0 + \beta_2 X_1 + \gamma_2 X_2$$

or:

$$(\gamma_1 + \beta_1)P = \beta_0 - \gamma_0 + \beta_2 X_1 + \gamma_2 X_2 \qquad (5.3)$$

This simplifies to:

$$P = \frac{\beta_0 - \gamma_0}{\gamma_1 + \beta_1} + \frac{\beta_2}{\gamma_1 + \beta_1} X_1 + \frac{\gamma_2}{\gamma_1 + \beta_1} X_2$$

With the structural equations rearranged and solved for price, we can substitute new parameters π as follows. Let:

$$\pi_0 = \frac{\beta_0 - \gamma_0}{\gamma_1 + \beta_1}$$

$$\pi_1 = \frac{\beta_2}{\gamma_1 + \beta_1}$$

$$\pi_2 = \frac{\gamma_2}{\gamma_1 + \beta_1}$$

Hence, we can say:

$$P = \pi_0 + \pi_1 X_1 + \pi_2 X_2 \tag{5.4}$$

Note that when we estimate the reduced form equation (5.4) then we will obtain estimates for the parameters π. We will not obtain estimates of the parameters from the structural equations (that is β_0, β_1, β_2, γ_0, γ_1 and γ_2) but from the combined effects of these parameters on price.

Example 1 demonstrates, using a very simple hypothetical example, how structural demand and supply functions can be combined and solved in order to arrive at a reduced form equation. In practice, most published models concern rent equations, that is, reduced form equations, that are constructed directly without first constructing the underlying structural equations. The chapter now turns to consider a number of published studies of commercial property rent determination that have followed this modelling approach. It is convenient to think of these models collectively as single equation rent determination models. In reality, there are other significant differences between many of them. As noted earlier, modelling approaches vary across space in relation to data availability and reliability and the level of aggregation relevant to the chosen study area. Single equation rent models tend to focus on one of three levels of spatial aggregation:

- national level
- regional level
- local (city) level

Early development of the UK commercial rent modelling literature is focused on regional rent models while the bulk of the literature is concerned with national level models. There are relatively few published models of rent determination focused on local study areas. This is primarily a consequence of the data limitations and unavailability together with the practical difficulties in conceptualising and defining boundaries for local markets. Markets appear less self-contained as the degree of disaggregation grows. If we examine, in turn, national, regional and local markets then we should expect to find a growing level of interaction between markets as we progress. This fact presents us with a range of difficulties since such interaction is suggestive that supply/demand in neighbouring markets should be accounted for in some way when constructing a local real estate market rent model. In addition, as noted by Hoesli and MacGregor (2000), market processes are likely to be inherently more difficult to model at local level since unmeasured partial determinants of economic prosperity, such as accessibility and the quality of road networks, are important at this level of aggregation.

Above all, the data limitations at local level are so severe in most cases that meaningful model construction and estimation is not possible (see Ball *et al.*, 1998; Hoesli and MacGregor, 2000, for a full review of the issues).

SINGLE EQUATION RENT MODELLING APPROACHES

One of the earliest documented reviews of time series rent explanation/prediction models in the UK is provided by Gardiner and Henneberry (1988). They postulate a relationship between a regional office rent index (RR_{it}), regional *GDP* (GDP_{it}) and regional floorspace (FSR_{it}):

$$RR_{it} = \beta_0 + \beta_1 GDP_{it} + \beta_2 GDP_{it-2} + \beta_3 FRS_{it} \qquad (5.5)$$

where

RR_{it} = the office rent index for the *i*th region in time period *t* divided by the rent index for all English regions in time period *t*
GDP_{it} = gross domestic product for the *i*th region in time period *t* divided by gross domestic product for all English regions in time period *t*
FSR_{it} = total commercial (office) floorspace in the *i*th region in time period *t* divided by total commercial floorspace in all English regions

The specification of the model is very simple. It contains one demand-side and one supply-side variable as shown. The rent equation contains contemporaneous *GDP* and *GDP* lagged two years. The authors justify this on the basis that regional changes to the level of economic output are likely to feed through to changes in occupation demand subject to a time lag. The variable GDP_{it-2} is included on the basis that it provides superior empirical results to GDP_{it-1}. Although the authors report inconclusive results for their tests for first order serial correlation, it is nevertheless possible that the lagged demand proxy minimises first order (or higher) serial correlation. The existence of serial correlation may signify that an important variable has been mistakenly omitted from the regression equation. In many cases it is not clear what this variable might be, but evidence of what should be a random error term behaving in a non-random way over time is suggestive that at least one significant determinant of the dependent variable has been neglected in the equation specification. In other words, there may be a stronger empirical than theoretical justification for the inclusion of the lagged demand proxy in this case.

The Gardiner and Henneberry (1988) model performs reasonably well for 'expanding' regions (defined by the authors as South East, South West, East Anglia and Yorkshire and Humberside). However, the results for 'declining' regions (North, North West, East Midlands and West Midlands) are poorer. Adjusted *R* squares for the expanding regions range from 0.754 to 0.968 compared with 0.397 to 0.893 for the declining regions. While these *R* squares are high, it must be remembered that the model is essentially estimated in levels rather than differences. The authors report that *GDP* lagged two years is statistically significant and correctly signed (positive) for all of the expanding regions. Contemporaneous *GDP* performs relatively poorly and is either incorrectly signed or not statistically significant for a number of regions. The floorspace ratio variable (*FSR*) is generally correctly signed but is not statistically significant for all regions.

In a development of their regional rent prediction model, Gardiner and Henneberry (1991) focus on improving their model by taking account of occupiers' expectations. They introduce the concepts of adaptive expectations and partial adjustment to UK rent determination models.

The adaptive expectations hypothesis is borrowed from mainstream economics, specifically the theory of consumption. It postulates that the current level of rent is a function of occupiers' expectation of the long-term trend or expectations level of demand for their output. The concept is closely related to the permanent income hypothesis of consumption which postulates that current consumption is based on households' perception of their permanent or long-term trend income levels rather than their current levels of income. The hypothesis is intuitively appealing. Graduates, for example, are likely to base consumption decisions on long-term expectations of earnings rather than their starting salary levels. Similarly, it may be argued, office occupiers are likely to base their decisions regarding the consumption or occupation of office space on their trend level of business rather than simply the level of business generated in the current year.

The adaptive expectations hypothesis, if appealing with respect to the level of household consumption, is more appealing still with respect to the commercial property user market. Although an upturn in economic demand will bring about a rise in the formation of new firms, existing firms are likely to experience a growth in business and may, in turn, develop a requirement for additional floorspace to facilitate business expansion. Yet, firms are unlikely to move premises continually in response to changing economic conditions. Aside from the fact that such behaviour would be disruptive to business, transactions costs in the property market are relatively high while transactions take time to complete. In addition, property is highly heterogeneous which reduces choice from the perspective of the occupier. Therefore, firms' levels of space consumption are likely to be based on firms' expectations about their trend level of business rather than their profitability in the current year. Gardiner and Henneberry (1991) express the rent bid by an office occupier as follows:

$$R_t = \alpha + \beta D_t^* + u_t \qquad (5.6)$$

subject to

$$D_t^* - D_{t-1}^* = (1 - \lambda)(D_t - D_{t-1}) \quad 0 \le \lambda \le 1 \qquad (5.7)$$

where

R_t = the occupier's rent bid in time period t
D_t = the occupier's observed level of demand
D_t^* = the occupier's expectation, in time period t, of their trend level of demand
D_{t-1}^* = last year's expectation of the occupier's trend level of demand
λ = an adjustment parameter
u_t = disturbance term

If the adjustment parameter λ is equal to zero then it is the case that the occupier's expectation of trend level demand responds fully to observed levels of demand. For low values of λ the occupier's expectations adjust rapidly in response to observed levels of demand. For high values of λ the occupier's expectations adjust slowly in response to observed levels of demand. Gardiner and Henneberry's (1991) operational rent prediction model is as follows:

$$R_t = \alpha(1 - \lambda) + \lambda R_{t-1} + \beta(1 - \lambda)D_t + (u_t - \lambda u_{t-1}) \qquad (5.8)$$

The parameters of the model are estimated using the Healey and Baker Regional Office Rent Index and Regional GDP at factor cost as a proxy for occupiers' demand. Hence, following Gardiner and Henneberry (1988) the equation becomes:

$$RR_{it} = \beta_0 + \beta_1 RR_{it-1} + \beta_2 GDP_{it} + (u_t - \lambda u_{t-1}) \qquad (5.9)$$

The model includes a first order moving average process and the authors report superior results compared with the simple supply and demand model reported earlier by Gardiner and Henneberry (1988) or a simple habit-persistence model with a specification as above but excluding the moving average (MA) disturbance term. The authors report adjusted R squares ranging from 0.463 to 0.978 for the habit persistence/MA model and report that values for λ above 0.6 produce the best empirical results. They argue that this is suggestive that occupiers are conservative in declining regions.

Key *et al.* (1994) provide a fairly complete single equation analysis of retail, industrial and office real estate market sectors. A detailed review of these models can be found in Ball *et al.* (1998) and Chaplin (1999) but, in general, their models (of real rent levels) include lagged real rents, demand proxies, the stock of floorspace, new construction starts and real interest rates. For several of the variables a range of lag structures are used, while the 'demand proxies' used are consumer spending, *GDP* and manufacturing output respectively for the retail, office and industrial sectors. Dobson and Goddard (1992) take the unusual step of including the price of housing in their modelling framework, arguing that the price of housing relative to commercial property should act as a supply proxy given that this relative measure will determine the incidence of property switching between use.

The single equation approach to modelling rent determination is also common outside the UK (with the exception of the US). D'Arcy *et al.* (1999) construct and estimate a single equation to explain and predict Dublin office rents using data on effective rents, volume of new office construction completions, gross domestic product and service sector employment. The sample period is 1970–97. The data are indexed (1990 = 100) with nominal financial variables converted to real variables using the consumer price index. The equation specification is relatively simple and is as follows:

$$\Delta RR_t = \alpha_0 + \Sigma\alpha_{1i}\Delta GDP_{t-i} + \Sigma\alpha_{2i}\Delta SSE_{t-i} + \Sigma\alpha_{3i}NC_{t-i} + \varepsilon_t \quad i = 0, 1, 2, 3 \tag{5.10}$$

where

ΔRR_t = change in the natural log of the real rental index in time period t from $t-1$ (first difference on the log of the real rental index)

ΔGDP_{t-i} = real *GDP* index (first log difference)

ΔSSE_{t-i} = service sector employment index (first log difference)

NC_{t-i} = volume of new office completions (log levels)

α_0 = constant

α_{1i} = parameters for the different lag structures on the real *GDP* index (first log difference)

α_{2i} = parameters for the different lag structures on the service sector employment index (first log difference)

α_{3i} = parameters for the different lag structures on the new office completions index (logs)
ε_t = error term

The model specification includes demand proxies and supply variables. Gross domestic product together with the level of service sector employment proxy for the profitability of occupying office premises. The supply of office space is measured directly using data on the volume of new office space completed for each year in the sample period. As the model specification suggests, the authors of this model experiment with different lag structures and include contemporaneous *GDP* and *SSE* as well as 1, 2 and 3 lags of these explanatory variables. This is generally regarded as acceptable practice. Theory indicates that *GDP* should be a reasonably good proxy for office occupiers' profitability which, in turn, should partly determine demand for occupying space, hence office rents. However, there is no consensus regarding the length of the time lag that should exist between changes in office occupiers' profitability, demand for occupying space and the level of office rents. Hence, analysts often include explanatory variables with several different lags in the first round of analysis. Similarly, theory indicates that an increase in the supply of new office space should have a negative effect on rents *ceterus paribus* but the property market is imperfect with poor information flows and a limited number of transactions. These facts tend to suggest that office rents need not adjust immediately in response to changes in supply.

The authors' empirical results indicate that *GDP* (with one lag, that is, one year behind) and *NC* with three lags are statistically significant and correctly signed. In keeping with prior expectations (which are derived from economic theory) the coefficient on the *GDP* variable is positive and the coefficient on the *NC* variable is negative. Clearly, we expect office rents to increase in response to an increase in office occupiers' profitability because the demand for occupying space is derived from the demand for office occupiers' output or services. Similarly, we expect that an increase in the supply of space should have a negative effect on rents. The authors' results indicate that the *SSE* variable is not statistically significant and this variable is not included in the final version of their model. The performance of the model itself is not particularly good. The authors report that the *R* bar square is 0.49. For a model estimated using data in log differences this is a reasonably good level of fit. However, the authors also report that the model consistently under-predicts rents between 1977 and 1985 when real GDP was on a downward long-term trend and over-predicts rents after 1985 when real GDP was on an upward long term-trend.

As noted by Ball *et al*. (1998) and Hoesli and MacGregor (2000), the commerical rent determination and modelling literature is in a state of evolution and development. Consequently, future developments and advances are likely and there is no universally accepted or 'state of the art' methodology in single equation rent equation construction and estimation. However, in a comprehensive review of the literature, Chaplin (2000) identifies broad consensus single equation rent determination explanatory variables as:

- Office sector: lagged dependent variable; financial and business services sector output; new office construction orders.
- Industrial sector: manufacturing sector output; manufacturing sector employment; new industrial construction orders.
- Retail sector: consumer spending; new retail construction orders.

Further examination of the predictive powers and empirical performance of single equation rent models is provided in the next chapter.

OVERVIEW OF THE SINGLE EQUATION RENT MODELLING APPROACH

Since single equation rent models tend to include variables such as gross domestic product and/or service sector employment as proxies for the demand for office space, these models do not contain a direct or explicit link between occupation demand and office rents (either in terms of levels or of changes). This means that the empirical results of such models can be difficult to interpret. For example, single equation models tend not to be particularly useful for predicting the result when the demand for, and supply of, office space are both increasing together, but at different rates.

A further weakness of single equation rent models is that the link between the supply of space (or changes to supply) and rent (or changes in rent) is often weak. This is demonstrated by the fact that the coefficients on supply-side variables are often not statistically significant or even 'incorrectly' signed. In part, this problem is the result of the fact that reliable and comprehensive data on the supply of office space over time are not always readily available. Single equation rent models often use data on new office completions as a proxy but, in reality, the supply of office space includes refurbished and second-hand space in addition to newly constructed space. The impact of new completions on office rents is likely to differ depending on the quantity of available refurbished and second-hand space.

A further reason for the fact that supply-side variables often perform poorly in single equation rent models is based on the fact that single equation rent models often do not contain a link to the capital markets. This criticism is also made by Ball *et al.* (1998) in their review of single equation rent models. Conditions in the capital markets are of importance because developers' decisions regarding new construction projects are not directly influenced by growth in occupation demand but by the investment demand for occupied commercial premises. It is beyond the scope of this book to examine the determinants of commercial property investment demand in any detail (see Fraser, 1993; Ball *et al.*, 1998; Brown and Matyisak, 2000; Hoesli and MacGregor, 2000). It is sufficient to note that 'trader' developers are primarily motivated by the likely price at which a fully let office development can be sold at completion. This price is determined by the rental value of the premises, and the yield. The yield is determined by investors' required returns on property investment which are derived from the prevailing and future expected returns on alternative investment classes such as gilts and equities, and investors' expectations of rental (income) growth. These relationships are too complex for a single equation rent determination model to realistically capture them. Thus, the supply of new office space is usually assumed to be exogenous, that is, an independent variable determined outside the relationship being modelled.

CONCLUSIONS

In summary, the construction of single reduced form rent equations is a common technique in rent determination modelling and the literature contains many examples of such models. As noted earlier, the literature is still developing in this area and it is likely that there will be future developments and advances in rent determination theory and modelling. Single equation rent models are grounded in economic theory although some of the models reviewed in this chapter accord more closely with theory than others. To a certain extent the single equation approach can be seen as something of a compromise since it permits the construction of a theoretically defensible model within the limits of data availability. As noted throughout this chapter, and as suggested by the specification of some of the models reviewed, reliable economic and property market data are not easy to come by and the problem worsens as the scale of disaggregation increases.

A real estate market researcher is likely to follow a number of steps in the construction and estimation of a single equation rent model:

(1) Carry out a detailed literature review in order to assess the value, validity and limitations of existing published models. The literature review will assist in deciding on the possible and preferred specifications of the model to be constructed and estimated. Some published models are accompanied by a discussion of the theoretical and empirical limitations of the models and an outline of possible ways in which the reported work might be further developed.

(2) Identify the real estate market sector that is to be modelled (office sector, industrial, and so on).
(3) Identify the study area. Most published models have a national focus although there are several models based on regional data. The literature contains very few examples of single equation rent models estimated using local market data.
(4) Construct structural supply and demand equations by drawing from accepted economic theory and the review of other published models. The purpose of this is to arrive at a theoretical view on the determinants of the supply of, and demand for, space in the chosen real estate market sector. At this stage, the specification is unlikely to be compromised in recognition of known data inavailability.
(5) Solve the structural equations in order to derive the reduced form rent equation. In practice, most researchers are likely to miss out the fourth step and construct a reduced form rent equation directly. If this approach is adopted then particular care must be taken in identifying the conjectured supply-side and demand-side determinants of rent and deciding *a priori* the sign and magnitude that the coefficients are likely to take on estimation.
(6) Review the model specification in order to identify the data requirements. At this stage it may become apparent that some of the variables cannot be measured directly and consideration should therefore be given to alternative variables (proxies) that are likely to be highly correlated with the unavailable variable(s). Where possible, alternative proxies should be identified in order to permit several alternative model specifications to be estimated and the results compared.
(7) Assemble the dataset and carry out preliminary analysis. Some researchers construct scatterplots in order to obtain a visual impression of the relationships in the data. Others combine this with statistical tests. For example, a unit root test may be employed to test the order of homogeneity of the data. As discussed in more detail in the next chapter, estimating a model using non-stationary data can lead to spurious results and it is good practice to reduce the data to stationarity prior to estimating the parameters of a model. Unit root tests are examined in the next chapter. Meanwhile, economic and financial data should be transformed to real figures using a suitable deflator as a matter of course.
(8) Estimate the parameters of the alternative model specifications using suitable time-series orientated statistics software. Estimation is likely to be an iterative process in which alternative model specifications are estimated in order to identify a robust specification with a good fit. Many researchers tend to select a specification with high R-bar square and F statistics and low standard errors.

(9) Carry out diagnostic testing in order to validate, or otherwise, the estimation results. As noted earlier, most researchers will carry out tests for serial correlation and heteroscedasticity as a matter of course. Tests for multicollinearity and misspecification may also be carried out. These are examined briefly in the next chapter.

REFERENCES

Ball, M., Lizieri, C. and MacGregor, B.D. (1998) *The Economics of Commercial Property Markets* (London: Routledge).

Barras, R. (1983) 'A simple theoretical model of the office development cycle', *Environment and Planning A*, vol. 15, 1381–94.

Brown, G.R. and Matysiak, G.A. (2000) *Real Estate Investment: A Capital Market Approach* (London: Financial Times).

Chaplin, R. (1999) 'The predictability of real office rents', *Journal of Property Research*, vol. 16, no. 1, 21–49.

Chaplin, R. (2000) 'Predicting real estate rents: walking backwards into the future', *Journal of Property Investment and Finance*, vol. 18, no. 3, 352–70.

D'Arcy, E., McGough, T. and Tsolacos, S. (1999) 'An econometric analysis and forecasts of the office rental cycle in the Dublin area', *Journal of Property Research*, vol. 16, no. 4, 309–21.

Dobson, S. and Goddard, J. (1992) 'The determinants of commercial property prices and rents', *Bulletin of Economic Research*, vol. 44, no. 4, 301–21.

Fraser, W.D. (1986) 'Supply elasticity and the rental value of investment property', *Journal of Valuation*, vol. 4, no. 4, 354–69.

Fraser, W.D. (1993) *Principles of Property Investment and Pricing*, 2nd edition (Basingstoke: Macmillan).

Gardiner, C. and Henneberry, J. (1988) 'The development of a simple regional office rent prediction model', *Journal of Valuation*, vol. 7, 36–52.

Gardiner, C. and Henneberry, J. (1991) 'Predicting regional office rents using habit-persistence theories', *Journal of Property Valuation and Investment*, vol. 9, no. 3, 215–26.

Hoesli, M. and MacGregor, B.D. (2000) *Property Investment: Principles and Practice of Portfolio Management* (Harlow: Pearson Education).

Key, T., MacGregor, B., Nanthakumaran, N. and Zarkesh, F. (1994) *Understanding the Property Cycle: Economic Cycles and Property Cycles* (London: Royal Institution of Chartered Surveyors).

6

Advanced Real Estate Rent Determination and Modelling Issues

INTRODUCTION

Chapter 5 provided a review and discussion of the single equation approach to constructing a rent determination model. In this chapter a number of alternative modelling strategies are examined. In particular, the chapter examines multi-equation rent determination models in some detail. More detailed aspects of commercial rent modelling approaches, including autoregressive and moving average models and diagnostic testing, are examined briefly. The chapter also provides a review on the sources and limitations of data used to estimate commercial real estate models.

RENT DETERMINATION MODELS BASED ON SYSTEMS OF EQUATIONS

An alternative approach to modelling rent determination and forecasting is to construct an interrelated set (system) of equations representing dynamics within, and interaction between, the different components of the real estate market. Keogh (1994) argues that there are three such components to the market: use, investment and development. The multi-equation modelling approach provides potential solutions to some of the difficulties encountered in single equation rent modelling by allowing direct confrontation with the fact that the use, investment and development sectors of the real estate market are, in reality, unlikely to be independent.

Most of the development in this area of real estate research has been carried out in the US although there are a few exceptions. An early example of a multi-equation modelling approach is provided by Rosen (1984). This system represents a set of equations that model the determination of the stock of office space, new supply (construction) and office rents.

The demand for office space is hypothesised as a function of employment in the financial and business sectors and office rents relative to wider macro price levels (real rents):

$$OS_t^* = f\,(E_t, R_t/P_t) \tag{6.1}$$

where

OS_t = stock of occupied office space in time period t. The superscript '*' signifies 'desired level of' or equilibrium level
E_t = employment in the finance, insurance and real estate sectors
R_t/P_t = rent level in time period t divided by the general price level in time period t

Meanwhile, service sector employment, as previously defined, is modelled in a separate equation in which it is postulated that the employment level is a function of economic output, corporate profits and (expected) growth:

$$E_t = f(O_t, \pi_t, G_t) \tag{6.2}$$

where

O_t = Gross National Product (economic output) in time period t
π_t = corporate sector profits level in time period t
G_t = growth in demand for service sector output in time period t

Equation (6.2) 'feeds' into equation (6.1) in the sense that the employment variable (E), while a partial determinant of the real rent level ($R \div P$), is endogenous. As noted earlier, an endogenous variable is one that is determined within the system of equations and the values of that variable are not given or independent. The variable (E) is itself a dependent variable in equation (6.2) even though it is an explanatory variable in equation (6.1). Taken together, the two equations predict that changes in economic output (O), corporate profit levels (π) and growth in demand for service sector output (G) combine to determine changes in service sector employment (E). Meanwhile, any such changes to the level of employment have a knock-on effect to the demand for office stock (OS).

As we have already noted, there are two basic determinants of the demand for office stock as specified in equation (6.1). So far we have examined the influence and determination of service sector employment (E). The influence and determination of the real office rental rate ($R \div P$) is a little more complex and is shown by way of a further three reduced form equations. The first introduces the concept of a natural or equilibrium vacancy rate:

$$V_t^* = f(i_t, R_t^e) \tag{6.3}$$

where
i_t = interest rates
R_t^e = expected or equilibrium rent levels

The natural vacancy rate concept is linked to the notion that landlords/investors hold an inventory of unoccupied office space such that the market is at equilibrium when there is a given proportion of office stock remaining unoccupied. In some ways this is a departure from the standard neoclassical view that markets clear through the price mechanism.

However, it is well established that producers in some industries may operate inventories in order to generate flexibility in production and to make it possible to react swiftly to short-run price changes. This is analogous to the idea of a natural vacancy rate which assumes that landlords withhold an element of their stock from the market in order to allow themselves flexibility in responding to changing market conditions. The specification of equation (6.3) suggests that Rosen (1984) sees the natural vacancy rate as a function largely of landlords' opportunity cost of holding vacant stock. Indeed, Rosen argues that higher interest rates lower the natural vacancy rate, presumably because the forgone return from an alternative investment resulting from holding vacant office stock is higher. The natural vacancy rate concept is firmly linked to the idea that there is an 'ideal' vacancy level. When the actual vacancy rate falls below this ideal then rents increase. Conversely, when the actual vacancy rate becomes higher than the ideal or natural vacancy rate then rental rates decrease. The actual vacancy rate is defined simply:

$$V_t = \frac{TS_t - OS_t}{TS_t} \quad \text{(note that this is an identity and not an equation)}$$

In Rosen's system, changes to the rental rate are determined by disparity between the natural and actual vacancy rates:

$$\Delta R_t = f(V_t^* - V_t, \Delta P_t) \tag{6.4}$$

Equation (6.4) is of particular importance because it defines the rental adjustment process. Since the dependent variable is defined as change in office rents, the equation describes a non-linear relationship between vacancy rates and rental rates. Clearly, an *a priori* assumption is that rental adjustments will be relatively large when disparity between actual and natural vacancy rates are large, and vice versa. This makes for quite an intuitively appealing model specification. The specification of the rental adjustment process is completed by introducing a construction or new supply equation:

$$\Delta TS_t = f(V_t, R_t^e, C_t, i, T) \tag{6.5}$$

Equation (6.5) describes the determination of office construction output as a function of the vacancy rate, expected rent level, construction costs, interest rates and tax laws. In summary, the user and development sectors of the office market are modelled using a set or system of equations rather than a single equation. Each equation models a separate process – rent determination, new construction, determination of an equilibrium or desirable office stock, and so on. Although the different equations have the appearance of being independent, they are linked together in the sense that some of the explanatory variables in the separate equations are in turn dependent variables in other equations.

A slightly different perspective on the idea of modelling rent determination using a system of equations is provided by Hekman (1985). The author uses data from 14 US cities over the period 1979–83.

The author argues, particularly in relation to the determination of construction activity, that national-level rent/construction determination models are inappropriate. Although it must be noted that this observation is of particular relevance to the US context in which the author presents his model, he rightly points out the fact that aggregation bias is likely to occur in national-level models since they essentially represent an aggregation of numerous local (city-level) user markets. The degree of aggregation bias is likely to increase with the spatial extent of the national market, and presumably the argument for steering clear of a national-level modelling framework is therefore stronger in the US context than in the UK or other European countries.

Hekman (1985) provides a system based on two regression equations as follows:

$$R_t = \alpha_0 + \alpha_1 V_t + \alpha_2 Y_t + \alpha_3 E_t + \alpha_4 U_t + \varepsilon_{1t} \tag{6.6}$$

$$Q_t = \beta_0 + \beta_1 \hat{R}_t + \beta_1 G_t + \beta_3 C_t + \beta_4 I_t + \varepsilon_{2t} \tag{6.7}$$

where

R_t = real rent per square foot in Class A office buildings still under construction. The GNP deflator is used to ensure the rental data are real rather than nominal.

V_t = the Class A office building vacancy rate.

Y_t = Gross National Product in constant prices.

E_t = total employment level in the standard metropolitan statistical area (SMSA).

U_t = unemployment rate in the SMSA.

Q_t = value of office building permits divided by construction costs per square foot.

G_t = expected market growth rate. Hekman proxies this using the ratio of the level of employment in finance, insurance, real estate, services and the public sector in 1980 to the 1970 level.

C_t = construction costs per square foot. Again, this series is deflated using the GNP deflator.

I_t = short-term interest rates. The data used are the difference between the 10-year government bond rate and the 3-month T-bill rate.

Equation (6.6) specifies the real rent level as a linear function of the vacancy rate, economic output, employment and unemployment. It should be noted that the data series are in levels rather than first log differences. Other interesting features of the system from a theoretical point of view are that the system does not include an equation for absorption or take-up. Consequently, there is an implied rather than specified link between the variables Q and V. To put this another way, presumably substantial changes in construction output (Q) feed back to affect the vacancy rate (V) but there is no equation to demonstrate this feedback effect.

R-hat represents predicted rent using equation (6.6). Hence, the fitted values of R become an explanatory variable in equation (6.7). Equation (6.7) is therefore generally known as a two-stage regression model. The parameters of both equations are estimated by pooling the data on the 14 cities. Although the time series is short (1979–83), pooling the 14 cross-sections in this way permits this essentially time series model to be estimated with a total of 70 degrees of freedom. As noted earlier, one use of panel models is to permit the estimation of a time series model with a small time series by obtaining the degrees of freedom of a longer time series essentially by stacking a number of different cross-sections together.

Hekman's empirical results show an adjusted R square of 0.37 for the rent equation and 0.61 for the construction output equation. In the case of the rent equation, the explanatory power is derived from the vacancy rate (V), economic output (Y) and employment (E) variables. These have t statistics of -2.41, 2.26 and 4.54 respectively. The unemployment variable is not statistically significant. For a pooled cross-sectional time series model estimated with data in levels, the degree of explanatory power of the model is relatively poor.

Hekman reports implied real rent elasticities of -0.08, 4.43 and 0.24 with respect to the vacancy rate (V), economic output (Y) and employment (E). Hence, using Hekman's example, the results indicate that rent levels should fall by 8 per cent following a doubling of the vacancy rate (say from 5 per cent to 10 per cent). Meanwhile, a 1 per cent increase in economic output leads to a real rent level increase of approximately 4.43 per cent and an increase in the employment rate of 1 per cent leads to an increase in the real rent level of 0.24 per cent. The coefficients (parameter estimates) for the rent equation are correctly signed and their magnitudes are plausible. Hekman notes that the large elasticity of rent with respect to economic output demonstrates the strongly cyclical nature of the user market.

When we turn to the construction output equation we can see (from the adjusted R square) that the explanatory power of the equation is superior to that of the rent equation (0.61). The rent (R), growth (G) and construction cost (C) variables are statistically significant with t statistics of 5.72, 9.51 and 3.51 respectively. The rent and growth coefficients are correctly signed (positive). This is in keeping with prior expectations since an increase in real rent levels or in expectations of future market growth should give rise to an increase in construction activity, all other things being equal. However, the construction cost variable is incorrectly signed positive. The short-term interest rate variable is not statistically significant.

The elasticities of construction output (Q) with respect to the real rent level, growth and construction costs are 3.64, 6.86 and 4.09 respectively. Clearly, these estimates suggest that construction output is strongly responsive to these explanatory variables.

Shilling *et al.* (1987) provide a further development of rent adjustment process modelling. In particular, they concentrate on the relationship between rental change and disparity between the actual and natural vacancy rate. They set out two equations as follows:

$$\delta R_t = \alpha_0 + \alpha_1 \delta EX_t + \alpha_2 V_t^* \qquad (6.8)$$

where

R_t = office rent level in time period t.
EX_t = operating expenses. Here, the authors have assumed that landlords grant gross leases such that their true returns are a partial function of commercial real estate operating costs.
V_t = vacancy rate in time period t. The superscript '*' denotes natural vacancy rate as before.

The authors estimate the natural vacancy rate for each of 17 US cities by regressing the vacancy rate on the mean time series values of annual change in office stock, non-manufacturing employment, population, property taxation rate and rent level. The time series spanned by the study is 1960–75.

Although not shown in the formal specification of equation (6.8), the authors also included an interaction term defined as the product of the rate of rental change and the vacancy rate. They argue that this term is included in order to take up non-linearity in the relationship between rental change and the difference between the actual and natural vacancy rates. In other words, as noted earlier, the magnitude of rental adjustment is unlikely to be linear with respect to vacancy rate disparity. When the difference between the actual and natural vacancy rate is small then we would expect relatively small rental adjustments to occur. When the difference is large then we would expect larger rental adjustments.

The authors' empirical results are quite impressive with adjusted R square statistics of between 0.66 and 0.98 for the 17 cities. The authors find that operating expenses (*EX*) is not statistically significant in any of the 17 equations but report that the vacancy rate variable (*V*) is statistically significant in 11 of the equations. However, they use the 10 per cent level of significance in interpreting their *t* statistics. Of slightly more concern is the fact that the authors report the interaction term ($R \times V$) to be statistically significant in all 17 equations. This finding is open to interpretation to a certain extent. The authors argue that this is evidence that the relationship between rental change and vacancy rate disparity is non-linear, or, in other words, that differences between the actual and natural vacancy rate is an important determinant of the magnitude of rental adjustment. However, given that the interaction term partially represents the dependent variable in the equation (*R*), it is not possible to conclude that the authors have not simply shown a spurious relationship. To put this another way: entering the same variable on both sides of the equation tends to guarantee some level of fit and the results should be interpreted with caution as a consequence.

Later studies (for example, Wheaton, 1987) have modelled the rental and stock adjustment processes more explicitly by estimating equations for absorption, construction and rent adjustment:

$$A_t = \alpha(OS_t^* - OS_{t-1}) \tag{6.9}$$

$$OS_t^* = f(E_t, R_t, E_t/E_{t-1})$$

$$C_t = f(R_t, V_t, S_t E_t/E_{t-1}, CC_t, I_t) \tag{6.10}$$

$$\frac{R_t - R_{t-1}}{R_{t-1}} = \lambda(V_t - V^*) \tag{6.11}$$

where

A_t = net absorption of office space in period *t*
OS_t^* = desired level of occupied office space
OS_t = level of occupied office space
C_t = quantity of new construction starts
CC_t = construction costs
R_t = real rents for office space
V_t = vacancy rate
V^* = natural vacancy rate
S_t = stock of office space
E_t = office employment
I_t = short-term cost of borrowing

An upturn in economic demand leads on to growth in office employment (*E*) and this gives rise to an increase in the desired occupied stock of space (OS^*). Actual occupied stock increases slowly subject to α, an adjustment parameter, and relative to the desired stock of occupied space.

New construction is determined by market conditions (measured by real rental rates and the vacancy rate or R and V respectively), construction costs and short-term borrowing costs. An upturn in demand leads to a reduction in the vacancy rate (as shown in the absorption equation) and this in turn leads to gradual rental adjustment. Rental change is a function of the parameter γ and disparity between the actual and natural vacancy rates.

Hendershott (1996) adopts an alternative approach to modelling rent adjustment. He argues that rents adjust to the gap between equilibrium and actual gross rents as well as the gap between the natural and actual vacancy rates. In essence, Hendershott's (1996) argument is that rents fall following a significant increase in supply but then return towards the equilibrium level more quickly than implied by the high vacancy rate. Hendershott's rental adjustment equation is as follows:

$$\frac{\Delta g_{t+j}}{g_{t+j-1}} = \lambda(v^* - v_{t+j-1}) + \beta(g^*_{t+j} - g_{t+j-1}) \qquad (6.12)$$

where
g^* = equilibrium gross rents
g = actual gross rents
v^* = natural vacancy rate
v = actual vacancy rate

SUMMARY

The multi-equation approach to modelling commercial rent determination is not common in the UK where data limitations and inavailability (with some exceptions) effectively preclude their use. Wheaton *et al.* (1997) and Hendershott *et al.* (1999) provide good examples of the application of the methodology to the London office market, but by far the majority of previous work on commercial real estate rent modelling in the UK has employed single equation methodology, largely, as noted earlier, as a result of poor data availability and reliability. For a brief general review of modelling rental adjustment processes, see Hendershott (1997) and Hoesli and MacGregor (2000). An excellent and detailed review of single and multi-equation rent modelling approaches can be found in Ball *et al.* (1998). Meanwhile, a comprehensive review of rent modelling approaches is provided by Tsolacos *et al.* (1998).

The main advantages of the multi-equation approach over the single equation approach are that there is no need to assume independence between the user, development and investor components of the real estate market while rent adjustment processes can be modelled over relatively long periods of time. Using a multi-equation approach, there is no need to assume that the market instantly adjusts to changes in supply and demand or that equilibrium is reached within a short period of time. These facts make it possible to construct and estimate more intuitively pleasing (with respect to the underlying economic theory) models of rent determination.

DATA AVAILABILITY AND LIMITATIONS

In previous chapters it has repeatedly been noted that strong theoretical foundations are a key component of a 'good' real estate market model, and in Chapter 5 it is argued that the first step to any real estate market modelling exercise should be a theoretical analysis. In other words, a model should be constructed from theoretical principles – well-rehearsed beliefs about how the market operates or behaves. In economics, most analysts, following on from this first theoretical discussion, are required to adopt a pragmatic approach. This is often necessary because in economics some of the explanatory variables included in model specifications cannot be measured directly. For example, information on commercial real estate occupiers' profitability would be so difficult and expensive to collect that this variable is effectively impossible to measure in practice. As noted in the previous chapter, profitability is normally measured by proxy (by using GDP or some other measure of economic output that is thought to be highly correlated with occupiers' profitability). Clearly, the validity and reliability of a model is likely to be partly dependent upon the quality and validity of the proxy data used to estimate the model and, hence, real estate market analysts are required to exercise a degree of judgement in the construction and estimation of models and particularly in relation to the choice of variables and data used for that purpose.

Until relatively recently, data on real estate market performance and dynamics were very difficult to obtain in the UK (for a detailed review of commercial real estate market data sources in the UK, see Dunse *et al.*, 1998). Furthermore, some of the data series that do exist suffer from gaps/discontinuities and even definitional changes, rendering them difficult and potentially misleading sources. Dunse *et al.* (1998) identify three main private sector sources of commercial real estate market data:

- Lasalle Investment Management/Jones Lang Lasalle Long Term Property Index (previously Jones Lang Wootton). The LIM index dates from 1967 and provides measures of capital and rental growth, net income and total returns. The indices are available on a quarterly basis from 1977. The indices are primarily used in the estimation of models focused on the national level of aggregation and are available for the offices, retail and industrial sectors. The indices are based on periodic valuations rather than transactions.

- CB Hiller Parker. These indices are available in annual form from 1965 and biannually from 1977. Indices measure rental values, capital values, average yields and rates of return. The indices are available for offices, retail and industrial and for both national and regional level. As with the LIM indices, these indices are based on periodic valuations rather than transactions.
- Investment Property Databank (IPD). IPD provides a subscription service to members in which members receive analyses of their portfolio performance in return for an annual subscription and subject to their depositing information on their own portfolio. IPD create several market indices using the information on all members' portfolios. Dunse *et al.* (1998) note that the number of properties fluctuates but stood at almost 14,000 in 1997. For a review of the IPD indices, see Morrell (1991).

Dunse *et al.* (1998) also note that the availability of real estate market information is more restricted at regional and local levels than national level. Several of the large surveying firms publish market reports in which rental values are reported for multiple local markets (centres). However, there are several potential problems with these sources of information. First, some reports give top achieved rents rather than mean effective rents, with the result that the rent series are 'sticky'. In other words, the volatility of the rent series is downplayed if the rental values are not adjusted to take account of the concessions granted to tenants on new lettings. In deteriorating market conditions the annualised value of such concessions (such as rent-free periods) is likely to increase as landlords become increasingly willing to sign on new tenants in the face of declining occupation demand.

Second, even if effective rather than top rents are reported, most local real estate markets other than the major centres do not witness a large number of transactions, with the result that reported rental values are essentially averages taken from very small samples. Clearly, the problem is exacerbated by the fact that even the large firms are unlikely to possess a dominant share of business in the letting market. In poor economic conditions, when occupation demand is declining, the number of transactions is likely to reduce further.

Third, property is highly heterogeneous and most surveying firms do not employ particularly advanced methods designed to mix-adjust transactions prices (reported rental values) prior to publication. Although firms often report figures for primary, secondary and tertiary property it is likely that there are differences between the properties represented in the sample used to calculate rental values each time period, with the result that some error is inevitable. Indeed, it is primarily as a result of this that most firms provide local market-wide information broken down into crude primary/secondary classifications. Information is not normally provided on different neighbourhoods within local markets.

Finally, most surveying firms do not possess data series that stretch back far enough to provide a sufficiently long time series useful for carrying out econometric analyses. There are some exceptions. For example, Jones Lang Lasalle possess information on office and industrial rents at local level stretching back to the late 1960s. However, this is the exception rather than the rule, with most of the other large firms possessing reliable indices from around the mid-1980s onwards. Dunse *et al.* (1998) report that the Jones Lang Lasalle data is annual prior to 1980 and are biannual thereafter, though the series are based on top achievable rents rather than effective rents.

SMOOTHING AND DESMOOTHING

A particular problem encountered by real estate researchers is the fact that the periodic valuations, on which commercial property indices are dependant, can introduce smoothing and lagging into the recorded performance of property. The problem arises due to the heterogeneous nature of property and the infrequency of trading. These facts, together with a general lack of freedom of information, combine to effectively preclude index compilation using market prices. Instead, published indices are normally constructed using valuation data.

There are convincing arguments and evidence indicating that valuation smoothing can cause successive index readings to under-record fluctuations of price and performance. In other words, indices are not a perfect proxy for property returns. In fact there are two issues that can introduce bias to commercial property indices – 'smoothing' and temporal aggregation (MacGregor and Nanthakumaran, 1992). The seriousness of temporal aggregation is partly a function of the frequency of the index readings since indices measured at annual level tend to disguise short-run fluctuations. Equally, an annual stock market index would disguise the day-to-day fluctuations in share prices. Smoothing, by contrast, is a problem that worsens as the frequency of index readings increases. Successive values of an index may under-represent movements in market prices partly because the time lag between market transactions and the availability of comparable evidence means that current valuations are dominated by past transactions (Blundell and Ward, 1987; Geltner, 1989). In addition, institutional leases with 5-yearly rent review structures mean that only rents achieved at review or in new lettings are responsive to occupier profitability. This tends to mean that commercial property indices measured at frequent intervals (monthly or quarterly series) will reflect market changes in previous time periods and, in other words, are biased. Some commentators argue that performance series (property indices) should be desmoothed as a matter of course prior to any further analysis (such as commercial rent modelling). For a discussion of this issue, refer to Barkham and Geltner (1994); Chaplin (1997).

SOME COMMON DIAGNOSTIC TESTS

Goodness of Fit

As noted earlier in the book, the adjusted *R* square statistic (*R* bar square) is the most commonly used indicator of goodness of fit, and where goodness of fit is the researcher's primary consideration, a model may be specified by selecting from a range of alternatives on the basis of maximum adjusted *R* square. Alternative measures, particularly useful in aiding the selection of lag specification, include the Akaike Information Criterion (AIC) and the Schwarz Information Criterion (SIC). Chaplin (1998), following Pindyck and Rubinfeld (1997), uses these two measures in conjunction with *R* bar square in order to select commercial rent determination equation specifications that maximise goodness of fit.

The AIC is defined as follows:

$$AIC = \log\left(\frac{\sum \hat{\varepsilon}_i^2}{N}\right) + \frac{2k}{N} \tag{6.13}$$

The SIC is defined as follows:

$$SIC = \log\left(\frac{\sum \hat{\varepsilon}_i^2}{N}\right) + \frac{k \log N}{N} \tag{6.14}$$

where

N = number of observations
k = number of independent variables

Pindyck and Rubinfeld (1997) note that it may be appropriate to use the *R* bar square, AIC and SIC statistics in order to aid selection of lag structures for cases in which theory offers insufficient guidance in the specification of a suitable lag structure. The AIC and SIC statistics penalise the addition of explanatory variables more heavily than the *R* bar square and, consequently, the maximum number of lags to be included in a model specification can be chosen by minimising the AIC and SIC and maximising the *R* bar square statistic. For example, a regression may be run first with one lag on the dependent variable, then with one and two lags, then with one to three lags and so on. Comparing the AIC, SIC and R bar square statistics for the successive rounds of analysis can assist in the selection of a parsimonious model specification if the specification with the lowest AIC/SIC and highest R bar square statistics is chosen.

Serial Correlation

A common test for serial correlation is provided by the Durbin–Watson (DW) statistic:

$$DW = \frac{\sum_{t=2}^{T} (\hat{\varepsilon}_t - \hat{\varepsilon}_{t-1})^2}{\sum_{t=1}^{T} \hat{\varepsilon}_t^2} \tag{6.15}$$

Pindyck and Rubinfeld (1997) note that the Durbin–Watson statistic can be difficult to interpret but indicate that the DW statistic ranges between 0 and 4 and will be close to 2 when there is no serial correlation present. Values close to zero indicate the presence of positive serial correlation and values close to 4 indicate negative serial correlation. Most statistical packages provide an estimate for the significance of the DW statistic. It should be noted that the DW statistic does not provide an appropriate test for serial correlation when the model specification includes the lagged dependent variable. Instead, a Breusch–Godfrey Lagrange multiplier (LM) test or Box–Pierce/Box–Ljung Q statistic test should be used. A detailed examination of these is beyond the scope of this book and readers are referred to Pindyck and Rubinfeld (1997) for a detailed review.

Heteroscedasticity

Common tests for heteroscedasticity include the Goldfeld–Quandt, Breusch–Pagan and White tests (see Pindyck and Rubinfeld, 1997). The Goldfeld–Quandt test is one of the easiest to conceptualise. The data are ordered with respect to one of the independent variables and separate regressions are run for low and high values. Sometimes a small number of middle observations may be omitted altogether. The ratio of the error sum of squares of the second regression (involving high values of the independent ordering variable) to the first is tested against the F distribution. When the ratio is higher than the critical value the null hypothesis of homoscedasticity is rejected (heteroscedasticity cannot be ruled out).

TIME SERIES METHODS

Autoregressive (AR) and moving average (MA) models do not draw heavily on economic theory. Instead, modelling strategies emphasise the predictability of a series based on its own past values. McGough and Tsolacos (1995) note that AR and MA models can provide good short-term predictions where short-term is defined as a few months or quarter years. They argue that MA models can be used to capture the gradual dissipation of demand or supply shocks. Such reasoning is not entirely inconsistent with economic theory, particularly in a commercial real estate market context, since significant changes in supply or demand are likely to be dissipated gradually rather than absorbed immediately in rent levels and growth.

A simple MA model takes the form:

$$Y_t = \mu + \varepsilon_t - \theta_1\varepsilon_{t-1} - \theta_2\varepsilon_{t-2} - \cdots - \theta_q\varepsilon_{t-q} \qquad (6.16)$$

This is referred to as an MA(q) process. In other words, Y_t is influenced by events that took place up to q periods in the past. If past shocks are hypothesised to persist for two periods then the model will be referred to as an MA(2) process. For more detail, refer to Greene (1997), Patterson (2000) or Pindyck and Rubinfeld (1997). A simple autoregressive model takes the form:

$$y_t = \phi_1 y_{t-1} + \phi_2 y_{t-2} + \cdots + \phi_p y_{t-p} + \delta + \varepsilon_t \qquad (6.17)$$

Note that the basic difference between the MA and AR processes is that in the former the value of the dependent variable in the current period is hypothesised as a weighted sum of past errors. With the latter the current value of the dependent variable is hypothesised as a weighted sum of the past values of the dependent variable together with a random error in the current period. Combining AR and MA processes in a model specification results in an ARMA model, denoted ARMA(p,q). Meanwhile, models can still be constructed for non-stationary series provided the data are first reduced to stationarity by differencing. For non-stationary series the model is referred to as an ARIMA model, and denoted ARIMA(p,d,q) where d refers to the order of homogeneity of the original series, or the number of times the data have been differenced in order to induce stationarity.

Specification of AR, MA and ARIMA models is primarily data driven and is beyond the scope of this book. For a full discussion, refer to Greene (1997), Patterson (2000) or Pindyck and Rubinfeld (1997). The preferred models chosen by McGough and Tsolacos (1995) are:

Retail:	ARIMA (1,2,0)
Office:	ARIMA (0,2,1)
Industrial:	ARIMA (3,2,0)

This indicates that the real rent series for all three sectors required differencing twice in order to induce stationarity. The specification of the retail and industrial models emphasise the autoregressive process while the specification of the office model emphasises the moving average process.

CONCLUSIONS

The purpose of this chapter has been to introduce, briefly, a number of more advanced modelling methods. The chapter begins with an examination of multi-equation rent determination models. In these, real estate market processes are explicitly modelled as a set of interacting or interdependent processes. Such models accord more closely with economic theory than single equation rent models. However, the data requirements of such a modelling strategy are significant and there are few such published models in the UK. The modelling approach is more common in US real estate market applications.

The commercial real estate rent determination literature is in a continual state of development and a number of concerns have been raised regarding existing published models and commonly accepted modelling methods. Drawing from a broad based survey of academics and practitioners in the real estate sector, Chaplin (1998) provides an analysis of the performance of a number of rent prediction/forecasting models. He identifies a consensus 'academic' single equation for predicting office rents as containing lagged rent, sectoral output and construction orders as explanatory variables. He argues that the consensus practitioners' model contains sectoral employees and GDP in place of sectoral output. Chaplin (1998) estimates parameters for the range of alternative models using, separately, data from Investment Property Databank (IPD), Jones Lang Lasalle/Lasalle Investment Management (JLL) and Hillier Parker (HP). He ranks the various models in terms of predictive power and goodness of fit. Disappointingly, he finds that few of the models that were ranked highly in terms of goodness of fit also scored well in terms of predictive power, and vice versa. Alarmingly, he also found that models selected on the basis of maximised goodness of fit criteria did not predict as well as a naive competitor around a third of the time where the naive competitor was defined as assuming that there would be no change in the dependent variable. Chaplin (1998, 1999, 2000) demonstrates the caution that should be used when considering predictions made using rent determination models. Estimating a range of office, industrial and retail rent determination models and simulating one step ahead predictions from the investor's perspective, he finds that models commonly fail to correctly predict the cyclical turning point, or else incorrectly predict one on several occassions for all the sectors examined.

These findings reinforce the argument that econometric modelling and forecasting can, at best, provide general guidance and improved information to real estate analysts and professionals. The complexity of economic, and real estate market, processes is such that market behaviour and dynamics cannot be reduced to a set of mathematical concepts and relationships that will perform perfectly well on empirical testing.

REFERENCES

Ball, M., Lizieri, C. and MacGregor, B.D. (1998) *The Economics of Commercial Property Markets* (London: Routledge).

Barkham, D. and Geltner, D. (1994) 'Unsmoothing British valuation based returns without assuming an efficient market', *Journal of Property Research*, vol. 11, 81–95.

Blundell, G. and Ward, C. (1987) 'Property portfolio allocation: a multi-factor model', *Land Development Studies*, vol. 4, no. 2, 145–56.

Chaplin, R. (1997) 'Unsmoothing valuation based indices using multiple regimes', *Journal of Property Research*, vol. 14, no. 3, 189–210.

Chaplin, R. (1998) 'An *ex post* comparative evaluation of office rent prediction models', *Journal of Property Valuation and Investment*, vol. 16, no. 1, 21–37.

Chaplin, R. (1999) 'The predictability of real office rents', *Journal of Property Research*, vol. 16, no. 1, 21–49.

Chaplin, R. (2000) 'Predicting real estate rents: walking backwards into the future', *Journal of Property Investment and Finance*, vol. 18, no. 3, 352–70.

Dunse, N., Jones, C., Orr, A. and Tarbert, H. (1998) 'The extent and limitations of local commercial property data', *Journal of Property Valuation and Investment*, vol. 16, no. 5, 455–73.

Geltner, D. (1989) 'Estimating real estate's systematic risk from aggregate level appraisal-based returns', *AREUEA Journal*, vol. 17, no. 4, 463–81.

Greene, W.H. (1997) *Econometric Analysis* (New Jersey: Prentice-Hall).

Hekman, J.S. (1985) 'Rental price adjustment and investment in the office market', *AREUEA Journal*, vol. 13, no. 1, 32–47.

Hendershott, P.H. (1996) 'Rental adjustment and valuation in overbuilt markets: evidence from the Sydney office market', *Journal of Urban Economics*, vol. 39, 51–67.

Hendershott, P.H. (1997) 'Uses of equilibrium models in real estate research', *Journal of Property Research*, vol. 14, 1–13.

Hendershott, P., Lizieri, C. and Matysiak, G.A. (1999) 'The workings of the London office market', *Real Estate Economics*, vol. 27, no. 2, 365–87.

Hoesli, M. and MacGregor, B.D. (2000) *Property Investment: Principles and Practice of Portfolio Management* (Harlow: Pearson Education).

Keogh, G. (1994) 'Use and investment markets in British real estate', *Journal of Property Valuation and Investment*, vol. 12, no. 4, 58–72.

MacGregor, B.D. and Nanthakumaran, N. (1992) 'The allocation to property in the multi-asset portfolio: the evidence reconsidered', *Journal of Property Research*, vol. 9, no. 1, 5–32.

McGough, T. and Tsolacos, S. (1995) 'Forecasting commercial rental values using ARIMA models', *Journal of Property Valuation and Investment*, vol. 13, no. 5, 6–22.

Morrel, G.D. (1991) 'Property performance analysis and performance indices: a review', *Journal of Property Research*, vol. 8, 29–57.

Patterson, K. (2000) *An Introduction to Applied Econometrics: A Time Series Approach* (Basingstoke: Macmillan).

Pindyck, R.S. and Rubinfeld, D.L. (1997) *Econometric Models and Economic Forecasts* (Boston: McGraw-Hill).

Rosen, K.T. (1984) 'Toward a model of the office building sector', *AREUEA Journal*, vol. 12, no. 3, 261–9.

Shilling, J.D., Sirmans, C.F. and Corgel, J.B. (1987) 'Price adjustment process for rental office space', *Journal of Urban Economics*, vol. 22, no. 2, 90–100.

Tsolacos, S., Keogh, G. and McGough, T. (1998) 'Modelling use, investment, and development in the British office market', *Environment and Planning A*, vol. 30, 1408–27.

Wheaton, W. (1987) 'The cyclic behaviour of the national office market', *AREUEA Journal*, vol. 15, no. 4, 281–99.

Wheaton, W.C., Torto, R.G. and Evans, P. (1997) 'The cyclic behaviour of the Greater London office market', *Journal of Real Estate Economics and Finance*, vol. 15, no. 1, 77–92.

7

Private Housing Market Analysis

INTRODUCTION

This chapter briefly examines methods that may be used to forecast, or predict, the demand for housing. It also examines methods of local housing market analysis including hedonic price modelling and testing for submarket (segmentation) effects. The chapter begins with a general discussion of housing as a commodity and an investment asset. This leads to an examination of hedonic price analysis and both macro and regional house price regression and forecasting models.

THE CHARACTERISTICS OF HOUSING

In some ways the housing market can be considered as being similar to other goods markets. However, there are a number of factors that distinguish the housing market from most other markets.

First, housing is not wholly a consumer good. Housing has a number of attributes including its most obvious function – the provision of shelter. Private housing may also be seen as bestowing status on its owners. However, it is the dual role of private housing as a consumer good and an investment asset that makes estimation of the demand for it potentially problematic (Maclennan, 1982). The demand for all buildings is a form of investment demand (Gruneberg, 1997) because buildings are durable and the economic life of a new building is normally many times the duration of the period required to construct it. In the housing market, the market price of owner occupied housing is normally equivalent to several times the annual income of those that purchase it (Maclennan, 1982). Most mortgage lenders are prepared to advance several multiples of a house purchaser's income. Households rarely have sufficient capital to purchase private housing outright and it is normally purchased on the basis of long-term mortgage agreements of between 15 and 25 years' duration. After the mortgage is repaid, a private house is likely to be one of the most valuable assets owned by a household. It is for these reasons that the demand for private housing must be considered as an investment, as well as a consumer, demand.

Second, as a direct consequence of the fact that housing is durable and has a long economic life, most of the demand for it is met not by the supply of new-build, but by the supply of second-hand units of housing. The private housing stock is considerably larger than the supply of housing for sale at any one time.

Third, private housing is a highly heterogeneous good. Different units of private housing traded in the housing market are not readily comparable since there will be differences between the physical and/or locational characteristics of the units. Housing is, in fact, a composite good (Rosen, 1974; Maclennan, 1982) and its demand is thus derived from the demand for its component attributes. As a consequence of the fact that each unit of housing is locationally fixed, Maclennan (1982) argues that the socio-economic and environmental attributes of a neighbourhood are traded with each private housing transaction. Importantly, it is worth noting that while the demand for a dwelling will be derived from the demand for its component attributes, the dwelling itself cannot be broken down into these components but must be traded as a composite good.

MICRO-LEVEL ANALYSIS

Hedonic Prices

As noted in the previous section, estimating the demand for housing is complicated by the fact that housing is a complex composite good. Different units of housing traded in the private market are likely to consist of different bundles and quantities of physical, locational and environmental attributes.

An extensive body of literature drawing on so-called hedonic price models has developed over recent years. Hedonic models, initially developed by Rosen (1974) following Lancaster (1966), may be used for the purpose of estimating the implicit (hedonic) prices of the individual attributes that comprise a composite good. Lancaster (1966) argues that consumer demand for a heterogeneous good is derived from consumers' demand for the constituent attributes of the good. According to consumer theory, consumers choose goods, and the quantities to consume, in order to maximise their utility or the satisfaction derived from the consumption of a good or service. According to Lancaster, consumers do not derive utility from the direct consumption of a complex heterogeneous good. Rather, their utility is derived from the attributes, or the services yielded by the attributes, of the good.

Rosen (1974) argues that the implicit prices of a good's attributes or characteristics can be estimated given knowledge of the market price of the good and a list of attributes and attribute quantities that comprise the good. Rosen's argument is that, in effect, consumers operate a production process the output of which is utility, or consumer satisfaction. The attributes yielded by heterogeneous goods are the inputs to individual consumers' utility production functions. Thus, consumers demand goods in order to consume their constituent attributes, and the price of a heterogeneous or differentiated good is a function of the good's implicit attribute prices and the quantities of the attributes present in the good.

Rosen's (1974) extension to Lancaster's modified consumer theory is based on a number of simplifying assumptions. Lancaster (1966) argues that combinations of goods could possess utility-bestowing attributes not present in any of the individual goods in isolation. Another way to put this is that the utility value of some combinations of attributes may be higher than the sum total of the individual attributes' utility values. However, Rosen assumes that this is not the case. His analysis assumes that a large number of differentiated goods are available to consumers such that consumers can acquire any combination of attributes by varying the combination and quantity of differentiated goods that they consume. Second-hand goods markets are assumed not to exist. Furthermore, all consumers are assumed to have identical evaluations of the different attributes, and their quantities, present in each differentiated good. The basic hedonic price model set out by Rosen is as follows:

$$p(z) = \sum_{i=1}^{n} p(z_i) \tag{7.1}$$

where

$p(z)$ = the known (observed) price of a differentiated composite good
$p(z_i)$ = the implicit price of the ith attribute present in the composite good

Hedonic regression has been widely applied for the purpose of modelling local house prices. Physically or structurally, housing is a heterogeneous good since individual houses may vary considerably in terms of size, layout, age, state of repair and the number and type of rooms present. Housing is always a heterogeneous good in terms of location since no two houses can share the same exact location. Thus, individual units of housing which are sold on the market are, at a minimum, spatially differentiated and are also frequently physically differentiated. The application of Rosen's implicit price model for differentiated goods to the purpose of modelling house prices is a logical step and the literature contains numerous examples of such applications.

The general hedonic price regression model for housing assumes that a linear, additive relationship exists between price and good attributes. The simple model takes the form:

$$P_i = \alpha + \beta' x_i + \varepsilon_i \tag{7.2}$$

where

P_i = observed price for the *i*th observation
α = constant term
β = vector of coefficients (parameters to be estimated) or implicit attribute prices
x_i = vector of physical (structural) and locational attributes for the *i*th observation
ε_i = random disturbance term for the *i*th observation

Equation (7.2) specifies that the price of the *i*th house is a function of the quantities of a set of attributes present in the house and their implicit (hedonic) prices. A disturbance term allows the relationship to be considered as an equality, since no model can hope to account for all the possible determinants of house prices. The simple model is cross-sectional, since it assumes that all observations relate to a single time period. Models based on observations encompassing more than one time period are generally adapted by including time-dummy variables. Thus:

$$P_i = \alpha_t D_t + \beta' x_i + \varepsilon_i \tag{7.3}$$

where

α_t = constant term for time period t
D_t = time-dummy variable, value 1 if the *i*th observation is in time period t, 0 otherwise

ESTIMATING AN HEDONIC HOUSE PRICE MODEL – BASIC PROCEDURE

The first step to the construction of any model based on economic relationships is a desk-based review of the objectives of the model, the objects being modelled and a theoretical review of the processes and dynamics to be captured by the model. For a simple hedonic house price model the goal of this step is to identify all possible partial determinants of house prices at the micro level, that is, the level of individual houses. As noted in the previous section, the following assumptions apply:

- Each observation of the complex heterogeneous good (each house in this case) represents a basket or bundle of simpler homogeneous goods or attributes.
- There is an implicit market for each of the homogeneous attributes such that their respective prices are determined by the interaction of supply and demand for that attribute.
- The price of an observation on the composite good (housing) is a function of its component attributes and their implicit market prices.

When compiling a list of all possible partial determinants of house prices, consideration should be given to physical, quality, locational and neighbourhood factors. Physical factors may include number of bedrooms, number of public rooms, total internal floor area, external space or plot area, number of bathrooms, house type, and so on. Quality factors may include aspects such as age and property condition. Locational factors may seem self-evident but can be difficult to adequately capture in appropriate variables. Clearly, if the model is being estimated to explain and predict house prices in a particular city or locality then locational factors are essentially neighbourhood factors. However, it may be possible to measure, or provide proxy variables for, aspects of neighbourhood quality such as local school quality, amenity or accessibility. After the list of theorised partial determinants has been compiled several fundamental questions must be addressed:

- Can the influences identified be measured or proxied by quantitative and/or binomial variables? In other words, are the variables actually measurable?

The fact that some influences on value are difficult, or even impossible, to measure and capture in quantitative variables is a recurring problem in the hedonic modelling literature. Neighbourhood quality provides a good example. It is not to be unexpected that one neighbourhood may be more attractive to house buyers than another similar neighbourhood. But what are the underlying factors that make this neighbourhood more attractive? Can these factors be captured in appropriate variables? There are no ready answers to such questions but it is important to note at the beginning of the modelling process that some of the partial determinants of prices or value will be difficult to conceptualise let alone model.

- Do the variables adequately capture the factors hypothesised to influence price or value? Are there any obvious partial determinants or possible determinants of value that have been omitted?
- Are any of the hypothesised relationships likely to be non-linear?

Since the use of OLS regression implicitly assumes that the relationship between the Y and X variables are linear, any non-linearity in these relationships must be removed or linearised. There is an argument, for example, that the relationship between price and internal area may be non-linear (for small houses additional square metreage may add value at a significant rate while for larger houses additional square metreage may add value at a lesser rate). We will come on to discuss linearising data later in this chapter.

- Are there likely to be any interactions between any of the variables?

There are often grounds for suspecting that there should be interaction between some explanatory variables. These possible interactions should be identified at the outset of the modelling process – before data are collected. Most hedonic house price models would be expected to include internal floor area and number of bedrooms as explanatory variables. Our *a priori* expectation would be that additional square metreage and additional bedrooms would both have the effect of adding value. However, it is also likely that there will be interaction between these two explanatory variables because additional large bedrooms should add more value than additional small bedrooms. Equally, it is plausible that a small number of very large bedrooms could be more valuable than a large number of small bedrooms.

HEDONIC EQUATION SPECIFICATION AND VARIABLE DESIGN

Hedonic price models are typically specified as linear additive equations with a combination of continuous and binomial explanatory variables. If a spreadsheet or database software package is used to compile the data prior to analysis then a typical (though highly simplified) example might be as shown in Table 7.1.

On importing the dataset into a suitable statistical package (such as SPSS) we can estimate the parameters of the equation. If the equation follows a simple linear, additive specification then the coefficients or parameter estimates (βs) will represent implicit prices (implied market prices of the attributes). We can estimate the parameters of a simple linear regression equation using the sample of data shown in Table 7.1. The results obtained are as shown in Table 7.2.

The size of the difference between the R square and adjusted R square statistics suggests that several of the explanatory variables are insignificant. Meanwhile, the standard error is high (more than £10,000) and the F statistic leads us to fail to reject the null hypothesis that all of the parameters of the equation are equal to zero. Table 7.3 shows the parameter estimates (coefficients) and t statistics.

Table 7.1 A simple hedonic price model dataset

P	*BRS*	*D*	*G*	*AR*	*DR*	*BR2*
39,500	2	0	0	44	0	0
65,750	3	0	0	55	1	0
41,750	2	0	1	59	1	0
44,500	2	0	0	62	1	0
49,495	2	0	0	65	0	0
30,000	2	0	0	70	1	0
70,211	3	1	0	72	1	1
31,040	2	0	0	78	1	0
48,550	3	1	1	79	1	1
33,060	2	0	0	84	1	0
38,500	3	0	0	85	1	0
51,020	3	1	0	90	1	0
58,595	3	0	1	100	1	0
57,595	3	1	1	109	1	1
49,995	4	1	1	129	1	0

P is the dependent or *Y* variable and refers to the observed transaction price for the *i*th house in the sample. The variable is discrete (with values measured to the nearest £1) with possible values for P_i ranging from zero to infinity.

BRS is a discrete explanatory variable measuring the number of bedrooms in the *i*th house.

D is a binomial or 'dummy' explanatory variable denoting whether the *i*th house is a detached house. If the *i*th house is detached then this variable takes the value 1. If the *i*th house is not detached then this variable takes the value zero.

G is a binomial explanatory variable denoting whether the *i*th house possesses a garage. If it does, then this variable takes the value 1 and zero otherwise.

AR is a discrete explanatory variable measuring the internal floor area (to the nearest square metre) of the *i*th house.

DR is a binomial explanatory variable denoting whether the *i*th house possesses a dining-room. If it does, then this variable takes the value 1.

BR2 is a binomial explanatory variable denoting whether the *i*th house possesses a second bathroom. If it does, then this variables takes the value 1.

Table 7.2 Regression statistics

R square	0.604
Adjusted *R* square	0.307
Standard error	10,122.05
F	2.034
Significance of *F*	0.174
Observations	15

Table 7.3 Parameter estimates and t statistics

Parameter	*Coefficients*	*Standard errors*	*t statistics*	*P*
Constant	22,365.12	16,862.30	1.3263	0.2213
BRS	18,142.11	7,270.57	2.4953	0.0372
D	−3,678.37	11,619.96	−0.3166	0.7597
G	249.33	7,085.45	0.0352	0.9728
AR	−259.67	207.54	−1.2512	0.2462
DR	−3,367.79	8,774.87	−0.3838	0.7111
BR2	11,378.28	10,812.15	1.0524	0.3234

The *t* statistics and their associated *P* values lead us to reject the null hypothesis that the parameter on the variable BRS (bedrooms) is equal to zero. In other words, this variable is statistically significant. The *P* value for this parameter estimate indicates that the estimate is significant at the 5 per cent level or with 95 per cent confidence. The estimates of the constant or intercept and the other five explanatory variables are not statistically significant. In general, if the *P* value is equal to, or greater than, 0.05 (5 per cent) then we fail to reject the null hypothesis. In some circumstances we might use the 1 per cent or even the 10 per cent significance level for these hypothesis tests, but this is rare.

If we were to take an overall view on the performance of the model, with the estimated parameters and regression statistics as shown above, it would be difficult to argue that the model we have is a good one. The explanatory power of the model is poor (the equation explains just over 30 per cent of variation in house prices in the dataset we have available). The *F* statistic is not significant, which means that we cannot be sure that the equation parameters are not all equal to zero. Most of the variables have proven to be statistically insignificant.

The most likely explanations for obtaining results such as those shown above are as follows:

(1) There is, in reality, no relationship between the dependent and independent variables as postulated in the specification of the regression equation. This possible explanation can be rejected in most cases. In the case of the example at hand it is unlikely that there really is no relationship between the price of housing and physical, locational and quality attributes of housing.
(2) The equation is misspecified. This is a more plausible explanation in many cases. It simply means that we have either incorrectly specified the equation (used the wrong independent variables) or not completely specified the equation (missed out some important influences on the dependent variable). In either case, the solution to the problem is to return to the business of specifying the equation from theory and then to collect data on the new or modified independent variables. The business of estimating the equation parameters is then repeated.
(3) Measurement error. If some or all of the independent variables are crudely collected, measured or have been collected from a potentially unreliable secondary source then we cannot rule out the possibility of measurement error. If this occurs then we are likely to obtain poor statistical results even if the equation is correctly specified.
(4) Insufficient data. If we attempt to estimate the parameters of a regression equation using a very small sample of data then we cannot rule out the possibility that the independent variables in the sample do not contain sufficient variance to explain the variance in the dependent variable. The solution here is to collect a larger sample of data and re-estimate the equation.

ESTIMATING PRICE, AMENITY OR NEIGHBOURHOOD EFFECTS WITH HEDONIC MODELS

Hedonic regression models have been used for the purpose of estimating the influence of amenity (disamenity) on the price of housing with considerable success. Typically, hedonic models constructed for this purpose include dummy variables denoting the presence or proximity of some amenity or disamenity effect. For example, we might include in the equation a dummy variable that takes the value 1 for houses situated next to busy main roads and 0 otherwise. When we estimate the parameters of the equation then we will obtain an estimate of the hedonic or implicit price of proximity to a busy main road. Our expectation would be to obtain a negative value for this coefficient. Alternatively, quantitative variables denoting the extent of some amenity or disamenity effect may be included. Such variables might include distance from a park or the quantity of traffic noise in a specific location. Another alternative is to estimate the parameters of identical regression equations for different samples of data representing groups of houses that are relatively homogeneous with respect to the amenity/disamenity effect(s) of interest. For example, we might estimate one equation for houses situated near parks and other green open spaces and another for houses that are not. There are several problems with this approach that will be examined later in the chapter.

The effects of airport noise on housing prices have been analysed by Mieszkowski and Saper (1978), Damm *et al.* (1980) and Uyeno *et al.* (1993). The analysis of Mieszkowski and Saper (1978), based on house sales data between 1969 and 1973, demonstrates that houses located in areas of high airport noise are associated with considerable sales price discounts. However, their analysis also demonstrates the susceptibility of the hedonic modelling approach to data and sampling inadequacies. The authors use several samples of data. For each sample, there is a test group consisting of houses situated in areas of high airport noise and a control group consisting of houses that are not situated in such areas. The analysis provides rather mixed results. As noted above, the analysis strongly suggests that houses situated in areas of high aircraft noise are associated with a price discount. Unfortunately, there is some inconsistency between the results obtained from the different data samples. For one of the samples, the results indicate that the discount increases with the level of noise. For the other sample, the results imply a discount that does not vary in relation to noise level – the discount applies to housing sold in the identified high airport noise areas at a flat rate.

The authors' model includes a total of 35 structural (physical) variables, 25 of which are dummy variables. Time-dummy variables are also included. Given the great physical detail described by the numerous variables, it is probable that multi-collinearity exists between sets of variables. This is not addressed explicitly by the authors and could account for some of the disparity between the results for the two different samples.

Similar analyses have been carried out to examine the influence of levels of air pollution on house prices. This approach is followed by Ridker and Henning (1968), Brookshire *et al.* (1982) and by Graves *et al.* (1988). Several of the studies exhibit subtle variations to the methodological approach adopted to test for amenity/disamenity effects on prices. The approach adopted by Graves *et al.* (1988), for example, is arguably more rigorous than that adopted by Mieszkowski and Saper (1978). Graves *et al.* (1988) identify variables as belonging to one of three categories: focus variables, free variables and doubtful variables. Focus variables are those that are of direct interest to the analysis at hand. In the case of Graves *et al.*, two focus variables identified the extent of air pollution (visibility and suspended particulate concentrations). Free variables are those which are not of direct interest to the analysis but which are known to be significant determinants of the dependent variable (locational and physical attribute variables, for example). Doubtful variables are those which may or may not be significant and/or for which uncertainty exists as to the expected sign of the parameters to be estimated.

Graves *et al.* (1988) devise a total of 16 different equation specifications and estimate the parameters for all 16 equations. In each case, all free and focus variables are entered into the equation. However, the 16 equations are differentiated by entering differing permutations of one, two, three, all or none of the doubtful variables into the regression equation. The authors select the specification that introduces the least bias, and the greatest estimated parameter stability. The analysis indicates that levels of air pollution are a highly significant determinant of house prices (second only to floor area for the authors' model and samples).

This section has provided a brief review of hedonic house price models. Hedonic theory is relatively simple: in constructing a model it is assumed that a unit of private housing (a dwelling) is analogous to a basket of goods such as those that might be purchased at a supermarket (Evans, 1995). The market price of the basket of goods is equal to the sum of the price of the *n* goods in the shopping basket. Possible uses for hedonic house price models include:

(1) A means of explaining and predicting the determination of housing prices at the micro level on the basis of physical, quality and locational characteristics.
(2) A means for exploring the spatial and structural boundaries of housing market areas and segmentation within markets (submarkets). The submarket hypothesis will be examined in detail later in the book.
(3) A means for identifying 'one off' positive and negative premia on house prices relative to amenity/disamenity effects. Hypothesised determinants of such premia are normally measured by way of binomial variables that measure the presence or otherwise of such effects.
(4) Constructing 'constant quality' house price indices. See the following section for a thorough discussion of this use of hedonic house price models.

MEASURING TEMPORAL HOUSE PRICE APPRECIATION

The purpose of a house price index is to provide a representative measure of price movements for a defined housing market area. They can provide a summary of market performance and are important primarily because housing is a highly heterogeneous good for which there is no single observable market price. Within any given housing market, demand is unlikely to rise and fall uniformly for all types of housing over time. Instead, it is likely that there are times when the price of properties of a certain type, or in certain sub-locations, will be growing faster than the price of other types of private housing or properties in other sub-locations within the market. To further complicate matters, the *relative* price growth rates of property types or sub-locations may change over time such that the property type or sub-location with the highest growth rate may be different in each time period or may change after several time periods. One of the effects of this phenomenon is the introduction of sample selection bias to estimates of typical (mean) price levels and growth rates. Sample selection bias can be demonstrated using a simple hypothetical example.

Example

Suppose that we wish to measure the mean house price over time in a given local housing market. For the sake of simplicity, assume that there are three types of private housing in the market and that we will describe them as 'lower end', 'standard' and 'upper end' houses. The stock of housing in the local market extends to 1,000 units of each property type. Around 300 units of housing come onto the market and are sold each year. However, this sample of 300 is not randomly drawn from the population of 3,000 units. Suppose that the composition of the sample is as shown in Table 7.4.

Table 7.4 Composition of hypothetical sample of private housing transactions

Year	*Lower end*	*Standard*	*Upper end*	*Sample size*
1	125	85	90	300
2	115	100	85	300
3	105	115	80	300
4	100	120	80	300
5	90	115	95	300
6	85	105	110	300
7	80	95	125	300
8	90	90	120	300
9	100	85	115	300
10	110	80	110	300

The figures in Table 7.4 have been deliberately selected to ensure that the sample is rarely representative of the population. Instead, the sample is over-representative of lower end followed by standard and, finally, upper end of the market properties. Although the figures shown here are contrived, there is evidence to suggest that private housing market activity does reflect such patterns, with the market being more driven by first-time buyers and cheaper properties at the beginning of an economic cycle compared with the late stages of a cycle. Suppose that annual price growth rates for the three property types are as shown in Table 7.5. If we happen to know that the values of the three property types are £50,000, £100,000 and £150,000 in year 1 then we can easily calculate their value, and the total value of the housing stock, in subsequent years (Table 7.6).

The value of the total private housing stock, from year to year, can and must be estimated using the sample of transactions data. The predictions are calculated as follows:

$$\text{Predicted stock value in year 1} = 10[(125 \times 50{,}000) + (85 \times 100{,}000) + (90 \times 150{,}000)]$$

$$\text{Predicted stock value in year 2} = 10[(115 \times 55{,}000) + (100 \times 106{,}000) + (85 \times 162{,}000)]$$

Hence, the predicted stock values (and implied predicted rates of price growth) are as shown in Table 7.7.

As the figures clearly show, our estimate of the growth rate is biased when we use a biased sample for the estimation. There is nothing surprising in this

Table 7.5 Price growth rates for the three property types (percentages)

Year	*Lower end*	*Standard*	*Upper end*
1	–	–	–
2	10	6	8
3	9	7	7
4	8	8	7
5	8	10	6
6	7	9	7
7	7	8	8
8	6	8	10
9	7	7	9
10	8	7	8

Table 7.6 Property values and stock value

Year	*Lower end*	*Standard*	*Upper end*	*Actual stock value (£m)*
1	50,000	100,000	150,000	300.00
2	55,000	106,000	162,000	323.00
3	59,950	113,420	173,340	346.71
4	64,746	122,494	185,474	372.71
5	69,926	134,743	196,602	401.27
6	74,820	146,870	210,364	432.06
7	80,058	158,619	227,194	465.87
8	84,861	171,309	249,913	506.08
9	90,802	183,301	272,405	546.51
10	98,066	196,132	294,198	588.40

Table 7.7 Predicted and actual growth rates

Year	*Predicted stock value*	*Implied growth rate*	*Actual growth rate*
1	282.50	–	–
2	306.95	8.65	7.67
3	332.05	8.18	7.34
4	360.12	8.45	7.50
5	404.66	12.37	7.66
6	449.21	11.01	7.67
7	498.73	11.02	7.83
8	530.45	6.36	8.63
9	559.87	5.55	7.99
10	588.39	5.09	7.66

finding and the example itself is a greatly simplified version of reality. Nevertheless, the example demonstrates that bias can be introduced to estimates of house prices and price growth when we use transactions data. This is for two essential reasons:

(1) The composition of the sample (with respect to property type, sub-location and so on) is unlikely to be constant and, worse, may change over time in a systematic way.
(2) Growth rates relating to different property types and sub-locations may change over time in a systematic way.

In this example we know very well that the housing stock comprises equal proportions of three distinct property types. In reality, the components of the housing stock (individual houses) would not be so easy to categorise. Nor would it be a simple task to estimate the number of properties in each defined property type or sub-location. If it were a straightforward task to define and identify a set number of property types and sub-locations, and to gather complete information on the composition of the housing stock, then we could correct for sample selection bias quite easily. However, in the absence of such an information set it is preferable to find an alternative method of estimating house price growth that is less susceptible to sample selection bias.

There are a number of different ways in which house price indices may be estimated but this chapter focuses on the hedonic regression and repeat-sales regression methods since these are particularly common. Over recent years a substantial body of literature has developed. The concern of much of this is the refinement of existing house price index estimation methods with the purpose of eliminating, or at least reducing, bias. This literature will be summarised briefly since the main interest in this section is on the mechanics of the two estimation methods mentioned above.

HEDONIC HOUSE PRICE INDICES

There are essentially two ways in which hedonic house price indices can be constructed and estimated. Both methods involve the specification and estimation of one or more hedonic regression equations in which house prices are regressed against a vector of physical and locational variables. The difference between the two methods relates to the temporal element of house price appreciation, that is, the treatment of time.

The first method is often referred to as the 'intertemporal hedonic method' (Gatzlaff and Haurin, 1997). The regression equation will, as usual, include variables that measure physical and locational characteristics of each unit of housing, and the dependent variable will be the observed transaction price (or possibly assessed value) of each unit. Additional time dummy variables (binomial variables) will indicate the year, quarter or possibly month in which each housing unit was transacted. If we return to the simple example set out in Table 7.1 then we can see that the temporal dimensions of a cross-sectional dataset covering three years in total can be measured by including an additional two dummy variables. This is shown in Table 7.8.

Table 7.8 repeats the information shown in Table 7.1 after including the two additional dummy variables (the last two columns of Table 7.8). For 1901 transactions the variable *YR1901* takes on the value 1. Otherwise this

Table 7.8 A simple hedonic price model dataset with time dummies

P	*BRS*	*D*	*G*	*AR*	*DR*	*BR2*	*YR1901*	*YR1902*
39,500	2	0	0	44	0	0	1	0
65,750	3	0	0	55	1	0	0	1
41,750	2	0	1	59	1	0	0	0
44,500	2	0	0	62	1	0	0	0
49,495	2	0	0	65	0	0	0	0
30,000	2	0	0	70	1	0	0	1
70,211	3	1	0	72	1	1	0	1
31,040	2	0	0	78	1	0	1	0
48,550	3	1	1	79	1	1	0	0
33,060	2	0	0	84	1	0	0	1
38,500	3	0	0	85	1	0	0	0
51,020	3	1	0	90	1	0	1	0
58,595	3	0	1	100	1	0	0	0
57,595	3	1	1	109	1	1	1	0
49,995	4	1	1	129	1	0	0	0

variable has the value 0. For 1902 transactions the variable *YR1902* takes on the value 1. The variables *Y1901* and *Y1902* are both equal to 0 for transactions that occured in 1900.

Constructing a housing price index from the coefficients is straightforward when the intertemporal method is used. The specification of the equation is such that physical and locational attribute parameters are assumed constant over time. In other words, assuming we had a dataset of housing transactions between 1980 and 2000 then the implicit price of, say, one bedroom is assumed constant irrespective of the year in which a given housing transaction took place. Although the coefficients (estimated parameters) are likely to differ from attribute to attribute, they will be constant for each attribute over time. The time dummy variables therefore measure nothing but temporal variation in house prices. This means that an index is formed by chronologically ordering the time dummy variable coefficients.

According to the second variation of the hedonic regression method, separate regression equations are estimated for each of a succession of cross-sectional datasets. Each dataset includes housing transactions that occured within one defined time period. Since parameter estimates are now obtained for all attributes and all time periods, the coefficients vary over time. In order to construct the price index, a chronologically ordered set of house prices is estimated for a given constant bundle of characteristics using each of the cross-sectional models. Thus, a predicted transaction price is obtained for an hypothetical house with a given, constant set of physical and locational attributes.

BIAS IN HEDONIC HOUSE PRICE INDICES

There are some practical difficulties with both variants of the hedonic regression method of estimating housing price indices. For example, the method is data-intensive. In order to estimate an index for one local housing market it is likely that several thousand observed housing transactions will be required. Each observation requires information on price as well as physical, locational and quality attribute information. Such data are, at best, time-consuming and expensive to collect. At worst, it may be impossible to collect an adequate data set for reasons of cost, the time required to do so or simply because price information is not readily available.

There are other, potentially more serious, problems with the hedonic regression method. As Meese and Wallace (1997) note, bias may be introduced to hedonic regression indices estimated by either variant if important physical or locational variables are mistakenly omitted from the analysis. This is likely to be a significant problem if the implicit prices of unobserved attributes change over time, particularly if the rate of change differs from that associated with the observed implicit price attributes. The likely outcome is that the estimated hedonic indices will give a misleading impression as to constant-quality house price changes over time.

A further source of potential bias, associated with the intertemporal hedonic method, is concerned with the necessary assumption that implicit physical and/or locational attribute prices are constant over time. The assumption is unlikely to be valid if rates of physical and locational attribute price appreciation differ over time. To a certain extent, the assumption of constant attribute prices over time confounds common sense: the purchasers of housing are, in part, consumers and are driven by tastes and preferences to a certain extent. It is likely that some locations, neighbourhoods and certain physical and design features of housing witness changing degrees of popularity over time. Certain features of housing move in and out of desirability over time.

Furthermore, Goetzmann and Spiegel (1997) note that there is a non-temporal component to house price appreciation. This occurs mainly because many house owners carry out improvements to their property just prior to their selling it or just after their purchasing it. The main benefit of estimating house price indices using a series of cross-sectional hedonic models is that the implicit prices of physical and locational attributes are permitted to change over time. Thus, the risk of bias is reduced using the cross-sectional method.

REPEAT-SALES REGRESSION HOUSE PRICE INDICES

Repeat-sales regression methods of constructing and estimating house price indices are an attractive alternative to the hedonic methods. As noted earlier, hedonic methods are data intensive and may be associated with high data collection costs. By contrast, repeat-sales regression methods do not rely on physical attribute variables in the regression equation. Consequently, data are relatively easy and inexpensive to collect. Using the RS method, house price growth is estimated from a dataset comprising pairs of house price observations. Each observation of the dataset describes the first and second sale price, and the transaction dates, for one given house. If the physical state of the house does not change between sales then the witnessed house price inflation can be assumed to be due wholly to constant quality price appreciation. In effect, constant-quality price appreciation is uncovered by calculating the price growth rates of individual (constant-quality) houses. The individual price growth rates of a sample of paired repeat-sale observations are used to estimate one price index over the period of the sample.

There are two main variants of the repeat-sales regression method of estimating housing price indices. These are the Bailey, Muth and Nourse (1963) method and the Case and Shiller (1989) method. These will be referred to as the BMN and CS methods hereafter. The general form of the repeat-sales regression model is as follows:

$$\ln\left(\frac{P_i^2}{P_i^1}\right) = \sum_{t=1}^{T} c_t(D_i^2 - D_i^1) + e_i^{21} \qquad (7.4)$$

where

P_i^1 = the initial sale price of the ith observation
P_i^2 = the subsequent sale price of the ith observation
D_i^1 = dummy variable relating to the date of the first sale
D_i^2 = dummy variable relating to the date of the subsequent sale

As noted earlier, the coefficients of the successive time dummy variables represent the log of the cumulative house price index. The main differences between the BMN and CS methods relates to the treatment of heteroscedasticity and estimation method. The BMN method makes no adjustment for heteroscedasticity. The dependent variable is the natural log of the second transaction price relative to the first (the log of the price relative). The explanatory variables are all time dummy variables. They are coded negative one to indicate the second transaction date and positive one to indicate the initial transaction date. Thus, for any given observation one of the time dummy variables will be coded negative one, one of them will be coded positive one and the remainder will be coded zero. The coefficients of the time dummy variables are estimated by ordinary least squares (OLS) regression. After estimation, the chronologically ordered time dummy variables represent the natural logarithm of the cumulative price index.

The CS method, as set out by Case and Shiller (1989), recognises that the price growth rates revealed by the repeat sales of individual properties are not necessarily independent of the length of time (the holding period) between those sales. Specifically, the residuals obtained from the ordinary least squares regression of log price relatives on time dummy variables may be heteroscedastic with respect to holding period. In other words, there may be some relationship between holding period and the residuals obtained from an OLS regression. The CS method accounts for the effect of holding period on the rate of price inflation. It involves weighting the dependent variable (log price relative) by dividing it by the predicted values obtained from a regression of squared residuals (obtained using the BMN method) on holding period. This method is also sometimes known as the 'weighted repeat sales method'. Essentially, the CS method has two stages, the first of which is the specification and estimation of a regression equation using the BMN method.

ESTIMATING A REPEAT-SALES REGRESSION EQUATION

The data requirements are simple for estimating a housing price index using the BMN method. A typical observation from such a dataset is likely to include the natural logarithm of the second sale price divided by the prior sale price (log price relative). This is the dependent variable. The independent variables are time dummies. If the dataset covers the period 1950 to 1955 and we wish to construct an annual house price index then there will be six time dummy variables (one for each year). A simple (hypothetical) example of such a dataset is shown in Table 7.9.

In Table 7.9 the first five columns are simply used to construct the dependent and independent variables and are not used in the statistical analysis. The dependent variable is *LPR* and the time dummies are the independent variables as noted above. The parameters of the time dummies are estimated using ordinary least squares. If this is done for the simple hypothetical dataset shown in Table 7.9 then the coefficients are obtained as in Table 7.10.

It should be noted that on estimating the coefficients shown in Table 7.10 a constraint is imposed such that the value of the first time dummy coefficient is equal to zero. When the antilog of the coefficient values are calculated this yields a housing price index, as shown in Table 7.11, with the first value equal to one. There are various ways in which to ensure that

Table 7.9 A simple repeat-sales regression model dataset

P1	*P2*	*Y1*	*Y2*	*PR*	*LPR*	*Y1950*	*Y1951*	*Y1952*	*Y1953*	*Y1954*	*Y1955*
50,000	54,500	1950	1951	1.090	0.0862	−1	1	0	0	0	0
45,000	52,500	1951	1953	1.167	0.1544	0	−1	0	1	0	0
80,000	106,500	1952	1955	1.331	0.2859	0	0	−1	0	0	1
49,000	69,000	1952	1955	1.408	0.3422	0	0	−1	0	0	1
76,000	104,000	1950	1954	1.368	0.3133	−1	0	0	0	1	0
38,000	46,000	1951	1953	1.211	0.1914	0	−1	0	1	0	0
54,000	64,000	1952	1954	1.185	0.1697	0	0	−1	0	1	0
84,000	90,000	1951	1952	1.071	0.0686	0	−1	1	0	0	0
66,000	83,000	1950	1952	1.258	0.2295	−1	0	1	0	0	0
41,000	53,000	1952	1955	1.293	0.2570	0	0	−1	0	0	1

P1	First sale price (dependent variable)	Y1950	Time dummy representing 1950
P2	Second sale price	Y1951	Time dummy representing 1951
Y1	First sale year	Y1952	Time dummy representing 1952
Y2	Second sale year	Y1953	Time dummy representing 1953
PR	Price relative	Y1954	Time dummy representing 1954
LPR	Natural log of price relative	Y1955	Time dummy representing 1955

Table 7.10 An example of repeat-sales coefficients

Time dummy	*Coefficient*
1950	0.000
1951	0.103
1952	0.189
1953	0.276
1954	0.336
1955	0.484

Table 7.11 Estimated housing price index

Year	*Index value*
1950	1.000
1951	1.108
1952	1.208
1953	1.318
1954	1.399
1955	1.623

the index starts with a value of one, but one simple method is to specify an ordinary linear (additive) equation and impose a constraint on the first coefficient. This can be done, for example, in SPSS (Statistical Package for Social Scientists) although the nonlinear regression function must be used in order to give access to the constraint options.

Estimating a housing price index using the CS method involves, as noted earlier, an additional step. The process can be broken down into a number of stages:

(1) Add a new variable to the dataset (holding period). This variable should measure time elapsed between the first and subsequent sale for each paired repeat-sale observation. Holding period may be measured in years, quarter years or months. In general, months would be preferable to quarters and quarters preferable to years.

(2) Estimate the time dummy coefficients using the BMN method as detailed above.
(3) Save the residuals (error term for each observation).
(4) Create a new variable by squaring these residuals.
(5) Estimate a regression equation in which the dependent variable is the new variable (squared residuals from the BMN estimation) and the explanatory variable is holding period.
(6) Save the predicted (fitted) values of this estimated regression equation.
(7) Divide the *LPR* variable by the saved fitted values.
(8) Estimate the BMN equation again. This time use the weighted version of the *LPR* variable rather than the original *LPR* variable.
(9) Transform the coefficients into a cumulative price index as previously described.

BIAS IN REPEAT-SALES REGRESSION EQUATIONS

As discussed earlier, the imperative for the creation of the hedonic and repeat-sales regression methods was the goal of reducing bias in housing price indices. However, this should not be taken as meaning that indices estimated using one or more of these methods are entirely free from bias. Bias in hedonic models was discussed earlier. In this section we examine sources of bias in repeat-sales regression models.

There are two main sources of bias in repeat-sales indices. First, the method does not explicitly take account of the influence of time on house prices. To estimate the model it is conventionally assumed that no physical changes have occured to a house between successive sales. Steps can be taken to ensure that information is collected on major physical alterations and improvements, but a problem with no simple cure is the fact that every house described in the sample dataset will have aged to some degree between its successive sales. For this reason, indices estimated using the RS method are thought, by some commentators, to understate house price appreciation (Clapp and Giacotto, 1992). There is a commonsense logic to this view because a property that increases in value by 50 per cent over a ten-year period has done so despite having aged by ten years. We assume here that housing declines in quality terms as it ages. So the 'constant quality' price appreciation must be more than 50 per cent.

Despite this argument, the empirical evidence is not conclusive that repeat-sales indices do understate house price inflation. Mark and Goldberg (1984) and Case *et al.* (1991) have found that their RS indices did predict lower than expected house price growth. By contrast, Crone and Voith (1992) and Gatzlaff and Ling (1994) did not find this to be the case.

Second, there is an argument that housing price indices estimated using repeat-sales data are not entirely free from sample selection bias. There are several published studies that suggest that datasets of repeat-sales transactions are unlikely to be representative of the underlying population (the private housing stock). Clapp and Giacotto (1992) argue that such datasets are likely to over-represent properties that trade frequently. They refer to such properties as 'lemons' or properties that are in some way substandard and are hence traded frequently. They go on to argue that using such a dataset may lead to biased index estimates.

According to Clapp *et al.* (1991), repeat-sales datasets are also likely to over-represent starter homes, which sell more frequently than other types of housing, and generally for lower prices. The implication is that RS indices are likely to give a better indication of house price appreciation relative to the lower end of the housing market than the full population of housing. Meanwhile, Steele and Goy (1997) hypothesise that repeat-sales datasets may include a large proportion of what they refer to as 'short-hold arbitrage transactions'. These are likely to be defective or run-down properties that are purchased relatively cheaply by entrepreneurial house buyers, upgraded and quickly re-sold for a profit. The argument is that this form of sample selection bias may introduce a tendency for repeat-sales indices to overstate price appreciation.

In conclusion, relatively sophisticated techniques such as hedonic and repeat-sales regression can be used effectively to reduce systematic bias in housing price indices. In fact, there is no reason why these methods cannot be used to create indices for other property types. However, it should be remembered that these methods do not give complete protection against bias. Researchers should bear potential sources of bias in mind. Furthermore, it is worth reiterating that every effort should be made to ensure, when sampling, that samples are as representative as possible of their parent populations.

MACRO-LEVEL ANALYSIS

There is a well-established literature concerned with modelling and forecasting UK house prices measured at the national level (for a review, see Muellbauer and Murphy, 1997; Meen and Andrew, 1998). Most published national house price models are derived from structural supply and demand equations and take the form of single reduced form equations. Over recent years macro-level models have become increasingly sophisticated and econometric models have proven suitable for estimating the effects of mortgage rationing on house prices (Meen, 1989, 1990, 1996; Muellbauer and

Murphy, 1997) and the effect of lumpy transaction costs on housing market activity and price inflation (Muellbauer and Murphy, 1997).

In general, variations in income over time are hypothesised as the primary determinant of cyclical house prices, although in some cases consumption rather than income is used (Pain and Westaway, 1996). Analyses of the UK housing market show that it tends to follow pronounced cycles that last approximately 7 or 8 years. Consequently, satisfactory results are obtained from econometric models of national house prices linked with income or consumption.

The process of specifying a macro-level house price model is similar to the process that should be followed when specifying a single equation commercial property rent model. The primary difference is that, on the demand side, house prices are derived from the level of disposable income. Other variables that are commonly included in such models include:

- The mortgage rate (borrowing rate)
- The household formation rate (an indicator of growth in demand)
- The number of households in certain age groups, often the 20–29 age group as such households are particularly economically active
- Expectations proxies

Since private housing has a dual role as an investment asset as well as a consumption good, it is logical that households' expectations about future house price growth rates will influence their present bids for the acquisition of housing. If future rates of growth are expected to be high then households are likely to be willing to pay more for housing. Expectations are difficult to proxy but some published models demonstrate satisfactory results by including lagged rates of house price growth. The assumption here is that households' expectations about future rates of growth are a function of recent rates of growth.

Many macro housing market models do not contain any supply-side variables. Others contain variables that measure the supply of new-build housing. However, supply-side variables are, in general, difficult to define and data are difficult to collect. Unlike commercial property market sectors, it is rare for a supply of vacant second-hand property to exist within the private housing market. Households with an intention to move home tend to remain until they have successfully sold on their existing house. It is therefore extremely difficult to conceptualise, let alone measure, second-hand supply in the private housing market. For this main reason, as noted earlier, single equation macro house price equations are often little more than inverted (rearranged) demand functions.

REFERENCES

Bailey, M.J., Muth, R.F. and Nourse, H.O. (1963) 'A regression method for real estate price index construction', *Journal of the American Statistical Association*, vol. 58, 933–42.

Brookshire, D.S., Thayer, M.A., Schulze, W.D. and D'Arge, R.C. (1982) 'Valuing public goods – a comparison of survey and hedonic approaches', *American Economic Review*, vol. 72, no. 1, 165–77.

Case, B. and Shiller, R. (1989) 'The efficiency of the market for single family homes', *American Economic Review*, vol. 79, no. 1, 45–56.

Case, B., Pollakowski, W.O. and Wachter, S.M. (1991) 'On choosing among house price index methodologies', *Journal of the American Real Estate and Urban Economics Association*, vol. 19, 286–307.

Clapp, J.M. and Giacotto, C. (1992) 'Estimating price indices for residential property: a comparison of repeat sales and assessed value methods', *Journal of the American Statistical Association*, vol. 87, no. 418, 300–6.

Clapp, J.M., Giacotto, C. and Tirtiroglu, D. (1991) 'Housing price indices based on all transactions compared to repeat subsamples', *AREUEA Journal*, vol. 19, no. 3, 270–85.

Crone, T.M. and Voith, R.P. (1992) 'Estimating house price appreciation: a comparison of methods', *Journal of Housing Economics*, vol. 2, 324–38.

Damm, D., Lerman, S.R., Lerner-Lam, E. and Young, J. (1980) 'The response of urban real estate values in anticipation of the Washington Metro', *Journal of Transport Economics and Policy*, September 1980.

Evans, A.W. (1995) 'The property market: ninety per cent efficient?', *Urban Studies*, vol. 32, no. 1, 5–29.

Gatzlaff, D.H. and Haurin, D.R. (1997) 'Sample selection bias and repeat-sales index estimates', *Journal of Real Estate Finance and Economics*, vol. 14, 33–50.

Gatzlaff, D.H. and Ling, D.C. (1994) 'Measuring changes in local house prices: an empirical investigation of alternative methodologies', *Journal of Urban Economics*, vol. 35, 221–44.

Goetzmann, W.N. and Spiegel, M. (1997) 'A spatial model of housing returns and neighbourhood substitutability', *Journal of Real Estate Finance and Economics*, vol. 14, 11–31.

Graves, P., Murdoch, J.C., Thayer, M.A. and Waldman, D. (1988) 'The robustness of hedonic price estimation: urban air quality', *Land Economics*, vol. 64, no. 3, 220–33.

Gruneberg, S.L. (1997) *Construction Economics: An Introduction* (Basingstoke: Macmillan).

Lancaster, K. (1966) 'A new approach to consumer theory', *Journal of Political Economy*, vol. 74, 132–57.

Leishman, C. and Watkins, C. (2002) 'Estimating local repeat sales house price indices for British cities', *Journal of Property Investment and Finance*, vol. 20, no. 1, 36–58.

Maclennan, D. (1982) *Housing Economics* (London: Longman).

Mark, D. and Goldberg, M. (1984) 'Alternative house price indices: an evaluation', *Journal of the American Real Estate and Urban Economics Association*, vol. 12, 30–49.
Meen, G. (1989) 'The ending of mortgage rationing and its effects on the housing market: a simulation study', *Urban Studies*, vol. 26, no. 2, 240–52.
Meen, G. (1990) 'The removal of mortgage market constraints and the implications for econometric modelling of UK house prices', *Oxford Bulletin of Economics and Statistics*, vol. 52, 1–24.
Meen, G. (1996) 'Ten propositions in UK housing macroeconomics: an overview of the 1980s and early 1990s', *Urban Studies*, vol. 33, 425–44.
Meen, G. (1999) 'Regional house prices and the ripple effect: a new interpretation', *Housing Studies*, vol. 14, no. 6, 733–53.
Meen, G. and Andrew, M. (1998) 'On the aggregate housing market implications of labour market change', *Scottish Journal of Political Economy*, vol. 45, no. 4, 393–419.
Meese, R.A. and Wallace, N.E. (1997) 'The construction of residential housing price indices: a comparison of repeat-sales, hedonic regression, and hybrid approaches', *Journal of Real Estate Finance and Economics*, vol. 14, 51–73.
Mieszkowski, P. and Saper, A.M. (1978) 'An estimate of the effects of airport noise on property values', *Journal of Urban Economics*, vol. 5, no. 4, 425–40.
Muellbauer, J. and Murphy, A. (1997) 'Booms and busts in the UK housing market', *The Economic Journal*, vol. 107, November, 1701–27.
Pain, N. and Westaway, P. (1996) *Modelling Structural Change in the UK Housing Market: A Comparison of Alternative Approaches to Modelling House Prices in the UK* (London: National Institute of Economic and Social Research).
Ridker, R. and Henning, J. (1968) 'The determinants of residential property values with special reference to air pollution', *Review of Economics and Statistics*, vol. 46, 246–57.
Rosen, S. (1974) 'Hedonic prices and implicit markets: product differentiation in pure competition', *Journal of Political Economy*, vol. 82, 34–55.
Steele, M. and Goy, R. (1997) 'Short holds, the distribution of first and second sales, and bias in the repeat-sales price index', *Journal of Real Estate Finance and Economics*, vol. 14, 133–54.
Uyeno, D., Hamilton, S.W. and Biggs, A.J.G. (1993) 'The density of residential land use and the impact of airport noise', *Journal of Transport Economics and Policy*, January, vol. 27, no. 1.

8

Modelling Real Estate Markets at the Local Level

INTRODUCTION

The purpose of this chapter is to set out methodologies for the analysis of real estate markets at the local level. Up to this point markets have been discussed in very general terms. The models and modelling approaches examined so far have been constructed on the principle that real estate markets exist as clearly identifiable, unambiguous entities. However, this assumption largely ignores the spatial characteristics of real estate and real estate markets. Clearly, it is the case that every property is fixed in terms of location and, furthermore, that only one property can occupy an exact given location. This suggests that, at the level of the individual property, location may be an important determinant of price or value. For example, real estate unit rentals are likely to be affected by proximity to consumers in the retail sector or transportation routes/nodes in the industrial sector. The spatial fixity of supply and the partly location-specific nature of demand are of particular importance to a micro-level (individual property) consideration of real estate markets. Indeed, these factors are a primary determinant of what may be termed 'local markets'.

As we have already noted, the user demand for real estate is a derived demand. Subject to a small number of rare exceptions, we can assume that users/occupiers of real estate demand it because it can either be used to produce utility (as in the case of occupiers of residential property) or to produce a profit (as in the cases of retail, office and industrial real estate occupiers). As noted in the previous chapter, private housing has (i) consumption good and (ii) investment asset properties. Households purchase housing because (i) it yields a flow of 'housing' services such as space, shelter, and so on, and (ii) it can be re-sold at some later date. This investment attribute of private housing complicates analysis somewhat since most occupiers are likely to hope to make a profit from later resale rather than simply recovering the capital invested. Meanwhile, commercial and industrial occupiers demand real estate because it may be used as an input to production processes which, in turn, may generate profit. Note that production processes refer to the production of both goods and services.

The remainder of this chapter focuses on the case of local office markets since the retail and residential sectors are each examined in more detail in separate chapters. The discussion begins with a consideration of what local markets are and how they may be defined. This conceptual and theoretical discussion then leads on to an examination of practical methods of identifying and analysing office markets at the local level.

DEFINING A MARKET

Probably the simplest conceptualisation of a market is provided by the idea of an auction house. Imagine an auction house that deals in the buying and selling of a slightly differentiated (nearly homogeneous) good, such as private motor vehicles. Since the example concerns an auction house we can assume that there are a large number of buyers and a large number of sellers (one seller for each item auctioned). The items (lots) are sold one by one, the prospective purchasers having had some time to view them in advance of the auction. Key characteristics of each lot are announced by the auctioneer prior to the commencement of the bidding. Let us assume that the features that matter to prospective buyers are fully described by:

- vehicle make
- vehicle model
- age
- physical condition (deterioration)
- engine size
- transmission type
- colour
- mileage
- service history

The market price of each lot is set by the bidding process and is a function of the vehicle's characteristics. Let us refer to the 9 features of characteristics as variables and denote them X_1, X_2, X_3 and so on through to X_9. If there are *n* lots and we denote the auction price as *Y* then we can say that the auction price of the first lot will be a function of that lot's characteristics:

$$Y_1 = f(X_{11}, X_{21}, X_{31}, \ldots, X_{91}) \tag{8.1}$$

where

Y_1 = the price that will be achieved for the first lot
X_{11} = the value of the first characteristic variable for the first lot

X_{21} = the value of the second characteristic variable for the first lot
X_{31} = the value of the third characteristic variable for the first lot
... and so on

This can be generalised further. We can say that the relationship between the auction lot characteristics and the auction price will hold for every lot:

$$Y_i = f(X_{1i}, X_{2i}, X_{3i}, \ldots, X_{9i}) \tag{8.2}$$

where

Y_i = the price that will be achieved for the *i*th lot
X_{1i} = the value of the first characteristic variable for the *i*th lot
X_{2i} = the value of the second characteristic variable for the *i*th lot
X_{3i} = the value of the third characteristic variable for the *i*th lot
... and so on

Since the auction house is attended by a large number of perfectly informed buyers and sellers and the lots are relatively homogeneous, there will be no such thing as a bargain where 'bargain' is defined as the sale of a lot for a price lower than its resale price should the lot be immediately re-auctioned. Suppose that we used the previous night's listing and sale prices to predict the price of a lot to be auctioned in today's auction. We calculate that lot A would have sold for £5,000 yesterday. So what will happen in today's auction? When lot A is auctioned the bid price will start low but will gradually rise as numerous prospective buyers bid the price up. While the price is rising bidders are still encouraged to bid because the prevailing price is lower than the inherent worth of the lot (£5,000). When the bid price reaches £5,000 there will be no further bids – the prospective buyers will become indifferent about whether they secure the lot or not. This is because the lot is not worth any more than £5,000 and prospective buyers would prefer to lose it and retain the ability to bid for one of the numerous other lots still to come.

DEFINING A LOCAL OFFICE MARKET: URBAN OFFICE MARKET DYNAMICS

One problem inherent in the conceptualisation and analysis of local office markets is the fact that the products of office occupiers are services rather than goods – they are 'intangibles'. This fact has impeded the rendering of a robust neoclassical office location theory. By contrast, a great deal of work has been done on industrial location theory. This has been assisted by the fact that manufacturers are in the business of producing finished or semi-finished goods using raw materials or other semi-finished goods as inputs to their own production process. This, in turn, accentuates the importance of location and transportation costs. According to early industrial location theories, occupiers choose their location in order to minimise their transportation costs. In a simple example of basic industrial location theory in which transportation nodes are assumed not to exist, firms are predicted to locate close to the destination market for finished goods where the ratio of input weight to finished good value is low. In other words, manufacturers whose production processes use relatively low transportation cost inputs to produce relatively high transportation cost outputs will tend to minimise the cost of transporting finished goods to the market for outputs (finished goods) by locating closer to that market. Firms whose production processes use relatively high transportation cost inputs to produce relatively low transportation cost outputs will tend to locate closer to the source of their inputs (raw materials).

Basic neoclassical location theory also recognises the importance of accessibility to the locational decisions of office occupiers, but in the office sector outputs are not physically transported to the market place and those outputs are not created using raw materials or semi-finished goods. Consequently, accessibility to input sources and output destinations are not strong influences on office occupiers' locational decisions. Instead, occupiers demand accessibility to the factors that partially determine the profitability of trading from offices, including, for example, accessibility to a skilled workforce. In view of the fact that service sector business practices are gradually changing over time, some authors have noted that the influence of agglomeration economies on the locational dynamics of commercial property markets may be declining (Ball *et al.*, 1998; Gibson and Lizieri, 1998; Egan and Nield, 2000). However, it is still widely accepted that accessibility to a ready pool of services, labour markets and possibilities for conducting 'face to face' business are still significant factors in attracting office occupiers to central business district locations (Dunse and Jones, 1998).

Dunse and Jones (1998) also note the importance of proximity to prestigious addresses as a partial determinant of office rental value. They argue that rents are likely to peak around such an address or street and decline with distance. They also note that there may be several rental value peaks in a central business district if it is the case that the benchmark prestigious address differs between the professions or subdivisions within the service sector. Other important partial determinants of office rental values include factor costs (the cost of capital, labour and development land) and the quality of the urban environment.

In a simple analysis framework derived from neoclassical economics, the central assumption is that office occupiers have an overwhelming preference for central locations. Hence, the boundaries of an urban office market are assumed to be coterminous with the boundaries of the central business district (CBD). Of course, this ignores the fact that occupiers can decentralise by taking on space in 'out of town' locations (business parks). This issue will be examined later in the chapter.

A sensible approach to beginning analysis of an urban office market is to consider the operation of the market from the perspective of an office occupier. In the simple neoclassical framework a prospective office occupier is assumed to arrive in the urban office market and begin searching among alternatives for suitable premises to take on. The occupier has an overwhelming preference for central locations such that the choice of exact location is something of a trade-off between cost (rent levels) and accessibility. Occupiers' preference for central locations coupled with a relatively fixed supply of space mean that rents are bid up for more central properties compared with slightly more peripheral alternatives. Detailed aspects of location such as proximity to public transportation facilities, car parking, prestigious addresses and competing firms have a secondary influence on the firm's locational choice.

Simple neoclassical approaches to theorising and conceptualising urban office markets are essentially derived from the work of Alonso (1964), Muth (1969) and others on residential location theory. In particular, the Access–Space model of residential location posits a household's locational choice as a trade-off between accessibility and space. On the assumption that travelling (for the purpose of work and to make shopping trips) reduces a household's utility (satisfaction), an equilibrium is reached in which the prices or rents of locations close to the CBD are bid up by households, and land/housing prices fall away at a decreasing rate with respect to distance. Simple neoclassical models of the urban office market follow the same principle, with rents decreasing at a decreasing rate with distance from a central point within the CBD. In the case of the residential Access–Space model the edge of the city is formed at some distance from the CBD where the cost of commuting is so high that householders are no longer willing to outbid farmers for the use of the land. In the case of the urban office market, firms (occupiers) base their bids on the profit they expect to make from occupying a given location. Since central locations are more profitable than less central ones, then unit rents will fall with distance, as noted earlier. Assuming a free market without land use planning controls, the furthest edge of the office district will be formed at the point at which office occupiers are no longer willing to outbid occupiers in the next most profitable real estate sector.

STOCK HETEROGENEITY AND NEIGHBOURHOODS

The rigid assumptions that underpin some neoclassical models, such as the Access–Space model, mean that their practical applications are of limited value (see Chapter 1 for a discussion on the attributes of real estate and real estate markets). In other words, the theoretical predictions often do not closely mirror 'real world' situations and outcomes. Some of the underlying assumptions are restrictive rather than fatal. For example, it is often the case in neoclassical location theory that the city centre (CBD) is assumed to be the only place of employment, business, consumption and leisure. Coupled with an assumption that cities lie amid extensive, flat, featureless plains, this leads on to a prediction that rents diminish with distance (irrespective of direction) from the CBD. In fact there is no reason to suppose that all economic activity should, in practice, take place in the CBD. Other assumptions are much more limiting still. For example, basic neoclassical models of urban office markets implicitly assume that markets are unitary entities. This means, among other things, that:

- All suppliers and demanders in the market have perfect information. This means, for example, that when a property comes onto the letting market all suppliers and demanders immediately have complete knowledge about the size, age, location, specification and market price (rental) of the premises.
- All properties are fairly close substitutes for each other. The concept of product homogeneity is important to the concept of a market. While products may be differentiated (slightly heterogeneous), it is implicit in the concept of a unitary market that all products on offer are essentially close substitutes for each other. In the context of the office market this means that a prospective occupier faced with a range of possible alternative premises would be able to carry out business in any of them. Small differences between the alternatives will, however, mean that the occupier will not be exactly indifferent between them.
- All locations (a given distance from the CBD) are fairly close substitutes for each other. To the applied real estate market researcher this assumption is a fatal flaw in the simple neoclassical approach to conceptualising urban office market dynamics and behaviour. Figure 8.1 provides a simple depiction of a monocentric city with two alternative properties (A and B) located at different points close to the edge of the CBD. According to the simple neoclassical approach a prospective occupier will be indifferent between these two alternatives because they are the same distance away from the CBD. An additional follow-on argument is that prices/rents will equilibriate at locations A and B. If, for whatever reason, properties around location A were to begin commanding higher rents then rents would follow suit in location B. This is because occupiers, indifferent between the two locations, would engage in an arbitrage process. In other words, some occupiers would choose to take advantage of the relative discount of location B and rents at location B would therefore be bid up to the level of location A.

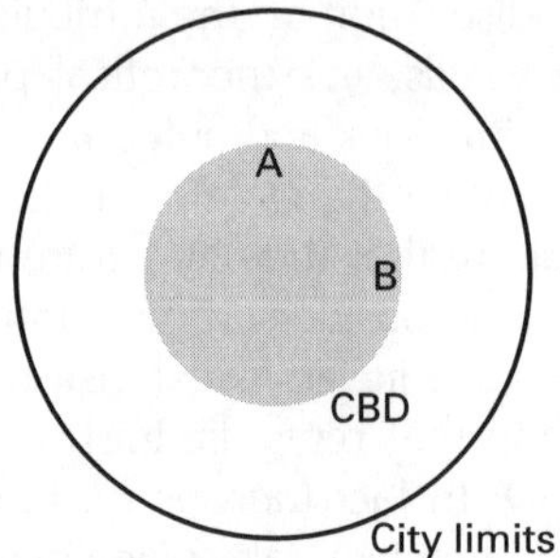

Figure 8.1 *Two alternative properties in a monocentric city*

There are a number of reasons why prospective office occupiers may not be indifferent between alternative urban locations even after controlling for distance from the CBD. Earlier it was noted that some commercial property occupiers are likely to have a preference for locations that are in proximity to other firms in the same line of business. For example, firms of solicitors may wish to locate close to other law firms if firms in this business sector share a perception that a certain street of neighbourhood has become associated with their line of business. To these firms, locational choice becomes a two-stage process. In the first stage, firms with a strong preference for locating near or next to like firms will select a commercial neighbourhood. In the second stage, firms will trade off physical attributes, quality and price in order to finalise their locational choice. These circumstances reduce the ability of the market to equilibriate through the arbitrage process. In other words, if firms of solicitors tend to locate in neighbourhood A then there is an argument that such firms will not be tempted to locate, instead, in neighbourhood B even if differences in occupation demand lead on to a relative discount in neighbourhood B. If occupiers employ a two-stage locational choice process then they are likely to exclude from consideration all properties outside the neighbourhood of choice.

If we extend the argument above and assume that there are several groups of occupiers that hold a preference for locating close to their competitors then we can predict that several neighbourhoods or 'submarkets' with quasi-independent market dynamics can evolve in an urban office market.

The 'submarket hypothesis' is borrowed from studies in housing economics dating back at least as far as the early 1970s (see, for example, Schnare and Struyk, 1976; Ball and Kirwan, 1977; Maclennan *et al.*, 1987; Bourassa *et al.*, 1999). The housing market differs from the urban office market in that the locational decisions of households are assumed to be driven by the goal of utility maximisation rather than profit maximisation. Schnare and Struyk (1976) demonstrate that spatial submarkets may be formed as the consequence of differences in neighbourhood quality. Specifically, they argue that demand for housing will become segmented spatially as a consequence of variation in the quality of some neighbourhood attribute (schools in their example) for which demand is price inelastic. In essence, the neighbourhood attribute whose demand is price inelastic leads to the creation of a two-step locational choice for households, the first step of which involves neighbourhood selection. The analogy is equally applicable to the commercial property user market, although firms (occupiers) seek to maximise profitability rather than utility as noted above.

The structure of the urban office market may be further complicated by the characteristics of office property as an economic commodity and the existence of a range of market imperfections. Office property is highly heterogeneous in terms of age, design, layout of internal space, external appearance, specification and size. So on the supply side of the market, the urban office stock can be thought of as being comprised of a set of 'property types'. Morrison (1994), for example, shows that the office stock in Glasgow is characterised by clusters of similar properties distinguished by the period in which they were constructed.

Market imperfections include information asymmetries and high transaction costs. Specifically, information is not widely and freely available in most urban office markets such that occupiers are likely to restrict their search for suitable premises. The fact that demanders will not have perfect information further reduces the possibility of arbitrage processes. In other words, demanders may have different preferences and business requirements which direct them towards particular subsets of the stock (see Powers, 1993).

These issues suggest that applied analyses of urban office markets should start with the assumption that an urban office market is a set of quasi-independent submarkets rather than a unitary market (Dunse and Jones, 1998, 2002; Dunse *et al.*, 2002). Such an analysis framework acknowledges the fact that interaction between segmented demand and differentiated stock (supply) of office units can lead to the co-existence of a number of interlinked submarkets associated with differential prices (even for a standardised unit) in different parts of the market. Furthermore, the quasi-independence of submarkets can be explicitly recognised. What this means, in practical terms, is that rental values throughout an office market are likely to respond to similar influences such as changes in occupation demand resulting from macroeconomic changes. However, rental values within the various submarkets of an urban office market will be, to some extent, independent of those in other submarkets. In particular, excess demand in one submarket cannot be completely offset by excess supply in another. Although some occupiers will be indifferent between similar properties in different submarkets, others will be prepared to pay a premium to locate in the submarket of choice, and disparities in rental levels will not therefore be 'arbitraged away'.

As a further complication to the submarket hypothesis, it should be noted that submarkets may also be conceptualised in terms of stock quality. According to this definition, submarkets are groups of properties that are relatively close substitutes for each other. While such groups may exist within spatially contiguous areas or office neighbourhoods, other groups may be market wide. Some firms (office occupiers) are likely to rate neighbourhood factors such as proximity to competitors, as discussed earlier. Other types of occupier are likely to be less concerned with neighbourhood factors but particularly concerned with stock quality. Some financial service firms, with a national or international market, are likely to seek out the most modern space with the highest specification wherever it may be found in an urban office market. In these circumstances, a price or rental division can form which cannot entirely be explained in terms of quality differences in the office stock. Such submarkets are difficult to conceptualise but are known as 'structural submarkets'. The likelihood is that most urban office markets represent interaction between spatial (neighbourhood) and structural segmentation.

A FRAMEWORK FOR THE ANALYSIS OF URBAN OFFICE MARKETS

Data inavailability and limitations are almost certainly the greatest impediments to undertaking analysis of real estate markets at the local level. The basic data requirements for constructing and estimating a rent determination/forecasting model include a long effective rent index series, information on vacancy stock over time, data on the completion of newly constructed space, and demand proxies. Long time series data on effective rents are not generally available at local level. Some of the leading property firms publish information on top rents for a selection of UK urban centres. However, stripping out the effects of different lease durations, rent review structures and tenants' incentives is difficult, particularly as a retrospective exercise. Furthermore, it is unlikely that a long time series of rent data can be obtained for more than a few UK cities. Meanwhile, information on vacant stock is notoriously difficult to obtain. Some incomplete information can be obtained from enterprise agencies and others in some parts of the country but there is no primary source for obtaining data on the quantity of vacant commercial real estate over time in the UK. Time series data on the volume of newly constructed commercial space may be available from planning authorities but, again, the availability and quality of data will vary from city to city since there is no actual requirement for planning authorities to maintain data in this form. Finally, demand proxies are difficult to construct at local level. Over recent years measures of economic output (GDP) have become available for smaller and smaller areas and they are now available, broadly, at county authority level in the UK. However, it is unlikely that the boundaries of these administrative areas will coincide with the boundaries of the chosen study area in every case. Furthermore, the time series of disaggregated economic data are, at present, too short for the estimation of good econometric models.

As a consequence of these facts, a pragmatic approach is normally taken when conducting an analysis of a local (urban) office market. Jones (1995) sets out a simple disaggregated or 'bottom up' methodology for the analysis of local office markets. There are six steps to the approach:

(1) Definition of study area
(2) Identification of demand structure
(3) Identification of stock characteristics
(4) Analysis of market dynamics
(5) Analysis of market performance
(6) Prediction

For most urban real estate market analyses the study area is likely to cover the inner urban area of one city encompassing several office neighbourhoods. One of the most important aspects to the Jones (1995) methodology is the identification of the demand structure within the market being studied. The essence of the disaggregated method is to build up a picture of how the market works from basic information. This involves identifying and grouping current office occupiers in order to quantify the significance of each demand stream to the local office market as a whole. Information can be obtained from a variety of sources, but in the UK the valuation roll can be a useful source. Examples of demand streams might include:

- Large financial service occupiers with a national market
- Professional service sector firms with a local market
- Professional service sector firms with a regional market
- Recruitment consultants with a local market
- Public sector offices

The objective is to identify a series of demand streams such that firms, and their space requirements, are relatively homogeneous within each of the streams. It follows that for each demand stream information should be collected on the typical, or spread of, property types, locations and sizes occupied by such firms. Information on property type should ideally include details of age, design, layout and specification, though collecting data of this type may involve some bespoke survey work.

The analysis of demand streams, and the typical, or spread of, occupation trends for each stream, should be reinforced by a thorough analysis of the urban office stock characteristics. The objective is to construct a profile of the stock, and this essentially entails devising a set of 'property types' described by age, design, layout, specification, size and location. This leads on to the identification of clusters of properties belonging to the same type of category previously defined as well as the identification of the boundaries of office neighbourhoods. When these exercises have been undertaken the following knowledge should be available:

- The boundaries of the urban office market.
- The number and location of office neighbourhoods or submarkets within the market.
- A typology of office types with a description of their characteristics.
- The location of the identified office types between and within the identified neighbourhoods.
- The quantity of each property type in the neighbourhoods or submarkets.
- A typology of demand streams relevant to the market under study.
- An understanding of the significance of each demand stream to the market as a whole.
- Identification of the location, property type and range of space requirements for each demand stream.

Jones (1995) suggests conducting a survey of recent movers in order to uncover more detailed aspects relevant to the analysis of market dynamics. For example, a trend of occupiers of a certain type moving gradually from one office neighbourhood to another might be investigated further in order to identify reasons for moving.

Analysis of market performance and prediction draws on the basic building blocks referred to above. The key to this methodology is to build up an aggregate forecast of occupation demand from a series of simple extrapolations of take-up rates for each identified demand stream. This is cross-referenced with information on future supply, which is largely drawn from planning authority records on the quantity of commercial floorspace under construction and expected completion dates.

Jones (1995) provides a practical example based on the Paisley office market (a large town just outside Glasgow on the west coast of Scotland) in which occupiers are classified:

- Finance and insurance
- Professional firms
- Business services
- Personal services
- Distribution/energy services
- Construction/property sector
- Transport/communication.

For each of these demand streams Jones (1995) calculates expected take-up for a future 5-year period by extrapolating each stream's trend over the previous 5 years. Assumed growth rates are permitted to vary between the different demand streams. This yields several predicted take-up figures or demand stream space requirements and these are then summed to give an aggregate expected requirement for office space for a future 5-year period.

INTERPRETATION OF HEDONIC MODELS

As outlined throughout this chapter, stock heterogeneity and the fact that the physical (quality) determinants of real estate prices are often difficult to separate from neighbourhood (locational) determinants impose significant difficulties in terms of the analysis of local real estate markets. Jones (1995) discusses a simple 'bottom up' approach to the analysis of local office markets for the purpose of prediction or extrapolation of market conditions into the medium-term future. However, if the study objective is concerned with the exploration and understanding of market dynamics, rather than production of a method for predicting ahead, then hedonic regression may provide a preferable alternative to the analysis of local markets (see Chapter 4 for a general review of regression models and Chapter 7 for a more specific discussion of hedonic regression models).

Hedonic regression models are well rehearsed in applied economics and real estate economics literature. Recent examples of hedonic studies of urban office markets are provided by Dunse and Jones (1998), Dunse *et al.* (2001, 2002) and Dunse and Jones (2002). Dunse and Jones (1998), for example, set out an hedonic regression of 477 asking rents on a vector of physical and locational attributes for a UK city (Glasgow). Their estimated equation has an adjusted R square of 0.79 and the coefficients and t statistics are as shown in Table 8.1.

The authors report a parsimonious model specification (all the variables entered into the final equation are statistically significant). Since the data on both sides of the equation are not transformed (for example, into logarithms), the equation has a simple linear functional form. The equation may be generalised as follows:

$$Y_i = \beta_0 + \beta_1 X_{1i} + \beta_2 X_{2i} + \beta_3 X_{3i} + \cdots + \beta_k X_{ki} + u_i \qquad (8.3)$$

Combining the estimated parameters (coefficients) with this model specification allows us to arrive at an operational equation that may be used to

Table 8.1 Dunse and Jones's (1998) hedonic model results

Variable	*Description*	*Coefficient*	*t statistic*
Constant		122.15	21.81**
SIZEM	Internal office area	0.01	3.09**
AGE2	Dummy; 1980–1989	−25.80	−5.22**
AGE3	Dummy; 1950–1979	−40.76	−7.43**
AGE3REF	Dummy; 1950–1979, refurbished	−24.80	−3.75**
AGE4	Dummy; Pre-war	−48.70	−6.06**
AGE4REF	Dummy; Pre-war, refurbished	−31.02	−6.84**
CA	Dummy; Central mid area of Glasgow	−12.15	−3.67**
CG	Dummy; Central outer area of Glasgow	−31.89	−7.89**
PARK	Dummy; Park area of Glasgow	−10.92	−2.07**
PERIPH	Dummy; Peripheral area of Glasgow	−19.36	−3.44**
DSTSTV	Distance from St. Vincent Street	−5.20	−3.33**
AIRCON	Dummy; air-conditioning	18.85	4.06**
AT	Dummy; acoustic tiling	−7.79	−2.95**
CARP	Dummy; carpeting	8.03	2.68**
CELL	Dummy; cellular layout	−7.18	−2.29**
DG	Dummy; double glazing	7.66	2.36**
PARKING	Dummy; internal parking	5.78	2.02**
RF	Dummy; raised floors	13.96	4.59**
TEAPREP	Dummy; tea preparation area	5.51	1.82*

* Significant at 1%; ** Significant at 5%.

predict the rental value, or asking rent in this case, of the *i*th office:

$$\begin{aligned}\hat{R}_i = 122.15 &+ 0.01SIZEM - 25.80AGE2 - 40.76AGE3 \\ &- 24.80AGE3REF - 48.70AGE4 - 31.02AGE4REF \\ &- 12.15CA - 31.89CG - 10.92PARK - 19.36PERIPH \\ &- 5.20DSTSTV + 18.85AIRCON - 7.79AT + 8.03CARP \\ &- 7.18CELL + 7.66DG + 5.78PARKING + 13.96RF \\ &+ 5.51TEAPREP\end{aligned}$$

If the *i*th office extends to 300 square metres, was constructed in the 1990s and is situated 0.5 km from St. Vincent Street (the designated central CBD point in the authors' study), then the basic asking rent per square metre can be predicted as follows:

$$\begin{aligned}\hat{R}_i = {} & 122.15 + (0.01 \times 300) - (25.80 \times 0) - (40.76 \times 0) - (24.80 \times 0)\\ & - (48.70 \times 0) - (31.02 \times 0) - (12.15 \times 0) - (31.89 \times 0)\\ & - (10.92 \times 0) - (19.36 \times 0) - (5.20 \times 0.5) \ldots\end{aligned}$$

or

$$\begin{aligned}\hat{R}_i &= 122.15 + (0.01 \times 300) - (5.20 \times 0.5) \ldots\\ &= 127.75\end{aligned}$$

This figure must be adjusted to account for the influence of various building and quality features on the asking rent per square metre. Suppose that the *i*th office has air conditioning, carpeting, a cellular layout, double glazing and parking. The full equation would be:

$$\begin{aligned}\hat{R}_i = {} & 122.15 + (0.01 \times 300) - (25.80 \times 0) - (40.76 \times 0) - (24.80 \times 0)\\ & - (48.70 \times 0) - (31.02 \times 0) - (12.15 \times 0) - (31.89 \times 0)\\ & - (10.92 \times 0) - (19.36 \times 0) - (5.20 \times 0.5) + (18.85 \times 1)\\ & - (7.79 \times 1) + (8.03 \times 1) - (7.18 \times 1) + (7.66 \times 1) + (5.78 \times 1)\\ & + (13.96 \times 0) + (5.51 \times 0)\end{aligned}$$

or

$$\begin{aligned}\hat{R}_i = {} & 122.15 + (0.01 \times 300) - (5.20 \times 0.5) + (18.85 \times 1) - (7.79 \times 1)\\ & + (8.03 \times 1) - (7.18 \times 1) + (7.66 \times 1) + (5.78 \times 1)\\ = {} & 183.04\end{aligned}$$

So the equation predicts the asking rent for the *i*th office (the particular office in the example given) to be £183.04 per square metre.

More sophisticated developments from the simple hedonic model discussed above are set out in Dunse *et al*. (2001, 2002) and Dunse and Jones (2002). Common developments from basic hedonic models include estimation of separate equations for defined submarkets rather than inclusion of dummy variables to represent neighbourhood effects and the use of interaction terms. Interaction terms measure the combined effect of groups of variables and may be entered together with variables that measure the effect of the variables individually. For example, the researcher might investigate the hypothesis that the effect of an office having air conditioning *and* raised floors is greater than the sum of the individual effects of (i) air conditioning and (ii) raised floors. The estimation of separate equations for defined geographical (spatial) or structural submarkets permits attribute parameters to vary between these defined segments. For example, it is plausible that the presence or absence of air conditioning will add/detract value at a different rate or level in one area compared with another, or in one type or age of property compared with another.

CONCLUSIONS

In the previous chapter, which was concerned with private housing market analysis, the hedonic regression model was introduced as an applied research tool that can be used to construct models of property price determination and price indices, and as building blocks for testing submarket effects and other forms of segmentation. While the focus of that chapter was on private housing, it should be noted that the commercial real estate literature often follows the housing economics literature closely and over recent years a number of papers have applied tools, drawn from the housing economics literature, to commercial real estate problems. The present chapter has focused on the office sector in order to provide a general framework for the analysis of urban real estate markets. Much of the content of this chapter has been concerned with the theoretical difficulties in conceptualising markets, and divisions within them, together with practical difficulties in obtaining relevant and reliable data. The chapter concluded with an exposition of a simple framework that can be used for the analysis of urban office user markets. These provide a 'commonsense' alternative to the construction and estimation of sophisticated econometric alternatives where data inavailability or methodological problems preclude their use.

REFERENCES

Alonso, W. (1964) *Location and Land Use: Toward a General Theory of Land Rent* (Cambridge (Mass): Harvard University Press).

Ball, M. and Kirwan, R. (1977) 'Accessibility and supply constraints in the urban housing market', *Urban Studies*, vol. 14, 11–32.

Ball, M., Lizieri, C. and MacGregor, B. (1998) *The Economics of Commercial Property Markets* (London: Routledge).

Bourassa, S., Hamelink, F., Hoesli, M. and MacGregor, B. (1999) 'Defining housing submarkets', *Journal of Housing Economics*, vol. 8, 160–83.

Dunse, N.A. and Jones, C. (1998) 'A hedonic price model of office rents', *Journal of Property Valuation and Investment*, vol. 16, no. 3, 297–312.

Dunse, N.A. and Jones, C. (2002) 'The existence of office submarkets in cities', *Journal of Property Research*, vol. 19, no. 2, 159–82.

Dunse, N.A., Leishman, C. and Watkins, C. (2001) 'Classifying office submarkets', *Journal of Property Investment and Finance*, vol. 19, no. 3, 236–50.

Dunse, N.A., Leishman, C. and Watkins, C. (2002) 'Testing the existence of office submarkets: a comparison of evidence from two cities', *Urban Studies*, vol. 39, no. 4, 483–506.

Egan, D.J. and Nield, K. (2000) 'Towards a theory of intraurban hotel location', *Urban Studies*, vol. 37, 611–21.

Gibson, V. and Lizieri, C. (1998) 'New business practices and the corporate property portfolio: how responsive is the UK property market?', *Journal of Property Research*, vol. 16, 201–18.

Jones, C. (1995) 'An economic basis for the analysis and prediction of local office property markets', *Journal of Property Valuation and Investment*, vol. 13, no. 2, 16–30.

Maclennan, D., Munro, M. and Wood, G. (1987) 'Housing choice and the structure of urban housing markets', in B. Turner, J. Kemeny and L. Lundquist (eds), *Between State and Market Housing: The Post-Industrial Era* (Gothenburg: Almquist & Wicksell International).

Morrison, N. (1994) 'The role of planning in the redevelopment process of Glasgow's city centre', *Planning Practice and Research*, vol. 9, no. 1, 31–41.

Muth, R.F. (1969) *Cities and Housing* (Chicago University Press).

Powers, R.T. (1993) 'Office submarket delineation in tenant location behaviour', in J.R. White (ed.), *The Office Building: From Concept to Investment Reality* (Counsellors of Real Estate, Society of Industrial and Office Realtors and Appraisal Institute, Chicago).

Schnare, A. and Struyk, R. (1976) 'Segmentation in urban housing markets', *Journal of Urban Economics*, vol. 3, 146–66.

9
Retail Gravity Models

INTRODUCTION

This chapter examines methods of predicting or assessing the sales potential, turnover and rental value of retail space. A separate chapter has been devoted to retail real estate owing to the relatively specialist nature of that sector. The chapter rehearses the theoretical foundations of the analytical methods identified subsequently, while there is a particular focus on so-called 'gravity' or 'spatial interaction' models. It should be noted that much of the content of the book so far has focused on the analysis of real estate markets at national and regional level. However, gravity and other spatial interaction models are almost exclusively concerned with market behaviour and interaction at the local level or, to be more specific, at the sub-regional and possibly even sub-centre levels. The result of this is, arguably, to enhance the practical value of the research tools examined in this chapter. However, a natural consequence is that the conceptual difficulty associated with such tools, together with relative empirical complexity, is increased.

SPATIAL INTERACTION

As already noted a number of times in this book, one of the distinguishing attributes of real estate is its spatial fixity and relative heterogeneity. Given the fact that occupiers and users of real estate (private, public and commercial alike) interact with each other during the natural course of economic activity, there is an automatic spatial dimension to real estate market dynamics and behaviour. At the simplest level, this could reflect nothing more than the fact that several firms (or a group of consumers and a firm) carrying out business transactions with each other are based in different locations. Of course, the magnitude and importance of this spatial dimension to real estate economic activity varies between the different use sectors. In the office sector, the spatial dimension to real estate activity is likely to be relatively unimportant compared with, for example, the manufacturing sector. This is simply because occupiers in the office sector produce intangibles rather than finished physical goods. In the manufacturing sector, occupiers produce physical goods, and hence the location of the manufacturing firm will reflect the spatial availability of raw materials or semi-finished goods together with the placement of primary markets or transportation nodes to those markets.

Further to this, spatial interaction is likely to become increasingly important as the level of spatial aggregation decreases. In other words, the spatial dimension to interaction between real estate users will be more important to an analysis focused on a local market than regional or national markets.

A distinction must be drawn between spatial interaction and other spatial/locational aspects of real estate market activity. As just noted, most real estate market processes have some spatial dimension even if this is simply because no two buildings can share the same exact site or location. As a consequence of this, there are many examples of real estate economic phenomena that are either trite examples of spatial interaction or that simply do not reflect spatial interaction at all. While all of the market processes and activities referred to above have a spatial dimension, the term 'spatial interaction' refers to a much more specific type of economic activity across space. The term implies that processes and outcomes in one market are partly determined, or at least influenced by, the processes and outcomes in another market.

In the disciplines of real estate and urban economics the research literature contains many examples of theoretical and empirical models of market processes that reflect spatial interaction. Almost all of these are concerned with (i) population/household migration, and (ii) households' consumption behaviour and retail real estate price (rent) modelling. The first of these areas is interesting in its own right – but it is a highly specialised subject to which justice cannot be done in anything less than a full chapter, possibly a complete book. In brief, household migration can be viewed as an outcome determined by 'push' and 'pull' factors. For example, it can be argued that households are more likely to leave (migrate out of) a local or regional housing market with poor economic growth and employment prospects. Migrant households are more likely to migrate to an area with strong growth, a high amenity environment and good employment prospects than to a less attractive area. Many household migration models treat migration as, at least, a two-stage process in which push factors determine the number of households that will migrate out of each local housing market and pull factors then determine the destination of these households. The focus of this chapter is on the second of the two main areas of spatial interaction modelling: the use of spatial interaction principles in the modelling of retail rents. It should be noted that the gravity modelling approaches reviewed here represent a relatively small proportion of all documented spatial interaction and gravity modelling approaches. For a detailed review of spatial interaction and gravity modelling in the contexts of human geography, spatial provision of healthcare, traffic generation and, to a lesser extent, retailing, readers are recommended to refer to Isard (1998). The techniques examined in this chapter initially follow Field and MacGregor (1987) and are developed with respect to more recently published academic studies of gravity and econometric modelling work.

SPATIAL INTERACTION AND RETAILING

It is relatively straightforward to construct an argument that economic activity will tend to form spatial clusters as a result of agglomeration economies. Recall that agglomeration economies are formed by the fusion of internal and external economies. So in the context of urban areas (cities) agglomeration economies represent firms' efficiency gains from aspects such as larger markets (economies of scale), larger and more diverse workforces, greater competition in input markets, and so on.

The constituents of agglomeration economies will vary between the various real estate sectors. In the industrial sector, agglomeration economies are likely to reflect economies of scale, access to a larger workforce and greater accessibility to better transportation links. In the office sector, agglomeration economies are likely to reflect access to a more highly skilled workforce and, in some sub-sectors, firms may experience enhanced levels of business simply by locating close to competitors. In some sub-sectors of the office market business may be carried out largely on a face-to-face basis (for example, firms offering professional services such as legal advice). Firms in this sector may actually increase business by locating next to their competitors in a quarter of the office market which has become synonymous with firms in that line of business. Furthermore, it is well rehearsed that some office occupiers will deliberately seek out a prestigious address, particularly for the location of their headquarters facility.

In the retail sector the tendency for firms to centralise, or cluster, is more pronounced still. In an excellent review of developments in retail real estate research, Eppli and Benjamin (1994) identify four strands of retail real estate research:

(1) Central Place theory following Christaller (1933)
(2) Homogeneous retailer agglomeration
(3) Shopping centre demand externalities
(4) Shopping centre valuation

In an examination of the first of these strands ('Central Place theory'), Eppli and Benjamin (1994) rehearse the theoretical basis for expecting retailer real estate occupiers to centralise and form clusters. Central place theory provides a basic understanding of consumers' shopping behaviour and retailers' locational choice. Developed from work by Christaller (1933), the theory rests on the assumptions that households make single-purpose shopping trips and will travel to the nearest outlet for their intended purchase. Christaller's work suggests that the result of this will be:

(1) The development of hexagonal trading areas which are each dominated by a single outlet (firm). Consumers travel to the outlet that is nearest to them and the shape of the trading/catchment areas is such that there are no overlaps.
(2) The development of an hierarchical system of overlaying trading areas. The logic is that consumers do not, or cannot, travel far in order to purchase everyday items (such as perishable foodstuffs) and a convenience store will therefore be sustainable with a relatively small catchment area. For more expensive or less frequent purchases retail outlets require a larger catchment or trading area. Meanwhile, consumers will be willing to travel further on such shopping trips as a result of the greater expense involved in the purchases and the longer time period between successive trips. This gives rise to an overlaying system of trading areas.

GRAVITY MODELS

The essential components of Central Place theory are that:

- On a single-purpose shopping trip consumers will travel further as the trip type frequency decreases. This is also an implication that consumers will travel further to purchase expensive items compared with cheaper items.
- Retailers choose their location in order to secure a catchment area whose size or extent is appropriate to the retailer's line of business. So, for example, a convenience store does not require a large catchment area, so such stores will locate in neighbourhood centres.

Since many different types of retailers are likely to decide that they require a larger, rather than a small, catchment area then it follows that retailers will tend to cluster together in the centre of urban, provincial or regional trading areas. A retailer whose business requires a catchment area of provincial size will not be able to stay in business by locating in the centre of an urban trading area (because a smaller trading area will bring lower turnover). Equally, there is no particular advantage for such a retailer to locate in the centre of a regional trading area since consumers will not travel further than the limits of a provincial trading area to make the purchases that can be provided by that retailer.

Central Place theory provides an explanation for the formation of spatial hierarchies of retailers but it does not explain why similar types of retailer also tend to cluster together. Indeed, Central Place theory suggests that this will not happen but rather that each trading area will be dominated by one retail outlet per shopping trip purpose. So, for example, one shoe shop, one clothing shop, one electrical store and so on may locate in an urban centre. The theory cannot offer a rationale for like stores locating in proximity to each other. Eppli and Benjamin (1994) describe this phenomenon as 'homogeneous retailer agglomeration'. They attribute this branch of retail location theory to Hotelling (1929). The essence of the Hotelling argument is that similar retailers that sell homogeneous goods can cluster together because consumers take into account a range of non-price factors when choosing where to shop. Such factors could include the design or layout differences between shops or small differences in the way in which different retailers conduct their business. This premise also accords well with the now widely accepted fact that consumers tend to 'comparison shop' when purchasing durable goods. That is, consumers tend not to purchase the first item they see at an acceptable price. Given the durability of some expensive manufactured goods, consumers prefer to compare prices and quality between retailers. Indeed, Eppli and Benjamin's (1994) review reports survey-based empirical evidence that consumer shoppers' satisfaction increases with the mix of different retailer types in shopping centres and that shoppers will bypass closer centres in order to access a more distant one with greater choice.

These considerations are important in the theoretical justification for the use of gravity models, and gravity concepts, in retail real estate research. Gravity models are so-called because they are formulated on the assumption that a spatial area, region or city exerts a force of attraction towards another concentration of population or spatial area. The force of attraction is assumed to be a partial function of the size of the area, region or city. The concept is analogous to Isaac Newton's Law of Universal Gravitation. This states that the force of attraction between two bodies is proportional to the sum of their masses and the inverse of the squared distance between them. This is adapted to predict the extent of spatial interaction between two areas or cities as a function of their respective size and the distance between them.

An early application of the gravity concept to retail property market research is reported by Reilly (1931). Reilly's 'law of retail gravitation' permits the estimation of a market boundary within a simplified framework in which two towns or cities compete for retail trade. According to Reilly, the delineation of the market boundary is a function of the distance between the towns or cities and their respective size:

$$d_B = \frac{d_{AB}}{\sqrt{\frac{P_A}{P_B}} + 1} \tag{9.1}$$

where

d_B = distance of boundary from city B
d_{AB} = distance between cities A and B
P_A = population of city A
P_B = population of city B

In formulating the expression shown above, Reilly (1931) makes the simplifying assumption that cities A and B are the only centres to which the local population may make shopping trips. Furthermore, the model only explicitly considers the position of the market boundary directly between A and B.

Despite its simplicity, Reilly's example is a useful demonstration of the gravity concept in real estate economics: all other things being equal, those that wish to travel to a town or city to make a shopping trip will tend to be drawn to the centre that exerts the strongest force of attraction. The force of attraction is a function of the size of the centre and its relative distance from consumers' residences.

PROBABILISTIC GRAVITY MODELS

Although Reilly's (1931) simple gravity 'model' concerns two cities, gravity models are readily applicable to the case of retail property and may be adapted to consider more than two areas or centres.

The applicability of the gravity concept to retail property is intuitively appealing. As briefly noted earlier, consumers of non-food shopping goods (the demand side of the retail market) are more likely to visit locations where numerous retailers have located together in clusters. For the consumers of durable goods (comparison goods) price is a key issue and consumers are generally willing to visit more than one shop in order to compare prices and quality (see Balchin *et al.*, 1995). In contrast to convenience goods, comparison goods yield a steady flow of services over a long period of time and are relatively expensive.

On the supply side, retailers tend to locate near to each other in main urban shopping streets or in shopping centres in order to harness the desire of consumers to visit numerous shops during a single shopping visit. In general, retailers tend to benefit rather than lose by locating close to competitors.

These facts tend to reinforce the theoretical validity of adapting the gravity model concept to retail property markets. Retail property is found in concentrations in towns, cities or out-of-town shopping centres. The force of attraction that a retail centre exerts on consumers can be expected to increase with the size of the centre. Meanwhile, the attractiveness of a retail centre to consumers is likely to decrease with distance.

In retail property research, gravity models are used for two main purposes:

(1) to estimate the sales potential for a proposed new shopping centre
(2) to estimate the effect of a proposed new shopping centre on existing, nearby shopping centres.

Gravity models are normally constructed on the assumption that either the number of visits by consumers to a retail centre, or the quantity of money spent in that centre, is determined by the centre's attractiveness to consumers relative to other competing centres. As a simplification to the analysis, models are normally focused on small residential areas or neighbourhoods rather than on individual consumers. If, for example, the focus of a particular study is on the shopping centre patronage of consumers from 100 residential neighbourhoods, then the objective of constructing and estimating a gravity model will be to predict the number of annual shopping trips from each of the 100 neighbourhoods to each of the shopping centres in the study area. Alternatively, the objective may be to predict, for every neighbourhood, the share of consumption expenditure that will flow to each of the shopping centres in the study area. Such models are often referred to as 'probabilistic gravity models'. An early example of such a model is set out by Huff (1964):

$$P_{ij} = \frac{\dfrac{S_j}{T_{ij}^{\lambda}}}{\sum_j \dfrac{S_j}{T_{ij}^{\lambda}}} \tag{9.2}$$

where

P_{ij} = the probability of the consumers living at location i shopping at shopping centre j
S_j = the size of shopping centre j
T_{ij} = the travelling time from residential location i to shopping centre j
λ = unknown parameter

The right-hand side of the expression represents the attractiveness of shopping centre j to the residents of i relative to the aggregate attractiveness of all shopping centres available to the residents of i. Hence, P_{ij} is the probability that the residents of i will frequent a shopping centre j which is a distance (expressed as travelling time) T_{ij} from residential location i. The application of this simple model can be demonstrated with reference to an example following Field and MacGregor (1987):

Example 1

Calculate the probability that consumers in each of three residential zones will patronise two shopping centres. The sizes of the centres are 2,000 square metres and 3,000 square metres respectively. The distances between the residential zones and the shopping centres are shown below. For the purpose of this example assume that the distance decay parameter (λ) is equal to 2.

Size of shopping centres A and B (square metres)

A	*B*
2,000	3,000

Distance between shopping centres and residential areas

Zone	*A*	*B*
1	4	9
2	5	7
3	11	5

Squared distance

Zone	*A*	*B*
1	16	81
2	25	49
3	121	25

Area of each shopping centre divided by squared distance from the residential areas

Zone	*A*	*B*	*Total*
1	125.00	37.04	162.04
2	80.00	61.22	141.22
3	16.53	120.00	136.53

Probability of consumers at i shopping at centre j

Zone	*A*	*B*
1	0.77	0.23
2	0.57	0.43
3	0.12	0.88

The results in this simple example indicate that the probabilities are:

77 per cent for consumers in zone 1 shopping at centre A
23 per cent for consumers in zone 1 shopping at centre B
57 per cent for consumers in zone 2 shopping at centre A
43 per cent for consumers in zone 2 shopping at centre B
12 per cent for consumers in zone 3 shopping at centre A
88 per cent for consumers in zone 3 shopping at centre B

One approach to the interpretation of these results is that consumers in zones 1 and 2 will patronise centre A while consumers in zone 3 will patronise centre B. However, this interpretation implicitly assumes that all consumers in each of the zones will patronise the same shopping centre (the most attractive one relative to their geographical position) and that all consumption expenditure will flow from a given residential zone to either one shopping centre or the other. This interpretation is not intuitively appealing. An alternative interpretation is that 77 per cent of consumers or consumption expenditure in residential zone 1 will flow to shopping centre A with the remainder flowing to centre B and so on. This interpretation is more appealing, since the flow of consumers or expenditure to each of the centres will reflect the relative attractiveness of them, while, at the same time, the model is sufficiently flexible to account for some incidence of consumers and expenditure flowing elsewhere.

Some researchers have made use of the probabilistic gravity model to predict the flow of consumers (shopping trips) to a set of alternative centres. Others have combined the basic probabilistic gravity model with supplementary data on households' spending patterns in order to predict the flow of consumption expenditure rather than consumers. An example of this approach is set out by Field and MacGregor (1987):

$$S_{ij} = \frac{C_i \dfrac{F_j}{d_{ij}^{\lambda}}}{\sum_j \dfrac{F_j}{d_{ij}^{\lambda}}} \qquad (9.3)$$

where

S_{ij} = the probable flow of consumer expenditure from the residents of location i to shopping centre j
C_i = the sum of money in location i which is available for consumption
F_j = the size of shopping centre j (total floorspace)
d_{ij} = the distance from residential location i to shopping centre j
λ = unknown parameter

The gravity model shown in equation (9.3) is a simple extension to that outlined by Huff (1964). For a given shopping centre j, the flow of expenditure from each of the i residential zones is equal to the sum of money for consumption in each i multipled by the attractiveness of the shopping centre j relative to the aggregate attractiveness of all shopping centres in the region.

Before the gravity model can be used to estimate the consumer expenditure that will flow from each of the i residential zones to each of the j shopping centres, the parameter λ must be estimated. A common way of achieving this is to carry out a household survey designed to yield a sample of data on households' consumption behaviour and, more importantly, information on where households spend money on comparison shopping goods together with the frequency with which they visit the alternative destinations (shopping centres). This information is used to 'calibrate' the gravity model. In other words, with a sample of data on households consumption patterns and the destination of their consumption expenditure, it is possible to work backwards using the gravity model equation to calculate the value of the distance decay parameter (λ). Clearly, carrying out a survey such as the one described above is an expensive business and, furthermore, the survey should be repeated periodically and especially following changes such as improvements to the transportation system, significant changes in travelling costs or further development of new competing retail centres.

After the distance decay parameter is estimated using a relatively small sample of household survey data, the gravity model can be operationalised by employing it to estimate expenditure flows using a more complete dataset describing the population, demographic profile and average consumption expenditure for a large number of census-based enumeration districts, wards or census tracts (roughly equivalent to a neighbourhood scale residential area).

Example 2

Calculate the total flow of consumer expenditure to each of three shopping centres ($j = 1, 2, 3$) from five residential zones (A, B, C, D, E). The geographical distribution of the shopping centres and the centre of each of the residential zones are shown in Figure 9.1. Table 9.1 shows the total amount of retail floorspace in each of the shopping centres.

In this example, suppose that the population and consumption figures are as given in Table 9.2. The first step to the analysis is to calculate the

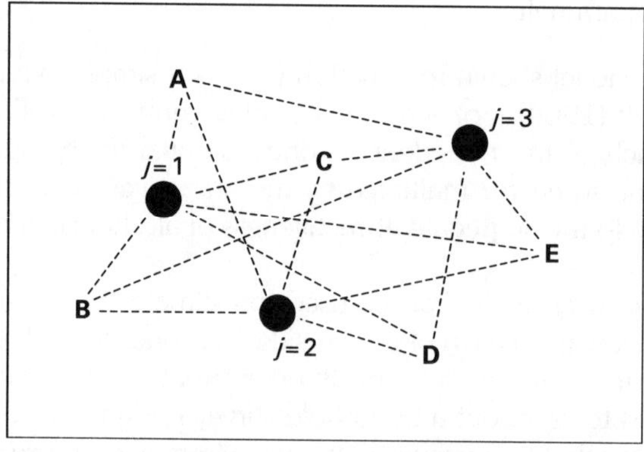

Figure 9.1 *Distribution of shopping centres and residential zones*

Table 9.1 Floorspace

Centre	*Floorspace*
1	22,500
2	11,200
3	18,400
Total	52,100

Table 9.2 Money available for consumption

Zone	*Expenditure per head p.a.*	*Population*	*Total expenditure*
A	£6,600	1,000	6,600,000
B	£6,100	1,200	7,320,000
C	£6,900	850	5,865,000
D	£4,800	1,700	8,160,000
E	£5,300	1,450	7,685,000
Total	–	6,200	35,630,000

Table 9.3 Distances from residential zones to shopping centres

	1	*2*	*3*
A	10	21	25
B	12	17	37
C	15	13	13
D	27	14	18
E	34	25	13

distances between each of the *i* residential zones and each of the *j* shopping centres (Table 9.3).

To simplify the analysis in this example we will assume that λ is equal to 1. The probable flow of consumer expenditure from the residential zones to shopping centres can now be estimated using the formulation examined earlier. For the case of shopping centre 1 the flow of expenditure from residential zone A is as follows:

$$S_{A,1} = \frac{C_A \dfrac{F_1}{d_{A,1}}}{\sum_j \dfrac{F_j}{d_{ij}}}$$

The figures can now be used to calculate the proportion of consumer expenditure from each residential zone that will flow towards each of the shopping centres. In Table 9.5, each cell is derived by dividing each cell of

Table 9.4 by the row total. Each cell can now be multiplied by the total available money for consumption for the *i* residential zones. This permits us to calculate the flow of expenditure from the residential zones to the shopping centres and the total flow of expenditure to each shopping centre (Table 9.6).

Table 9.4 Shopping centre floorspace divided by distance from residential zones

	1	*2*	*3*	*Sum*
A	2,250	533	736	3,519
B	1,875	659	497	3,031
C	1,500	862	1,415	3,777
D	833	800	1,022	2,656
E	662	448	1,415	2,525

Table 9.5 Proportional expenditure flow from residential zones to shopping centres

	1	*2*	*3*
A	0.63933	0.15154	0.20913
B	0.61858	0.21735	0.16406
C	0.39715	0.22811	0.37475
D	0.31381	0.30126	0.38494
E	0.26207	0.17742	0.56052

Table 9.6 Expenditure flow from residential zones to shopping centres

	1	*2*	*3*
A	4,219,549	1,000,189	1,380,261
B	4,528,028	1,591,025	1,200,947
C	2,329,277	1,337,841	2,197,882
D	2,560,669	2,458,243	3,141,088
E	2,014,004	1,363,436	4,307,559
Total	15,651,528	7,750,734	12,227,738

OPERATIONALISING A GRAVITY MODEL

An important element of constructing and estimating a gravity model involves the estimation of the model parameters. This is done using empirical evidence (actual data) and permits a model, constructed from theoretical principles, to be operationalised. This process if often referred to as model calibration. Field and MacGregor (1987) note that OLS regression cannot be used to estimate the parameters directly from the gravity model specifications shown so far since they do not postulate linear relationships between a dependent and a set of independent variables. They note that a generalised gravity model can be linearised by taking logarithms and the parameters estimated using regression analysis. They suggest two alternative generalised model specifications:

$$T_{ij} = \frac{KP_i^{\beta_1}H_j^{\beta_2}}{d_{ij}^{\lambda}} = KP_i^{\beta_1}H_j^{\beta_2}d_{ij}^{-\lambda} \tag{9.4}$$

or

$$T_{ij} = KP_i^{\beta_1}H_j^{\beta_2}e^{-\lambda d_{ij}} \tag{9.5}$$

where

T_{ij} = trips between zone i and destination j
K = constant
P_i = population of zone i
H_j = 'opportunities' at destination j
d_{ij} = distance between i and j

Note that this specification is a simple, generalised, unconstrained gravity model that may be used as a starting point for developing a probabilistic model for shopping centre patronage, traffic generation, household migration and a range of other gravity model applications. The simple specification can be used, after linearisation, to estimate the parameters α, β and λ. On taking logs, the two specifications shown above linearise to:

$$\begin{aligned} \ln T_{ij} &= \ln K + \beta_1 \ln P_i + \beta_2 \ln H_j - \lambda \ln d_{ij} \\ &= \alpha + \beta_1 \ln P_i + \beta_2 \ln H_j + \beta_3 \ln d_{ij} \end{aligned} \tag{9.6}$$

or

$$\begin{aligned} \ln T_{ij} &= \ln K + \beta_1 \ln P_i + \beta_2 \ln H_j - \lambda d_{ij} \\ &= \alpha + \beta_1 \ln P_i + \beta_2 \ln H_j + \beta_3 d_{ij} \end{aligned} \tag{9.7}$$

Using regression analysis the parameters can now be estimated using either equation (9.6) or (9.7). Field and MacGregor (1987) argue that specification (9.7) is preferable since equation (9.6) can yield a downward-biased estimate of λ. Specifically, they note that the estimate of T_{ij} tends towards infinity as d_{ij} tends towards zero, or, in other words, equation (9.6) provides an upward-biased estimate of T_{ij} when the distance between i and j is very small.

Using equations (9.6) or (9.7) and a suitable dataset of observations on T, P, H and d, the parameters can be estimated using regression analysis and the known parameters substituted in the gravity model equation(s) to form an operational model.

The real estate market literature contains few examples of constrained gravity model estimations, possibly since such models are difficult and expensive to estimate and have commercial value. The literature does, however, contain many examples of econometric models that are specified along gravity model lines. These are examined briefly in the next section.

ECONOMETRIC MODELS OF RETAIL RENTS

The focus of this section is on econometric cross-sectional models of retail rents. As noted earlier, a cross-sectional model is one in which numerous observations are collected within a single time period. Panel datasets possess some of the characteristics of both time series and cross-sectional datasets. Typically, panel datasets include a number of observations within each of several time periods. The time span covered by panel datasets is normally smaller than for time series datasets such that the use of 'pure' time series techniques is not possible. Models estimated using panel methods are, in essence, cross-sectional models that include variables intended to measure inter-temporal effects.

There are two basic approaches to modelling the retail property user market econometrically. First, a retail rent model may follow the general form of a gravity model, as discussed earlier. Second, the model may be specified as a function of the interaction of supply and demand. If the first approach is adopted then the underlying assumption in the construction of the econometric model is that retail rents in a given market are a partial function of the size of that market in terms of total retail floorspace. The logic is as follows:

Retail markets (particularly High Street retail centres) become more attractive to consumers as they increase in size according to the retail gravity model shown earlier. According to Fraser (1993), the supply of High Street retail space is price inelastic since planning restrictions prevent central urban shopping centres from expanding easily. In any event the supply side of the property market cannot respond quickly to price signals because new space must be constructed before it can be brought onto the market. As a consequence, retail rents are essentially demand-determined, at least in the short run.

Retailers bid up rents through a competitive bidding process. Their willingness and ability to bid up rents are a function of their own turnover. According to Fraser (1993), the rent paid by a retailer is therefore a geared residual representing the retailer's turnover less operating costs.

Since retailers' turnover increases with the size of the retail market in which they are located, the rents paid by those retailers also increases with the size of the retail centre. Thus, the gravity model based approach to predicting retail rents uses retailers' turnover as a primary input.

The econometric-gravity model approach is demonstrated by Robertson and Jones (1999). They estimate total retail turnover for each of 29 retail centres in Scotland in 1989 using a gravity model specified as follows:

$$S_{ij} = \alpha(C_i F_j) \exp(\beta d_{ij})$$

This is a variant of the gravity model formulation referred to earlier.

Robertson and Jones (1999) also measured the total length of retail frontage in each of the 29 retail centres. Two variables (turnover and turnover ÷ frontage) were entered as explanatory variables in an ordinary least squares regression on retail rents. The second variable (turnover ÷ frontage) represents the degree of constraint in each shopping centre. On the assumption that the stock of retail floorspace is relatively fixed, the greater the ratio of retail turnover to retail floorspace for a centre, the greater the implied level of excess retail occupation demand. The authors report an adjusted R^2 of 0.91 with both variables statistically significant at the 5 per cent level of significance.

The approach followed by the authors can be broken down as follows:

Step 1 Estimate the total flow of consumer expenditure to each of *j* shopping centres. This is done using a gravity model in which the flow of expenditure from a residential zone *i* to a shopping centre *j* is a function of its size (total retail floorspace) and the distance from *i* to *j*.

Step 2 Specify and estimate a multiple regression model in which the average retail rent for a shopping centre is a linear function of the total turnover (consumer expenditure) of the shopping centre and the ratio of turnover to floorspace for each centre.

There are numerous other econometric models of shopping centre rents, primarily in the US literature, that embody elements of Central Place theory, positive demand externalities and gravity model principles. The concept of 'demand externalities' is an important real estate economics principle in the retail sector. Just as the concept of comparison shopping can explain homogeneous retailer agglomeration, as discussed earlier, image or retailers' identity can help explain seemingly irrational consumer behaviour such as travelling past a nearby shopping centre in order to shop at a more distant one. Research in the area of 'shopping centre demand externalities' is almost entirely focused on the concept of 'anchor stores' or anchor tenants.

There is empirical evidence to support the fact that the brand image of some retailers is sufficiently powerful to draw in potential consumers from relatively great distances. At the same time, recognition that consumers make multipurpose shopping trips leads to a hypothesis that anchor stores may be associated with positive externalities for lower order retailers. Sirmans and Guidry (1993), following Ghosh (1986), note that lower order retailers tend to benefit most from the fact that consumers make multipurpose shopping trips and that retailers that are 'known traffic generators' tend to receive rental discounts. This is consistent with the idea that anchor store occupiers are associated with positive externalities.

Meanwhile, Gatzlaff *et al.* (1994) estimate the effect of anchor tenant loss on shopping centre rental levels for the remaining retailers. Their analysis is based on a dataset of 36 shopping centres described as 'smaller to moderately sized' and with an average size of 104,000 square feet. The authors conclude that there is a large and statistically significant diminution in rental levels following the loss of an anchor tenant.

Sirmans and Guidry (1993) set out a rent determination equation in which shopping centre rents are hypothesised to be a function of variables that can be described in four different categories:

(1) Customer drawing power (labelled as DRAW)
(2) Shopping centre design (labelled as DESIGN)
(3) Location
(4) Market conditions

The customer drawing power variables in the equation include shopping centre total area, age and anchor tenant type. Clearly, total shopping centre area is expected to be a 'pull' factor, while shopping centre age can be expected to act as a repellant on the assumption that consumers are likely to be drawn to more modern centres with a contemporary design. Design variables included in the equation primarily reflect the design layout of shopping centres. Sirmans and Guidry (1993) identify malls, shop clusters, L-shaped centres, U-shaped centres and linear or strip centres. According to the authors, L- and U-shaped centres are configured to reduce pedestrian walk times between shops but are less visually appealing than shopping malls. Meanwhile, cluster centres do not offer pedestrians shelter from weather conditions and, the authors argue, tend to offer less choice.

In terms of locational variables, the authors categorise their sample by 4 regions defined on the basis of population density, growth potential and income level. Meanwhile, the equation includes variables on vacant space levels and past economic trends as proxies for market conditions. Interestingly, work by other authors (see Jackson, 2002, for example) suggests that retail rental growth rates in the UK tend to be similar in individual centres (towns or cities) with similar population, demographic and economic drivers.

Using data on 55 shopping centres in Baton Rouge, Louisiana, Sirmans and Guidry (1993) estimate the equation parameters using weighted least squares (the authors report heteroscedasticity with respect to shopping centre size). The results are in keeping with theoretical expectations. Shopping centre size, anchor tenant classification, design and traffic count are statistically significant and positive. Centre age and vacant space are statistically significant and negative. The design variable parameter estimates suggest that the mall design is superior to the cluster design, while both are superior to L, U and linear designs (the differences between these last three are not statistically significant). Overall, the authors' model appears to yield impressive results with an R square of more than 0.85 and no evidence of heteroscedasticity or multicollinearity.

CONCLUSIONS

Gravity models have proven a particularly powerful tool in real estate research, particularly in relation to the retail sector. As noted earlier, there are good theoretical reasons for supposing that areas, neighbourhoods, shopping centres and settlements will interact with each other. In the case of consumers and shopping centres, it is possible to identify attractive and repellant factors and, in many cases, to measure these quantitatively for the purpose of yielding data to assist with model construction.

Finally, it should be noted that although it may be relatively straightforward to establish a strong empirical relationship between potential expenditure, attractive forces, repellant forces and final expenditure, the relationship between expenditure and rents is by no means so straightforward. In theory at least, it should be possible to extend gravity models for the purpose of predicting shopping centre rental levels and there are some published studies that report some measure of success in achieving this. However, shopping centre rents are likely to diverge from retail sales in the short run (Chun *et al.*, 2001) as a result of the fact that retailers enter into lease contracts that effectively fix their rent for several years at a time. Furthermore, there is still considerable scope for the improvement of gravity models used to explain consumption expenditure let alone retail rent determination. Ownbey *et al.* (1994) note that design, layout, traffic, trade area congruity, tenant mix, competition, visibility, access and demographic factors can be expected to influence retail centre patronage over and above the basic factors size and distance. They suggest the inclusion of variables such as anchor store type, a measure of parking provision relative to centre size, daily traffic count for adjacent streets and percentage visibility of tenants' signs from the primary street and parking area.

REFERENCES

Balchin, P.N. *et al.* (1995) *Urban Land Economics and Public Policy*, 5th edition (Basingstoke: Macmillan).

Christaller, W. (1933) *Central Places in Southern Germany*, translation by C.W. Baskin (1966) (Englewood Cliffs, NJ: Prentice-Hall).

Chun, G.H., Eppli, M.J. and Shilling, J.D. (2001) 'A simulation analysis of the relationship between retail sales and shopping center rents', *Journal of Real Estate Research*, vol. 21, no. 3, 163–86.

Eppli, M.J. and Benjamin, J.D. (1994) 'The evolution of shopping center research: a review and analysis', *Journal of Real Estate Research*, vol. 9, no. 1, 5–32.

Field, B.G. and MacGregor, B.D. (1987) *Forecasting Techniques for Urban and Regional Planning* (London: Hutchinson).

Fraser, W.D. (1993) *Principles of Property Investment and Pricing*, 2nd edition (Basingstoke: Macmillan).

Gatzlaff, D.H., Sirmans, G.S. and Diskin, B.A. (1994) 'The effect of anchor tenant loss on shopping center rents', *Journal of Real Estate Research*, vol. 9, no. 1, 99–110.

Ghosh, A. (1986) 'The value of a mall and other insights from a revised central place model', *Journal of Retailing*, vol. 62, 79–97.

Hotelling, H. (1929) 'Stability in competition', *Economic Journal*, vol. 39, 41–57.

Huff, D.L. (1964) 'Defining and estimating a trading area', *Journal of Marketing*, vol. 28, 34–8.

Isard, W. (1998) 'Gravity and spatial interaction models', in W. Isard, I.J. Azis, M.P. Drennan, R.E. Miller, S. Saltzmann and E. Thorbecke (eds), *Methods of Interregional and Regional Analysis* (Aldershot: Ashgate).

Jackson, C. (2002) 'Classifying local retail property markets on the basis of rental growth rates', *Urban Studies*, vol. 39, no. 8, 1417–38.

Ownbey, K.L, Davis, K. and Sundel, H.H. (1994) 'The effect of location variables on the gross rents of neighbourhood shopping centres', *Journal of Real Estate Research*, vol. 9, no. 1, 111–23.

Reilly, W.J. (1931) *The Law of Retail Gravitation* (New York: Knickerbocker Press).

Robertson, M. and Jones, C. (1999) 'A cross-sectional model of rents in urban retail centres', *Journal of Property Research*, vol. 16, no. 1, 51–66.

Sirmans, C.F. and Guidry, K.A. (1993) 'The determinants of shopping center rents', *Journal of Real Estate Research*, vol. 8, no. 1, 107–15.

10
Option Pricing Theory and Real Estate Research

INTRODUCTION

The main focus of this book is on quantitative methods in applied real estate market research although the next chapter also provides an overview of quantitative methods and some more specialised statistical methods. The focus of this chapter is on the use of quantitative methods to evaluate the cost or value of uncertainty. Option pricing theory applications represent a growing area and a developing research agenda in real estate research. Unlike many of the regression and statistics based methods and studies reviewed earlier in the book, option pricing theory is borrowed almost directly from the finance literature. Many of the other applied research methods examined so far are developed from the economics literature. The primary applications of option pricing theory and option pricing models are in guiding and shaping investment decisions and in the valuation of risk and uncertainty. However, the relatively recent emergence of published studies with real estate research and option pricing foci means that the development of a research agenda based around the valuation of risk in real estate investment and development is still continuing. This fact is the primary inspiration for the inclusion of this chapter in the book.

Investment in financial, real estate and construction markets is often associated with considerable uncertainty (risk). However, legal mechanisms (contracts) may be used by an investor to lower risk or transfer an element of it to another party in a transaction. Clearly, a contract that transfers more risk to another party is worth more to the investor than an alternative form of contract that has the effect of transferring less risk. Thus, returns from the former should be lower or a premium should be paid by the investor in return for securing such a contract. The question is: how can such contractual differences be valued?

Some answers are found in option pricing theory, which is itself borrowed from the finance discipline. There has been use of option pricing theory in real estate research since at least the early 1970s. Over recent years, the application of such theory to real estate research problems has grown apace. This chapter begins with a brief examination of option pricing theory before moving on to examine examples of real estate research applications.

WHAT ARE OPTIONS?

Most real estate professionals and researchers will be familiar with the concept of explicit options. Options are often used, for example, in the development land acquisition process. Unfortunately, this fact can give rise to some confusion. The word 'option', in the context of the development land acquisition process, typically refers to a contract between a site vendor and a prospective purchaser. The option either compels or permits the prospective purchaser to purchase the site either on or before a given date. A financial consideration will normally be paid by the prospective purchaser in exchange for this 'right of first refusal'. Meanwhile, the eventual purchase price is often set out in advance, in the wording of the option.

There are a number of reasons why developers enter into option agreements with site vendors. The justification that we are interested in here is that options have the effect of reducing risk from the point of view of the option purchaser. As a result, developers are more likely to use options to acquire 'risky' sites than 'safe' ones. Let us simplify matters somewhat by assuming that there are two sources of risk from the point of view of the developer:

(1) The likelihood of obtaining planning permission/a development permit/ a building permit (regulatory uncertainty).
(2) The likelihood that market conditions will remain strong or improve beween site acquisition and development completion (market uncertainty).

Suppose that a developer purchases a site that is suitable and viable for office development. The site is situated in a market which is subject to strong regulatory development control and it does not have planning permission/ a development permit. Prior to developing the site the developer must obtain planning permission/a development permit. There are two outcomes to the developer's application for this permission:

(1) Permission is granted (the site is valuable to the developer).
(2) Permission is not granted (the site is not valuable to the developer but may retain some 'hope' value).

When this source of uncertainty is combined with the fact that market conditions may stay constant, improve, or decline between site purchase and development completion, we can see that developers may face significant risks in purchasing sites outright. Options allow developers to secure a supply of suitable sites while reducing risk.

Non real estate professionals will be more familiar with financial options than land options. In fact, real option pricing theory is developed from models designed to price (value) options to buy and sell ordinary shares (call and put options). Financial options are contracts that allow their owner to buy or sell ordinary shares in the future at a previously agreed price. Call options give the owner the right to purchase shares at a given price (the exercise price) on or before a given date. Since the exercise price is determined when the option is purchased, the value of an exercisable call option is simply equal to the difference between the market share price and the exercise price. If the exercise price is greater than the prevailing market share price (for example, if share prices have dropped since the option was purchased) then a call option has no exercise value. The option may still have a value, however, if there is some time to go before the exercise date (the last date on which the option can be exercised). Put options give the owner the right to sell shares at a given price. The exercise value of a put option is equal to the difference between the exercise price and the market share price. If the exercise price is lower than the market share price then the put option has no exercisable value. As before, the option may still have some value if there is some time to elapse before the exercise date.

WHAT ARE REAL OPTIONS?

In the last section we noted that an option is a contract that gives the owner the right to buy or sell an asset at a previously negotiated price (the exercise price) on or before a given date (the exercise date). Real options, by contrast, can be thought of as implicit options. They are not formal agreements to buy or sell assets but tend to follow on as consequences of investment decisions. For example, a residential development company might purchase a site well in advance of its current land requirements. When it does so, it is in effect purchasing the option to build at some point in the future. Owning the site can be likened to owning a call option with an infinite life. The exercise price is equivalent to the price paid for the site at the time of its acquisition. The market price is a function of (unknown) future housing prices, interest rates and construction costs. The site may have a present market value derived from the expected profitability of developing it now. It also has an option value because the developer can choose to postpone development until some point in the future. The site may therefore be valued as a real option.

Other examples of real options include ownership of natural resources, the ability to make follow-on investments and ownership of property rights.

For example, owning an unviable natural resource (such as an oilfield which is very expensive to operate) is like owning an option to pump oil in the future. If, in the future, oilfield operating costs were to drop and market oil prices were to rise then the oilfield would become profitable to operate. The oilfield therefore has a present value (a real option value) despite the fact that it is presently unprofitable to operate it.

The complexity and multiplicity of regulations and contractual interests are important factors in distinguishing real estate markets from other types of factor, investment or goods markets. Land use planning policies and building regulations are examples of policy, or intervention, that influence the efficiency and profitability of occupying, procuring and investing in commercial real estate. Meanwhile, the wording and provisions of commercial leases, planning agreements and construction contracts can be used to minimise or transfer risk and uncertainty between different real estate market actors and agents. Contractual arrangements that modify or transfer risk, or modify flexibility, are 'option like' in the sense that their financial implications are unknown, as determinants such as future rents, prices, interest rates and construction costs are subject to uncertainty. Real option pricing is intended to provide answers to questions over the value of such contractual arrangements through the application of modified financial option pricing theory. Before examining real option pricing methods, financial option pricing methods are examined.

VALUING SIMPLE CALL AND PUT OPTIONS

The value of an option to buy ordinary shares is a function of its exercise price, the future (unknown) market share price and the length of time between the purchase of the option and its exercise date. Clearly, lack of knowledge about future market share prices presents the only real difficulty. Since this variable is unknown, valuing the option requires us to use probability.

If the number of possible outcomes – in terms of possible future market share prices – is limited then the task of valuing the option is simplified. Suppose that there are only two possible outcomes – high price and low price – and that these lie either side of the exercise price. We can value the option using the concept of riskless arbitrage.

Example 1

What is the value of an option to buy 1 share at an exercise price of 100 when the present market share price is 90 and the exercise date is one year hence? The possible outcomes are a low price of 80 and a high price of 120. Interest rates are 10 per cent per annum. The starting point for the analysis is to consider the possible options values at the end of 1 year (just before the exercise date):

Low price option value: 80–100 = −20 (≡0)
High price option value: 120–100 = 20

The next step is to calculate the option delta:

Delta = possible option value spread ÷ possible share price spread
= (20–0) ÷ (120–80)
= 0.50

In order to complete the analysis and arrive at a valuation for the option we must first recognise that an option can be replicated by combining borrowing (or lending) with straight share purchasing (selling). Specifically, a call option equivalent can be made by purchasing a quantity of shares equivalent to the option delta and borrowing the capital to enable this. This is shown below:

Current market price of 1 share	= 90.00
Option delta	= 0.50
Current market price of 0.50 share	= 45.00
Spread of possible option returns	= 20–0
Spread of possible share returns	= 60–40
	(based on 50 per cent of a share)

The amount of money that should be borrowed to complete the option equivalent can be calculated in relation to the low share price outcome assuming that shares are purchased in line with the option delta. This is shown as follows:

Low share price 1 year from now = 80.00
Low price × option delta = 40.00

The amount that should be paid back to the bank 1 year from now is therefore 40.00. Since interest rates are 10 per cent per annum, we can discount this sum back to a present value in order to find the amount that should be borrowed from the bank today:

Amount to be borrowed = 40.00 × PV 1 year @ 10%
= $40.00 \times (1 \div 1.10^1)$
= 36.36

	Low share price outcome 1 year from now	Cash flow	Discount factor	PV, cash flow	High share price outcome 1 year from now	Cash flow	Discount factor	PV, cash flow
Call option equivalent	Buy 50% of a share	−45.00	1.000	−45.00	Buy 50% of a share	−45.00	1.00	−45.00
	Borrow money from the bank	36.36	1.000	36.36	Borrow money from the bank	36.36	1.00	36.36
	Sell 50% of a share	40.00	0.909	36.36	Sell 50% of a share	60.00	0.909	54.55
	Pay money back to the bank	−40.00	0.909	−36.36	Pay money back to the bank	−40.00	0.909	−36.36
	Present value of investment			**−8.64**	Present value of investment			**9.55**
Call option	Buy a call option	−*x*	1.000	−*x*	Buy a call option	−*x*	1.000	−*x*
	Do not exercise option	0.00	0.909	0.00	Exercise option	20	0.909	18.18
	Present value of investment			**−*x***	Present value of investment			**18.18−*x***
	Call option value = 8.64				Call option value = 8.63			

Figure 10.1 *Possible outcomes for the call option and call option equivalent investment strategies*

The possible outcomes of both investment strategies are shown in Figure 10.1. It is easy to see that the combination of borrowing and buying delta proportions of shares completely replicates the possible pay-offs of buying the call option. Since the pay-offs are the same, a rational investor would be indifferent about the two alternative investment strategies. It follows that both investments should have the same present value. This permits us to value the call option at 8.64 (as a consequence of rounding, the figure works out to 8.63 if we use the high share price figures).

In summary, to find the present value of a call (or put) option, we employ the concept of riskless arbitrage. We can construct an alternative investment strategy with a known price and pay-offs that exactly replicate the option. Since the two investments (option and replicant) are equivalent in terms of risk and pay-off, a rational investor would be indifferent between them and they must therefore have the same present value (price).

REAL ESTATE APPLICATIONS OF THE BINOMIAL OPTION PRICING METHOD

An interesting real estate application of the simple, binomial option pricing method is set out by Titman (1985). The author sets out to provide an explanation for the existence of land which, although suitable for development and situated in high density urban areas, remains vacant. An explanation is provided by way of analysis based on an option pricing model. The model considers the value of vacant urban land, which is suitable for residential development, and the development timing decision of land owners. The land owners' decision is defined as:

$$\max\Pi(p_0) = p_0 q - C(q) \tag{10.1}$$

where

Π = residual site value or development profit
p_0 = the current price or capitalised market rental value of space
q = quantity of space constructed (number of building units)
C = construction costs – a function of q, the quantity of space constructed

In other words, land owners are assumed to maximise the value of their land by selecting from a range of development possibilities in order to maximise the residual site value (the positive remainder after construction costs are deducted from development values). This is subject to two constraints:

(a) $\frac{\partial C}{\partial q} > 0$

(b) $\frac{\partial^2 C}{\partial q^2} > 0$

The constraints indicate that construction costs are assumed to (a) increase with building size and (b) increase more than proportionately with building size. The model predicts that the land owner will have selected the optimal building size when ($\partial C \div \partial q = p_0$), that is, when the marginal cost from building more units is equal to the marginal revenue. This is a standard condition for profit maximisation.

The model, shown as equation (10.1), explains land owners' choice of development density. The author goes on to expand this simplistic model in order to account for the phenomenon of market uncertainty. The model is based upon several simplifying assumptions:

(1) Owners of vacant urban land face a choice between developing now, or deferring development for one year.
(2) Current and future construction costs, and current capital values, are known to the land owner.
(3) Land owners believe that capital values at the deferred development date will be at one of two possible levels.

The value of a vacant site, upon which development will be deferred one year, is:

$$V = \Pi(p_h)s_h + \Pi(p_l)s_l \tag{10.2}$$

where

$\Pi(p_h)$ = the profit (residual value) from deferring development for one year and selling buildings for the higher of the two possible prices
$\Pi(p_l)$ = the profit (residual value) from deferring development for one year and selling buildings for the lower of the two possible prices
s_h = the opportunity cost of deferring development for one year and selling buildings for the higher of the two possible prices
s_l = the opportunity cost of deferring development for one year and selling buildings for the lower of the two possible prices

Titman (1985) concludes that the model is capable of explaining why vacant urban sites sometimes remain vacant despite high demand for space. Uncertainty over future development values means that a vacant urban site has an option value. Exercising the option value can be done by developing the site. However, developing the site means realising current development value and forgoing option value. Paradoxically, sites are worth more undeveloped (because of their option value) than developed in conditions of uncertainty and option values increase with uncertainty.

VALUING OPTIONS WHEN THERE ARE MULTIPLE PRICE OUTCOMES

The binomial method of valuing options clearly has it limitations. However, it provides the basic building blocks for valuing more complex options. So far, this chapter has established that the value of a call option is equal to the value of a share holding and borrowing whose proportions are devised so as to yield the same potential returns as the option. In other words, the value of a call option is:

$$V = (d \times P) - L \tag{10.3}$$

where

V = call option value
d = option delta
P = current share price
L = borrowing

This simple model can be expanded to render it capable of valuing a call option when the share price is expected to move from its value at the time of option purchase to some other position on a continuum of possible prices. Assuming that the share price is Normally distributed, the

Black–Scholes (1973) formula can be used:

$$V = [N(d_1) \times P] - [N(d_2) \times (E \div (1 + r)^t)] \tag{10.4}$$

where

$$d_1 = \frac{\ln\left[\frac{P(1+r)^t}{E}\right]}{\sigma\sqrt{t}} + \frac{\sigma\sqrt{t}}{2}$$

$d_2 = d_1 - \sigma\sqrt{t}$
V = call option value
$N(d_1)$ = the probability that a Normally distributed random variable is less or equal to d_1, the option delta
P = current share price
E = the exercise price
r = the risk-free interest rate (cost of borrowing/lending)
t = periods (years) to exercise date

As noted earlier, the Black–Scholes (1973) formula can be used to value a call option when there are multiple future stock price outcomes. More accurately, the stock price is a continuous random variable and can assume any value between zero and infinity. The variability in the stock price is accounted for since it is effectively proxied by the standard deviation of stock returns (σ).

The Black–Scholes formula looks complex and unwieldy. However, it is relatively straightforward to set up a simple Excel spreadsheet to calculate call option values, as shown in Figure 10.2 (Example 2).

The spreadsheet shown in Figure 10.2 can be used to value a call option simply by changing the parameters in Column C. However, note that at this point no consideration has been given to the fact that dividends are paid on most shares and, in some cases, may be significant. The formula shown above does not account for this fact.

REAL ESTATE APPLICATIONS OF BLACK–SCHOLES AND RELATED FORMULAE

The use of option pricing theory in real estate research stems from the recognition that some real estate rights bestow the owner with potentially valuable option-like assets. Clearly, real estate developers and land traders frequently make use of options in their own right. Land options typically

Excel spreadsheet							Column F formulae
	A	B	C	D	E	F	
1	Current stock price	P	90.00		$(1+r)^t$	1.1000	=(1+C4)^C5
2	Exercise price	E	100.00		$\sigma\sqrt{t}$	0.3000	=C6*(C5^0.5)
3	Risk-free interest rate	r	0.10		d_1	0.1165	=((LN((C2*F2)/C3))/F3)+(F3/2)
4	Periods (years) to exercise date	t	1.00		d_2	–0.1835	=F4–F3
5	Standard deviation of stock returns	Sig	0.30		$N(d_1)$	0.5464	=NORMSDIST(F4)
6					$N(d_2)$	0.4272	=NORMSDIST(F5)
7					$P \times N(d_1)$	49.1734	=C2*F6
8					$N(d_2) \times [E \div (1+r)^t]$	38.8366	=F7*(C3/F2)
9					V	10.3368	=F8–F9

Figure 10.2 *Example 2: a simple Excel spreadsheet design to calculate Black–Scholes call option values*

give their owner the right, or sometimes compel them, to purchase a development site on the reaching of a given date or the completion of some event. In the UK, speculative house building firms use options to purchase land without planning permission. Typically, the option matures if, or when, planning permission is obtained over the land.

In a real estate research context, financial option pricing theory has many more potential applications than simply the valuation of land options. Lucius (2001) sets out a broad categorisation of real options with a real estate focus. This includes the option to:

- Abandon
- Shut down
- Contract
- Expand
- Defer
- Invest in stages

The best way to demonstrate what these valuable option-like rights are is by way of anecdotal examples or scenarios:

Scenario 1

Suppose that a manufacturing firm considers purchasing a large development site in order to construct a manufacturing facility. The site is sufficiently large to house two such facilities, or to build one facility with the possibility of extending it in the future. If the firm purchases the site then it is acquiring a real option as well as a site suitable for the construction of its manufacturing facility. Supposing that the surplus land could be used only for the purpose of extending the original facility, then the firm will have acquired the option to expand in the future on purchasing the site.

If the firm purchases an alternative site, one which is just large enough to accommodate its proposed new facility, then future expansion on site will be impossible. In these circumstances the firm will either acquire an additional facility elsewhere or abandon the existing facility in favour of another with a greater capacity. If we assume that this course of action would be more expensive than extending on site then it is clear that the option to expand is valuable to the firm.

Scenario 2

A firm enters into a 15-year lease over a city-centre office block. The lease includes a break option at the end of the fifth year. This lease clause gives the firm the right to end the lease prematurely by serving an appropriate notice to the landlord just prior to a given date. This clause is potentially valuable to the tenant for a number of possible reasons:

- The firm may become profitable and seek to expand rapidly. The break clause, if exercised, will allow the firm to quit the premises and take on larger premises 10 years earlier than possible without the break clause. Without the break clause the firm would be obliged to take on additional rather than alternative premises to allow expansion.
- The firm may lose market share or its market may contract. Either of these outcomes are likely to lead the firm to contract its business. It may wish to take on smaller premises in order to reduce unnecessary costs after contraction. Without the break clause the firm will be obliged to occupy, and pay rent over, larger premises than required for an additional 10 years.

It is therefore fairly clear that the firm, by taking on the premises with a lease that includes a break clause, is acquiring an option to expand and an option to contract in the process. These are potentially valuable rights.

Scenario 3

A landlord grants a 10-year lease which includes an 'upwards only' rent review at the end of the fifth year. At the end of five years, the clause gives the landlord the right to invoke a rent review. This is something that the landlord will choose to do if it seems evident that market rents have risen since the granting of the lease. If rents have not risen, or have decreased, then the landlord will not invoke the rent review clause and the rent will continue as before. The rent review clause in this particular lease is therefore very much like a call option.

These hypothetical examples, or scenarios, are far from exhaustive but they demonstrate that some rights and obligations over real estate are similar to call or put options. Before developing a general approach to the pricing treatment of such rights and options it is worth examining some of the real estate option pricing literature in more detail.

Much of the literature is focused on the application of option pricing models on the problem of valuing development land (sites). A transaction to acquire land suitable for development can be likened to the purchase of an option to own a building in the future, and some authors argue that owning a site is therefore a bit like owning an American call option to buy common stock. Note that the difference between American options and European options is that the former can be used to buy stock on or before the exercise date while the latter can be used only to buy on the exercise date.

There is a close link between the literature focused on real estate application of option pricing theory and a separate literature concerned with the application of the theory to the problem of pricing natural resources (Brennan and Schwartz, 1985; Paddock *et al.*, 1988; Morck *et al.*, 1989).

The owner of a site with development potential may choose to construct a revenue-bearing building at some later date rather than develop it immediately. In order to acquire the building and its associated rental income stream, the land owner will incur development costs. The analogy of development sites compared with financial call options is logical. Development costs can be likened to the exercise price of a financial call option. The development site can be likened to the option itself. Meanwhile, developers rarely possess certainty about the level of the rental income stream that might be achieved on completion of development and subsequent letting. The volatility of new-build commercial real estate rental income streams is likely to vary significantly depending on country, region, local market characteristics, sector and market conditions. Similarly, there is considerable variation among the market prices of different stocks depending on similar factors.

Titman (1985), Williams (1991, 1993) and Grenadier (1996) demonstrate that the price of an option to develop (i.e. the price of development land) can be found by solving a partial differential option valuation equation derived from the Black and Scholes financial option valuation equation (Black and Scholes, 1973). The example provided by Williams (1991) is of particular interest:

$$0 = \frac{1}{2}\sigma_1^2 x_1^2 V_{11} + \sigma_{12} x_1 x_2 V_{12} + \frac{1}{2}\sigma_2^2 x_2^2 V_{22} + \upsilon_1 x_1 V_1 + \upsilon_2 x_2 V_2 - iV + \beta x_2 \qquad (10.5)$$

where

x_1 = development cost per unit
x_2 = development revenue per unit
υ_i = expected growth rate for the *i*th security
V_i = value of the *i*th security
i = riskless rate of interest
$V(x)$ = option price (the value of development land), where $x = (x_1, x_2)$
βx_2 = cash inflow from undeveloped land (per unit of time)
σ = standard deviation of the developed property price changes

Thus, Williams (1991) demonstrates that the present value of an option to own developed property is a function of development revenues and costs, time and the riskless rate of interest. As with Titman (1985), Williams (1991) shows that the effect of increasing uncertainty is to increase the present value of an option. Just as the option pricing equation predicts a higher option price for stocks with greater volatility, *ceteris paribus*, the price of a site with development potential increases as the volatility of development revenues over costs increases.

One of the difficulties faced in applying the Black–Scholes formula to the valuation of development sites is the fact that the (unknown) future market price for the site is itself derived from several other 'key' development variables. In the Black–Scholes formula the market stock price can be viewed as an exogenous variable. In a development site context the market price is determined by the interaction of construction costs, market rental values and interest rates.

Aside from the valuation of development sites, financial option pricing theory is argued by some authors as suitable for the pricing of leases with option-like features (Grenadier, 1995; Ward and French, 1997; Ward *et al.*, 1998). Simple options with two states or outcomes can be priced using the binomial method (see example 1). For example, Ward and French (1997) demonstrate that the premium for a lease with an upwards-only rent review clause rather than an upwards/downwards rent review clause can be calculated using this method. A similar example, and its solution according to the binomial option pricing method, is shown below as Example 3.

Example 3

What should be the premium attached to a lease with an upwards-only rent review clause rather than an upwards/downwards rent review clause? The lease has a duration of 10 years and makes an allowance for a rent review at the end of five years. The current market rent is £50,000 and the two possible state prices (rents) at the end of the fifth year are £44,000 and £60,000. Cash can be borrowed at the riskless rate of 6 per cent while the all risks yield is 10 per cent.

As before, the starting point for the analysis is to consider the possible options values at the end of the fifth year. However, before doing this we need to calculate the possible market prices of the underlying asset at the end of five years. This can be done simply using term and reversion valuations as follows:

First term			
Rent	50,000		
YP 5 years @ 8%	3.9927		
Value	199,636		
Second term	Low rent	No change	High rent
Rent	44,000	50,000	60,000
YP 5 years @ 8%	3.9927	3.9927	3.9927
PV £1 5 years @ 6%	0.7473	0.7473	0.7473
Value	131,278	149,179	179,015

These simple investment valuations yield the following possible (notional) rental income present values (ignoring rental income streams after the 10-year period of the lease in question):

Lease type	Rents fall	No change	Rents rise
Up/down rent review clause lease	306,957	324,859	378,651
Upwards-only rent review clause lease	324,859	324,859	378,651

The range of values of the asset (the lease with upwards and downwards rent review clause) is £306,957 to £378,651 – a difference of £71,694. The value of the put option (the option to keep the rent at £50,000 even when market rents have fallen to £44,000) can be seen by considering the potential outcomes when the investor purchases an asset with an upward-only rent review clause.

If market rents increase then the asset increases in value from £324,859 to £378,651 – an increase of £53,792. If market rents decrease then the investor can avoid a decline in value from £324,859 to £306,957 – a saving of £17,902.

The option pay-off range is therefore £35,892 (53,792 less 17,902) while the asset value range is £71,694 as discussed earlier. This means that the option delta is 0.5006. The possible outcomes of both investment strategies are shown in Figure 10.3.

Low share price outcome 1 year from now

		Cash flow	Discount factor	PV, cash flow
Upwards only r/r lease equivalent	Buy 50.06% of an assset	–162,628	1.000	–162,628
	Borrow money from the bank	114,828	1.000	114,828
	Sell 50.05% of an asset	153,666	0.7473	114,828
	Pay money back to the bank	–114,828	0.7473	–85,806
	Present value of investment			**–18,778**
Upwards only r/r lease	Buy a call option	$-x$	1.000	$-x$
	Do not exercise option	17,902	0.7473	13,377
	Present value of investment			**13,377–x**

Option value = 32,155

High share price outcome 1 year from now

		Cash flow	Discount factor	PV, cash flow
Upwards only r/r lease equivalent	Buy 50.06% of an asset	–162,628	1.000	–162,628
	Borrow money from the bank	114,828	1.000	114,828
	Sell 50.06% of an asset	189,557	0.7473	141,648
	Pay money back to the bank	–114,828	0.7473	–85,806
	Present value of investment			**8,042**
Upwards only r/r lease	Buy a call option	$-x$	1.000	$-x$
	Exercise option	53,792	0.7473	40,197
	Present value of investment			**40,197–x**

Option value = 32,155

***Figure 10.3** Possible outcomes for the call/put option combination and an equivalent investment strategy*

CONSTRUCTION ECONOMICS APPLICATIONS OF OPTION PRICING THEORY

Real option models have also become a fairly common feature in construction economics related research over recent years. For example, Boukendour and Bah (2001) examine the application of option pricing theory for the purpose of valuing, from the perspective of construction clients, the reduction of uncertainty arising from the use of 'guaranteed maximum price' (GMP) contracts rather than 'cost plus fee' contracts. Specifically, the authors consider the GMP contract as a combination of a cost reimbursement contract and a call option. Cost reimbursement contracts oblige the client to pay the contractor's actual incurred costs together with a prearranged fee. The GMP contract follows the same lines except that the client benefits from a known cost ceiling or guaranteed maximum price. Boukendour and Bah (2001) point out that the GMP contract permits clients to pay the lower of actual costs (including agreed fee) or the guaranteed maximum price, and argue that the GMP contract carries with it a legal right similar to a call option. On completion of the contract, if the actual construction costs are greater than the guaranteed maximum price then the client can invoke their right to pay the GMP. This act is similar to exercising a call option since the contractual right effectively gives the client the right to acquire the completed project below cost. The authors calculate the call option value as follows:

$$C = Ee^{-rt}[N(d_1) - N(d_2)] \qquad (10.6)$$

where

$$d_1 = \frac{\ln\left(\frac{Ee^{-rt}}{E}\right) + \left(r + \frac{1}{2}\sigma^2\right)}{\sigma\sqrt{t}}$$

$d_2 = d_1 - \sigma\sqrt{t}$
E = exercise price (GMP)
t = contract duration (time to exercise)
r = risk-free interest rate
σ = continuously compounded rate of return (proxied by standard deviation on a building cost index)

The call option value represents the additional value of the GMP contract to the client as compared with the standard cost reimbursement contract. An alternative way to interpret this is that the call option value represents the maximum additional amount that the client is able to pay to the contractor in respect of fees in order to reflect the transfer of risk to the contractor.

In contrast with real estate there has been relatively little research focused on the use of option pricing theory to value risk and uncertainty in construction projects. Other recent examples are provided by Sing (2002), Ho and Liu (2002) and Ford *et al.* (2002). In particular, Sing (2002) notes that most real option models focused on real estate development projects assume that the procurement of a building is instantaneous. This is clearly not the case and in fact construction clients are exposed during the construction period of a real estate development project. Legal mechanisms designed to transfer risk from the client to contractor or occupier (such as different procurement contracts and pre-leasing arrangements) carry with them 'option-like' features. The implied market value of these contractual differences can be valued using option pricing models. It is likely that this area of construction economics and management research will develop extensively over the coming years.

REFERENCES

Black, F. and Scholes, M. (1973) 'The pricing of options and corporate liabilities', *Journal of Political Economy*, vol. 81, 637–59.

Boukendour, S. and Bah, R. (2001) 'The guaranteed maximum price contract as call option', *Construction Management and Economics*, vol. 19, 563–7.

Brennan, M.J. and Schwartz, E.S. (1985) 'Evaluating natural resource investment', *Journal of Business*, vol. 58, no. 2, 1135–57.

Clarke, H. and Reed, W. (1988) 'A stochastic analysis of land development timing and property valuation', *Regional Science and Urban Economics*, vol. 18, 367–82.

Ford, D.N., Lander, D.M. and Voyer, J.J. (2002) 'A real options approach to valuing strategic flexibility in uncertain construction projects', *Construction Management and Economics*, vol. 20, 343–51.

Grenadier, S. R. (1995) 'The valuation of leasing contracts: a real options approach', *Journal of Financial Economics*, vol. 38, no. 3, 297–331.

Grenadier, S.R. (1996) 'The strategic exercise of options: development cascades and overbuilding in real estate markets', *Journal of Finance*, vol. 51, no. 5, 1653–79.

Ho, S.P. and Liu, L.Y. (2002) 'An option pricing-based model for evaluating the financial viability of privatized infrastructure projects', *Construction Management and Economics*, vol. 20, 143–56.

Lucius, D.I. (2001) 'Real options in real estate development', *Journal of Property Investment and Finance*, vol. 19, no. 1, 73–8.

Morck, R., Schwartz, E. and Stangeland, D. (1989) 'The valuation of forestry resources under stochastic prices and inventories', *Journal of Financial and Quantitative Analysis*, vol. 24, no. 4, 473–87.

Paddock, J.L., Siegel, D.R. and Smith, J.L. (1988) 'Option valuation of claims on real assets – the case of offshore petroleum leases', *Quarterly Journal of Economics*, vol. 103, no. 3, 479–508.

Sing, T.F. (2002) 'Time to build options in construction processes', *Construction Management and Economics*, vol. 20, 119–30.

Titman, S. (1985) 'Urban land prices under uncertainty', *American Economic Review*, vol. 75, no. 3, 505–14.

Ward, C. and French, N. (1997) 'The valuation of upwards-only rent reviews: an option pricing model', *Journal of Property Valuation and Investment*, vol. 15, no. 2, 171–82.

Ward, C., Hendershott, P.H. and French, N. (1998) 'Pricing upwards-only rent review clauses', *Journal of Property Investment and Finance*, vol. 16, no. 5, 447–54.

Williams, J.T. (1991) 'Real estate development as an option', *Journal of Real Estate Finance and Economics*, vol. 4, 191–208.

Williams, J.T. (1993) 'Equilibrium and options on real assets', *Review of Financial Studies*, vol. 6, no. 4, 825–50.

11

Behavioural and Qualitative Methods in Real Estate Research

INTRODUCTION

So far, the overriding focus of this book has been on quantitative methods in real estate research. In the application of many of the methods examined so far it is implicitly assumed that real estate markets are relatively simple entities consisting of groups of firms (occupiers, investors or developers) or individuals (households). Through their interaction, these groups of suppliers and demanders give rise to the real estate market processes and dynamics that are the subject of investigation in many research projects. Some of the quantitative methods examined so far really assume that such processes can be boiled down to abstract models employing generalised concepts and subject to sets of simplifying assumptions.

The purposes of this chapter are to relax some of the rigid assumptions about market behaviour and dynamics and to introduce some basic qualitative and behavioural research methods that may be used in real estate market research. The chapter is inspired by the fact that the complexity of real estate market processes, the importance of the behaviour of actors in real estate markets and the well-documented imperfections in real estate markets (particularly relating to heterogeneity, transactions frequency and the role of information), suggests that applied research examining many real estate market processes and issues may not be best served by quantitative methods underpinned by rigid assumptions about market efficiency and the role of actors in real estate markets. The chapter begins by discussing behavioural issues in real estate market research and analysis. It then provides a brief overview of some well-documented qualitative research methods.

QUALITATIVE AND BEHAVIOURAL RESEARCH IN REAL ESTATE

In both the US and, to a greater extent, the UK, there has been relatively little qualitative based real estate market research since around the 1960s. However, over recent years there has been a gradual shift in the focus and methods employed in some published real estate economics research.

The emphasis of this book has been on quantitative applied real estate research methods. These methods are in common usage in studies that adhere to the quantitative paradigm. The implicit assumptions that underpin the theoretical reasoning in such studies are that market processes can be explained through logical extensions to the accepted theories subject to simplifying assumptions. Clapp and Myers (2000) refer to this form of deductive reasoning, that has dominated real estate economics research since the 1960s, as the New Urban Economics paradigm.

Many of the empirical papers cited in this book provide classic examples of research studies in the New Urban Economics paradigm. Quantitative models are developed in accordance with accepted economic theory and subject to simplifying assumptions. Empirical analyses are designed to test out the validity of and limits to the deductive reasoning, and results flow into the body of evidence and thence influence accepted theory. Some commentators generalise this dominant paradigm in real estate research by referring to studies in this tradition as 'neoclassical analyses'. Such studies typically focus on the construction of sophisticated models, using quantitative techniques, that can be used to explain and predict market outcomes such as price determination and spatial interaction. Proponents of institutional and structure and agency approaches to analysing real estate markets are particularly sceptical about what they describe as an overly restrictive approach to analysing and researching real estate markets (see Ball, 1998; D'Arcy and Keogh, 2000; and Diaz, 1999, for example). Other commentators argue that institutional and structure and agency orientated research provides a complement to, rather than a substitute for, neoclassical analyses (see Guy and Henneberry, 2000, 2002).

The idea that the behaviour of firms and individuals is important to real estate market outcomes is at the forefront of a developing agenda in behavioural real estate market research. Research belonging to this paradigm is described by Ball *et al.* (1998) as 'Behavioural Institutionalism' and is typified by an explicit acknowledgement that misleading results may be obtained from analyses in which market efficiencies and differences between the behaviour of different types of agent, firm or individual are assumed away.

The literature contains several examples of such behavioural analyses focused on urban land and housing markets. Such behavioural approaches tend to address the operation of the development process by focusing on the roles and behaviour of its key actors: land owners, developers (house builders) and planners (the planning system). The behavioural approach recognises that the development of land for private housing is a result of the interaction between these key actors. In relation to the land market, the implication of behavioural models is that land values, as well as the level of development activity, are at least partially determined by the decisions of, and interaction between, key actors in the development process. For example, Drewett (1973) examines seven methods by which house builders acquire land for the development of private housing. The methods have a varying emphasis on local contacts, analysis of development plans, lobbying local real estate professionals, interaction with planning professionals and presence at auctions. The diversity of the house builders' land acquisition methods implies that the price of land will not be consistent between different methods of acquisition. Rydin (1984) notes that the involvement of builders in the land allocation process is likely to depend on their land banking activities. She contends that volume builders with land banks lobby actively for the release of land within their control for development whilst actively seeking to prevent the release of land which they do not own. By contrast, small builders, who usually do not own land banks, actively lobby for the general release of all suitable development land.

Others, for example Goodchild and Munton (1985), emphasise the importance of the route that a site takes through the planning and development process in determining the outcomes, where 'outcomes' may be taken to include the land price realised and the speed and form of development. They identify six routes that vary with respect to the emphasis on the role of the land owner, developer and planning system in taking the site through the development process. They point out that the behaviour of land owners is diverse: some are likely to be professional land traders or developers in their own right, others may be farmers or urban site owners with little property market knowledge and little interest in the property market itself except in the short term. They identify six land owner characteristics that affect the behaviour of land owners in relation to the development process, including legal personality, occupancy status, sources of income, personal characteristics, means of acquisition and knowledge of and attitude to risk (see Adams, 1994, for a detailed review). Meanwhile, Adams (1994) concentrates on distinguishing between active and passive behaviour as a means of describing land owners. Active land owners are defined as 'those who develop their own land, enter into joint venture development or make their land available for others to develop' (Adams, 1994, p. 103). More specifically, active land owners are described as those 'who obtain planning permission, tackle development constraints or offer their land for sale without undue influence from developers' (Adams, 1994, p. 103). Passive land owners are taken as those who make no attempt to develop their land or market it as suitable for development.

Fairly recently a number of studies have examined behavioural influences on market outcomes in the context of land price determination (Antwi and Henneberry, 1995; Leishman *et al.*, 2000). These studies are essentially neoclassical in nature but are driven by a desire to improve the validity of neoclassical analysis by relaxing the rigid assumptions that all firms and agents are identical and the market is informationally perfect. Both studies mentioned consider a range of alternative sets of decision-making behaviour and simulate land prices according to these scenarios. Meanwhile, analyses of real estate investors' perceptions have been carried out by Adair *et al.* (1999), and the importance of office occupiers' locational decision-making behaviour to real estate market outcomes has been argued by Leishman and Watkins (2002).

The term 'Behavioural Institutionalism', as defined by Ball *et al.* (1998), might be argued by some as being too restrictive since it emphasises the role of firms and agents and downplays the role of individuals. A recent series of papers examining the role of human behaviour in the introduction of bias to the real estate valuation process emphasises the potential significance of human behaviour in the determination of real estate outcomes. For example, in an hypothetical valuation study in which students and real estate professionals carried out valuations, Northcraft and Neale (1987) found that asking prices significantly affect valuations. Specifically, the valuations produced by their participants were biased towards the asking price supplied by the researchers, suggesting that undue consideration was given to this information even when ample comparable evidence was supplied. Building on descriptive work by Diaz (1990), Black and Diaz (1996) also find evidence that heuristic behaviour in the valuation process may lead to valuations biased towards 'anchors' such as asking price. Meanwhile, Gallimore (1994, 1996) investigates 'anchoring and adjustment', 'recency', 'dilution' and 'confirmation bias' as four possible sources of valuation bias.

Anchoring and adjustment is a process in which valuers are conjectured to carry out a valuation with some *a priori* notion of value. The argument is that the final valuation will be biased towards this anchor. Asking prices may also become anchors. The concept of 'confirmation bias' is closely related. This describes an unconscious tendency for professionals to calculate an answer that tends to ratify their own *a priori* view. Meanwhile, the phenomenon of 'recency' describes a tendency for individuals to overweight the most recently acquired information. In the context of valuation, the hypothesis would be that valuers place too much emphasis on the most recently acquired comparable evidence, while 'dilution' describes a tendency for valuers to disregard or down-weight comparable evidence that is not supportive of their *a priori* view.

Whether the focus is on individuals, firms, households or agents (actors), a key feature of most behavioural research is that the assumption of rationality is dropped or, at a minimum, modified to permit a more realistic and/or accurate analysis to be undertaken. In a simplistic neoclassical analysis it is assumed that producers and consumers are rational. This may be taken to mean that, all other things being equal, a producer would always prefer to sell a unit of its output at a high price than a low price while consumers will always prefer to purchase a unit of a good at a low price than a high price. More detailed aspects of rational behaviour (on the supply side) might include the idea that producers will seek to expand output when profit levels are high and contract or stockpile when profits are low, and so on. A behavioural analysis would not necessarily contradict these notions. Rather, such an analysis might be constructed in accordance with the idea that producers' output decisions and consumers' consumption decisions are more complex than described by these simple rules. Such an analysis might also recognise that heterogeneous producers and consumers can be grouped in some way, to form more homogeneous groups, and that their behaviour will vary between these groups.

The economics literature contains various examples of ways in which such an approach can improve understanding of economic phenomena such as consumption and production decisions and firms' location decisions. For example, the competing relative, absolute and permanent income hypotheses of consumption vary primarily in terms of the emphasis placed on prestige, today's income level and a consumer's expectations of income over his/her working life in arriving at decisions regarding current consumption. On the supply side, even relatively simplistic microeconomic theories of the firm are capable of recognising that the motivation of the firm may be market penetration or development of market share rather than simply profit maximisation. Meanwhile, other commentators have recognised the role that seemingly 'irrational' factors may play in firms' location decisions. For example, the location decision of a newly formed small firm may be unduly influenced by the forming managing director's travel to work preferences (see Balchin *et al.*, 1995, for a general discussion on firms' location decisions and the potential role of seemingly irrational factors).

Recently, some commentators have argued for the use of qualitative empirical methods as a complement to quantitative methods (see Philip, 1998, for an interesting discussion on the use of alternative methodologies and approaches). The logic of this argument is that such an approach permits the testing of some of the assumptions that underpin the use of the quantitative methods reviewed earlier in the book. The essence of a behavioural approach to applied real estate market research is not that producers and consumers are irrational but that their decision-making processes are more complex than implicitly assumed in many published quantitative studies. The use of qualitative techniques permits background research into the factors that shape decision-making processes. Consequently, there is an argument that drawing on qualitative methods should permit the construction and estimation of more accurate quantitative models that better reflect the real estate market realities that are being modelled. The remainder of this chapter sets out a brief overview of a selection of commonly used qualitative methods in social science research.

QUALITATIVE METHODS

In the real estate discipline, qualitative methods are, arguably, under-used by practitioners and over-used by students. This probably stems from the fact that there are two main misconceptions regarding qualitative research.

The first misconception is that qualitative methods are easily employed – that they are an 'easy option'. This is a particularly popular misconception among undergraduate students, probably because at the start of an undergraduate research project the mental image of working with interview and questionnaire results may be more appealing than the mental image of wrestling with large quantitative datasets and barely comprehended quantitative methods. However, an experienced researcher would argue that it is often simpler to conceptualise, construct and estimate a quantitative model in order to test a hypothesis rather than design a robust qualitative strategy that permits a hypothesis to be tested rigorously and scientifically.

Secondly, there is a general scepticism, among researchers and practitioners, about the rigorousness and scientific merit of qualitative research methods. Yet, as noted earlier in the book, research is scientific or not depending on the rigour of the process and the methods used during the research. Well-conceptualised and designed qualitative research can yield robust and rigorous results. Equally, of course, unscientific and unreliable results can be obtained from an analysis that uses even the most demanding of quantitative methods if the research process followed is ill-conceived and/or carelessly executed. The common misconception that qualitative methods are not rigorous is probably related to the first misconception, mentioned above, that employing qualitative methods is an 'easy option' when undertaking a research project.

Having briefly addressed two popular misconceptions about qualitative research, it must be reiterated that the choice of empirical methods should be closely linked with the research questions and/or hypotheses and should be appropriate methods for investigating or testing these rather than the easiest or least daunting of the range of possible methods. While a great deal of real estate market research is of a quantitative nature, from time to time most researchers are faced with circumstances in which quantitative methods are inappropriate for the research questions or hypotheses at hand. In other circumstances the research questions will call for an appropriate blend of qualitative and quantitative methods. Common circumstances that suggest a need for qualitative methods include:

- The research question cannot be tested directly because data do not exist and cannot be collected.
- The conjectured cause and effect relationship is sufficiently complex that a quantitative test cannot be devised.
- The focus of the research question or hypothesis is on individuals (for example, consumers or practitioners) rather than markets or some other abstraction of individuals on aggregate.
- The goal of the research is to collate information on the operation or dynamics of a complex process which cannot directly be observed.
- The subject area is not well understood, there are few or no published studies relating to it and the proposed research project is of an investigative nature.
- The proposed empirical research requires the collection of information on views, opinions, attitudes or decisions rather than economic or financial data.

As this list demonstrates, researchers are often faced with circumstances in which qualitative data collection methods may be appropriate. It should be noted that the term 'qualitative' is just as wide-ranging as the term 'quantitative'. Quantitative analysis may describe methods as simple as the calculation of means and variances and the construction or the estimation of a complex econometric model. Qualitative methods encompass techniques as diverse as the analysis of dialogue, text and behaviour through to quantitative analysis of qualitative data (for example, a large dataset on voters' socio-economic characteristics and their expressed political opinions might be analysed statistically).

RESEARCH ETHICS

The role of research ethics takes on a renewed importance when undertaking research using qualitative methods. Field work will normally involve the collection of data from individuals while empirical analysis will involve working with data that often includes personal and confidential information. Ethical issues are examined throughout the remainder of the chapter during the course of reviewing different qualitative data collection methods.

In terms of working with qualitative data there are some general rules that should always be followed. For example, questionnaire, interview and focus group responses should be anonymised. Individuals should not be identified for ethical reasons, while there should be no need to in any event since any sample chosen should be representative of its parent population. Where there is a diversity of response types within the sample it is perfectly acceptable to segment the sample and provide representative responses for each of the sub-samples. For example:

'Mr Brown thought that....'	This is not ethically acceptable.
'The responses of practitioners in small firms tended to believe X while practitioners in the large firms surveyed thought Y.'	This is ethically acceptable.
'Mr Smith paid £200,000 for his house.'	This is not ethically acceptable.
'Young professionals paid up to five times their income for their house while the remainder of the sample paid, on average, up to three times their income.'	This is ethically acceptable.

Clearly, these rules are largely common-sense and adhering to them is unlikely to cause many problems for the researcher in most cases. There are occasional instances in which the results may indicate a need for further information on a particular individual. For example, a sample of interview responses may contain an outlier or unexpected response that can be explained with reference to the background or characteristics of the individual. In these circumstances it is permissible to give sufficient additional information to demonstrate the argument that the observation is not representative but confidentiality and sensitivity to the respondents should still be maintained. Normally, there will be a way in which to provide the information ethically. For example:

> 'This respondent had been in practice for a shorter period of time than the other respondents.'
>
> or
>
> 'This respondent did not have much experience of living in the UK.'

When writing-up the results of field work and qualitative analysis researchers are required to summarise, and sometimes provide an interpretation on, the views, opinions and attitudes of others. This is another issue that requires firm adherence to research ethics. The researcher's job is to report the results as found and not to construct or massage the results in such a way as to lend weight to the argument, hypothesis or thesis under investigation. This may seem too obvious to make it worthwhile making the point but the real problem is that qualitative data are easily, and unconsciously, biased. Many qualitative datasets are collections of views and opinions and, as such, they are highly susceptible to the introduction of bias in the form of the researcher's own views, conscious or otherwise. The problem is particularly pronounced when the researcher is motivated to carry out the research project out of interest, as in the case of almost all student and academic research projects. With a strong interest in the matters under investigation it is likely to be very easy for a researcher to introduce bias when analysing and writing-up qualitative results. A sensible strategy is for the researcher to dissociate him/herself from the project while undertaking the analysis and writing-up the results by suppressing his/her own interest in the matter until after completion.

GENERAL GUIDANCE FOR QUALITATIVE RESEARCH

Clearly, questions should be designed in such a way that respondents are in a position and have the authority to provide the information. Furthermore, it is an inviolable principle that information only has value if it has been volunteered by the respondent rather than extracted unwillingly. The latter is to be regarded as a breach of research ethics.

Considerable care must be taken in constructing questions in order to avoid unnecessarily complex or jargony phrasing as well as ambiguous words and phrases. Since language forms part of the data collection tools in qualitative research, questions should be constructed so as to be objective and neutral. Data collected using unobjective or leading questions are likely to be biased and are therefore of little value. Simple questions are to be preferred to lengthy complex ones, as the latter are associated with a greater risk of misinterpretation and ambiguity. Few researchers would argue that an accurate sensor is not preferable to an inaccurate one since the former reduces the risk of measurement error. In qualitative research, questions are, in effect, devices that permit the collection of data. The risk of misinterpretation and miscomprehension can be reduced by ensuring that questions are specific rather than general and relate to non-hypothetical matters. Hypothetical questions, by definition, encourage respondents to become conjectural.

Qualitative research almost always involves primary data collection through field work. Common data collection methods include direct observation, observation based on group interaction, interviews and surveys.

Direct observation is a common data collection technique in some social science disciplines but is unlikely to be a useful method in applied real estate market research. Observation based on group interaction can be semi-structured (focus groups) or structured (workshops). Meanwhile, interviews are also referred to as either semi-structured or structured depending on the degree of control exerted by the researcher over the data collection. Surveys include commissioned surveys such as household surveys, postal questionnaire surveys and telephone surveys. Several possible data collection methods will now be examined in turn.

FOCUS GROUPS AND WORKSHOPS

Running focus group sessions is a popular, and often very productive, method of collecting qualitative data. When running focus groups the interviewer (known as a moderator in the context of focus group work) will be dealing with a number of people simultaneously, and in some ways a focus group can be thought of as an informal group interview. One of the main reasons for running a focus group rather than a series of individual interviews is to allow the collection of more detailed, and sometimes more diverse, information through the use of group dynamics. Group dynamics are present when interviewees (focus group participants) give fuller and more detailed responses as the result of being prompted by, agreeing with, disagreeing with or empathising with other focus group participants. Focus groups are therefore a good way of gathering information on collective experiences, shared opinions and, to a lesser extent, differences of opinion.

As the term suggests, the moderator's role is to facilitate rather than force discussion and a good moderator will follow a thin line between questioning too much and failing to exercise sufficient control. This task is normally assisted by using a topic list or a set of broad questions or topics around which the focus group discussions will be based. Moderators often ask a question from the topic list in order to begin discussion and then remain silent for a few minutes, or longer, to allow several participants to give answers or venture opinions. This often leads on to a discussion among participants. Depending on the nature of the particular group and the personalities of the participants, group discussion can go on for too long and begin drifting too far from the issue of interest. One of the moderator's tasks is to gently redirect discussion when required and, if an issue has been exhausted or the discussion is moving in an unhelpful direction, the moderator may cease discussion by asking a new question from the topic list. Other focus groups are more difficult to motivate towards a discussion and it is wise to ensure that a sufficiently long and detailed topic list is available should a particular group require significant prompting.

Focus groups tend to work best when there are between five and eight participants and the participants are fairly homogeneous. Discussion and group interaction are unlikely to be particularly successful if the group is heterogeneous. Focus groups are valuable as an investigative tool since discussion and group interaction may lead to the identification of new issues that were not thought *a priori* to be of importance by the moderator. For this reason, it is not uncommon to run a series of focus groups. Sometimes the topic list may be modified or expanded after several focus groups have been run to take account of the new issues uncovered in the focus group discussions.

SEMI-STRUCTURED AND STRUCTURED INTERVIEWS

At the outset of the project there will often be a fairly clear understanding of the issues to be addressed and it may be possible to take a more formal approach to the qualitative data collection by embarking on a series of interviews rather than undertaking focus group or workshop sessions. This is also likely to be the case during investigative research in which the importance of group interaction is not thought to be of importance in helping to generate discussion with interviewees. For example, consumers are not necessarily likely to be forthcoming about discussing their tastes, preferences and spending habits, while professionals, being questioned about matters relevant to their own profession, are likely to be forthcoming about their views. In the latter case the significance of group dynamics in the generation of discussion will be limited. In addition, there is a pragmatic argument in favour of carrying out interviews where possible since it is generally easier to arrange a series of individual interviews than to co-ordinate the availability of several individuals for the purpose of arranging a focus group or workshop. However, this is a secondary consideration – of primary importance is the assessed significance of group interaction to the generation of the qualitative data.

As noted, interviews are likely to be used when there is some prior knowledge about the issues – that is, the research question or hypothesis is already fairly well specified before the qualitative data collection begins. Yet interviews need not be heavily structured or formalised. In real estate economics research most interviews are likely to follow a semi-structured or structured approach. In other social science subjects unstructured interviews may be used but such an approach is rarely used in real estate economics research.

Semi-structured interviews are akin to focus groups in that discussion loosely follows the structure of a pre-prepared topic list that details issues or broad questions to be addressed during the interview. Unlike a focus group, semi-structured interviews normally involve one interviewer and one interviewee although there are circumstances in which this may be altered. Questions are normally open-ended and designed to open up discussion rather than closed questions that require short, specific answers.

Structured interviews are more formalised in the sense that questions tend to be more specific and closed. Interviews tend to be organised to the structure of a questionnaire or detailed topic list rather than a loose topic list. In many ways, structured interviews have more in common with questionnaire surveys (see below) than focus groups, workshops and semi-structured interviews.

The choice of whether to use a semi-structured or a structured approach will depend largely on the depth of information that is required together with the homogeneity of the population/sample and the required sample size. If the population is fairly homogeneous and a relatively small sample is required then semi-structured interviews may be chosen in order to maximise the depth of information gathered. If the population is heterogeneous and/or a large sample is required then structured interviews are more likely to permit the subsequent analysis to highlight areas of consensus and difference between the different sub-samples identified.

COMMISSIONED AND POSTAL SURVEYS

Questionnaire surveys are at the very structured end of qualitative data collection methods. Surveys are unlikely to be investigative since their arm's-length nature reduces the researcher's control over the conditions in which the data are collected and, more important, almost completely eradicates the researcher's ability to re-state or clarify questions. This fact alone emphasises the importance of good question and questionnaire design, since discovering, after the fact, that some questions were ambiguous or were frequently misinterpreted can spell disaster for a research project. Most projects are run to tight budget and time limits, with the result that there will be insufficient money or time to repeat a failed survey. There are other complexities, because there is an argument that the views of respondents will change slightly even as a result of participating in a survey and so there is no guarantee that the results of a revised survey will not be biased with respect to the first survey, unless an altogether new sample is chosen.

Questionnaire surveys are used when a larger sample of responses is required and when the population is difficult to reach (sample). A large sample is likely to be needed when the population itself is large (for example, if the population is all UK households rather than London-based surveyors) or if the population is thought to be highly heterogeneous. If the latter applies then the significance of potential sample selection bias is increased and a stratified random sampling technique may be used in conjunction with a large-scale survey.

The exact choice of data collection method will depend on the size of the budget, time constraints, the homogeneity and accessibility of the population and the complexity of the survey. If the budgetary restrictions are not severe or if the survey is complex then commissioning a market research firm to carry out a specified number of face-to-face interviews could be the best option. All reputable market research firms are able to offer advice on survey/question design and sampling requirements in addition to providing the time and labour necessary to carry out a large number of standardised interviews. Commissioned surveys have the added advantage that market researchers are able to clarify questions. It is generally preferable to request that market research firms carry out a small-scale pilot survey in order to highlight any remaining ambiguities prior to releasing the final questionnaire design and beginning the real data collection. Further advantages to using a market research firm to collect data include the fact that this option effectively guarantees that a dataset with a specified number of observations will be available on completion of the work, while typical response rates associated with face-to-face surveys are generally much higher than for other common alternatives such as postal and telephone surveys.

Postal questionnaire surveys, much loved by undergraduate students, are a cost-effective means of collecting qualitative data since the labour requirements are reduced to the time needed to design, print, duplicate and send out the questionnaires in addition to inputting data derived from completed and returned questionnaires. With the removal of the laborious tasks of finding and surveying respondents face-to-face, postal questionnaire surveys can usually be carried out by in-house research teams, or personally in the case of student research projects.

One of the most important issues in relation to postal questionnaire surveys relates to the size of the response rate. Typical response rates on questionnaire surveys are considerably lower than for other forms of qualitative data collection. The actual response rate is likely to be related to the complexity of the survey and the characteristics of firms and individuals surveyed, so it is difficult to formulate guidance on good and bad response rates. However, it is unlikely that a response rate above around 50 per cent will be achieved with even a very well-designed survey, and rates of 10 to 25 per cent are not uncommon. The size of the response rate is important for two reasons. The first point is obvious: large samples are better than smaller samples and most researchers are likely to be pleased with a good response rate purely from the point of view that a good response rate delivers a large dataset. The second reason is that the risk of sample selection bias increases as the response rate decreases. Postal questionnaires involve an element of self-selection on the part of respondents since recipients of a questionnaire can choose whether or not to complete and return it. When a low response rate is received in relation to a postal questionnaire survey this poses the question of whether the characteristics of respondents are in any way different from the characteristics of non-respondents. In other words, a low response rate raises a question over the randomness and representativeness of the sample. Clearly, this problem is exacerbated if the population is fairly heterogeneous and a stratified random sampling approach has been used.

Common methods of boosting response rates are rooted in common sense. These include using good-quality stationery and including a stamped, addressed reply envelope. The latter may help to increase the response rate not because it removes a financial penalty for responding but simply because it indicates that the researcher values the responses and is prepared to make an effort to obtain them. Equally, sending questionnaires to a named individual in a firm or household may help. It is well worth investing some time on some background research to assist with the identification of target individuals. Finally, covering letters, reminder letters and reminder telephone calls all act to increase the response rate. However, it is worth reiterating that response rates will rarely exceed 50 per cent even if all of these measures have been taken, and if there is a requirement that a minimum number of observations are collected then it is obviously prudent to take a pessimistic view on the likely response rate.

As noted earlier, the importance of good question and questionnaire design is increased when an arm's-length data collection method is used. Questionnaire design may affect both bias and response rate. Bias can be introduced by biased, leading, misleading or unobjective question wording and, as mentioned earlier, it is important to use short, clear objective questions as far as possible. Apart from the wording of individual questions the very structure of the questionnaire can also contribute to the introduction of bias. It is a plausible hypothesis that some respondents' views will evolve during the course of completing the questionnaire. Furthermore, a respondent's answer to a particular question may be influenced by the preceding questions. This can be demonstrated by a trite example shown in Table 11.1.

There is an argument that responses to questions 7 and 8, as shown in Table 11.1, will be subject to bias with respect to answers to question 6. It is widely accepted, in any event, that some questions do not attract truthful answers – people often over-estimate income and aspects such as fruit and soap consumption while under-estimating other aspects such as the amount of time they spend watching television or the amount they spend on tobacco and alcohol. The placement of question 7 may induce a further downward bias since it is likely that some respondents will wish to 'play down' their spending on alcohol relative to their spending on food.

Table 11.1 Bias and order effects

Q	*Question*	*Answer*
6	How much, to the nearest £5, does your household spend on food in an average week?	
7	How much, to the nearest £5, does your household spend on alcohol in an average week?	
8	How much, to the nearest £5, does your household spend on soap in an average week?	

Common solutions to the 'order effect' include randomising the order of the questions, while testing for an order effect can be facilitated by reversing the order of half the questionnaires. Other solutions to the minimisation of bias include splitting up the most important questions and using less important questions in between.

Questions on academic qualifications, age, gender, time spent in current employment, time spent in current address, income, and so on, are often used to permit segmentation of the results and to allow a judgement to be made on the appropriateness/ability of each respondent to answer the questions set in the survey. Such questions also tend to reduce the incidence of 'joint efforts' among respondents in filling out questionnaires. As mentioned earlier, the response rate can be influenced by respondents' difficulty in filling out the questionnaire. In order to engage respondents early, questionnaires are often designed with easy or general questions at the beginning and more complex or more difficult to answer questions towards the end (the 'funnel' technique). The logic is that respondents are less likely to stop filling out a questionnaire halfway through than they are to decide not to fill out the questionnaire at all. In addition, there is an argument that answering simple and unthreatening questions builds up a form of trust between the respondent and the unseen researcher. The counter-argument is that difficult or threatening questions should be asked early in the questionnaire, particularly if answers to these are a crucial part of the questionnaire response. This may be a valid approach if semi-complete questionnaires are of no value to the research.

Finally, questionnaire design requires careful consideration of the form of the questions. At one extreme, questions can be open-ended in the sense that the respondent is left free to contribute an answer of his/her choice. At the other extreme, questions may be completely closed and request a YES/NO answer. Other questions are likely to require respondents to choose from a list of possible answers or to indicate preference for a list of items by indicating on a numerical or graphical scale. As general guidance, it is preferable to avoid too many open-ended questions but, at the same time, a highly prescriptive questionnaire with tightly specified closed questions may miss some of the issues under investigation. As in the case of market research, it is advisable to pilot a questionnaire before using it to launch a full-scale survey.

CONCLUSIONS

The main objective of this book is to provide a theoretical and practical foundation for practising, and for those interested in practising, real estate market research and analysis. The focus of the book is on quantitative research methods. This chapter has provided a short overview on a widening, and developing, real estate research agenda. The focus of this particular chapter is on behavioural research. Earlier it was argued that the developing behavioural real estate research agenda might best be served by employing a blend of qualitative and quantitative research methods and techniques and much of this chapter has been devoted to an examination of some commonly used qualitative research techniques. It should be noted that many qualitative research techniques are well-rehearsed and a single chapter in a book such as this cannot hope to provide complete coverage of the subject. Interested readers are therefore advised to refer to a more detailed qualitative research methods text for more detail, particularly with regard to the theory underpinning the use of qualitative techniques, together with a wider range of qualitative techniques and applications.

It should be noted that the purpose of this chapter is not to promote the use of qualitative and behavioural research as a substitute for the well-rehearsed and accepted research methods reviewed throughout this book. Rather, the issues and methods examined in this chapter should be viewed as a potential complement to other methods reviewed here. A number of alternative paradigms have a bearing on real estate market economics and research. These include the Marxist, 'Structures of Provision' and 'Structure and Agency' approaches. A thorough analysis of these is beyond the scope of this book and readers are advised to refer to Ball *et al.* (1998) for a discussion.

REFERENCES

Adair, A., Berry, J., McGreal, S., Deddis, B. and Hirst, S. (1999) 'Evaluation of investor behaviour in urban regeneration', *Urban Studies*, vol. 36, no. 12, 2031–45.

Adams, C.D. (1994) *Urban Planning and the Development Process* (London: UCL Press).

Adams, C.D. and May, H.G. (1991) 'Active and passive behaviour in land ownership', *Urban Studies*, vol. 28, no. 5, 687–705.

Antwi, A. and Henneberry, J. (1995) 'Developers, non-linearity and asymmetry in the development cycle', *Journal of Property Research*, vol. 12, 217–39.

Balchin, P.N. *et al.* (1995) *Urban Land Economics and Public Policy*, 5th edition (Basingstoke: Macmillan).

Ball, M. (1998) 'Institutions in British property research: a review', *Urban Studies*, vol. 35, 1501–17.

Ball, M., Lizieri, C. and MacGregor, B.D. (1998) *The Economics of Commercial Property Markets*, (London: Routledge).

Black, R.T. and Diaz, J. III (1996) 'The use of information versus asking price in the real property negotiation process', *Journal of Property Research*, vol. 13, no. 4, 287–97.

Clapp, J. and Myers, D. (2000) 'Graaskamp and the definition of rigorous research', in J.R. Delisle and E. Worzala (eds), *Essays in Honour of James A. Graaskamp: Ten Years After* (New York: Kluwer).

D'Arcy, E. and Keogh, G. (2000) 'Graaskamp, institutional economics and the real estate market', in J.R. Delisle and E. Worzala (eds), *Essays in Honour of James A Graaskamp: Ten Years After* (New York: Kluwer).

Diaz, J. III (1990) 'How appraisers do their work: a test of the appraisal process and the development of a descriptive model', *Journal of Real Estate Research*, vol. 5, no. 1, 1–15.

Diaz, J. III (1999) 'The first decade of behavioural research in the discipline of property', *Journal of Property Investment and Finance*, vol. 17, no. 4, 326–32.

Drewett, R. (1973) 'The developers: decision processes', in P. Hall, H. Gracey, R. Drewett and R. Thomas (eds), *The Containment of Urban England*, Volume 2. (London: Allen & Unwin).

Gallimore, P. (1994) 'Aspects of information processing in valuation judgement and choice', *Journal of Property Research*, vol. 11, no. 2, 97–110.

Gallimore, P. (1996) 'Confirmation bias in the valuation process: a test for corroborating evidence', *Journal of Property Research*, vol. 13, no. 4, 261–73.

Goodchild, R. and Munton, R. (1985) *Development and the Landowner: An Analysis of the British Experience* (London: Allen & Unwin).

Guy, S. and Henneberry, J. (2000) 'Understanding urban development processes: integrating the economic and the social in property research', *Urban Studies*, vol. 37, 2399–416.

Guy, S. and Henneberry, J. (2002) 'Bridging the divide? Complementary perspectives on property', *Urban Studies*, vol. 39, no. 8, 1471–8.

Leishman, C. and Watkins, C. (2002) 'The decision-making behaviour of office occupiers', *Journal of Property Investment and Finance*, forthcoming.

Leishman, C., Jones, C. and Fraser, W. (2000) 'The influence of uncertainty on house builder behaviour and residential land values', *Journal of Property Research*, vol. 17, no. 2, 147–68.

Northcraft, G.B. and Neale, M.A. (1987) 'Experts, amateurs and real-estate – an anchoring and adjustment perspective on property pricing decisions',

Organizational Behaviour and Human Decision Processes, vol. 39, no. 1, 84–97.

Philip, L.J. (1998) 'Combining quantitative and qualitative approaches to social research in human geography – an impossible mixture?', *Environment and Planning A*, vol. 30, no. 2, 261–76.

Rydin, Y. (1984) 'The struggle for housing land: a case of confused interests', *Policy and Politics*, vol. 12, no. 4, 431–46.

12 Conclusions and Further Reading

As noted in many places in this book, real estate market economics is a relatively young discipline and the literature is in a continual state of evolution. The catalogue of accepted and commonly used methods of research and analysis will continue to grow and evolve with the research agenda. The purpose of this book is not to set out everything that is known about real estate market economics or to cover every possible aspect of research in the discipline. Instead, the book aims to draw together a disparate literature in order to provide a useful single reference for students and practitioners of real estate market research and analysis. Readers unfamiliar with basic principles of urban land economics are advised to read this book in conjunction with an appropriate urban economics text such as Balchin *et al.* (1995), Harvey (2000) or, for a stronger real estate market focus, Ball *et al.* (1998). This book does not cover real estate investment analysis and readers with an interest in this area are directed to Fraser (1993), Brown and Matysiak (2000) or Hoesli and MacGregor (2000).

This book is designed to provide a general background on quantitative methods together with a detailed review of a range of, mainly quantitative, methods in real estate market research and analysis. The early part of the book (Chapters 1 and 2) is intended to demonstrate the real estate context of the material covered in the book. Those chapters examine the nature of research, different types of research project and, most importantly, set out the issues that are specifically important to research in the real estate market economics discipline. Subsequent chapters provide a brief review of inferential statistics, sampling theory and hypothesis testing. Some of the techniques and forms of statistical testing contained in those chapters are unlikely to be used directly in applied real estate market research and analysis. However, an understanding of this background theory is essential to gaining an understanding of the more complex, and arguably more useful, applied research methods examined later in the book.

Chapters 5 and 6 are focused on commercial real estate rent determination models based on single equations and on systems of equations.

Chapter 6 also provides a discussion on empirical difficulties that are often encountered in applied real estate market research and analysis, and the chapter introduces several more complex empirical issues and empirical methods that are not reviewed in detail in this book. Chapter 7 is concerned with private housing market analysis. However, the review of hedonic regression models and index estimation methods is also of value to readers with an interest in real estate market research in sectors other than housing. Hedonic regression models and index estimations methods may be applied to office, retail and industrial property as well as housing. Equally, Chapter 8 examines methods of local real estate market research and analysis. Although the chapter is focused mainly on the urban office market, the methods and discussion set out in the chapter will be useful to those with an interest in the analysis of local markets in other real estate sectors.

The material contained in Chapters 9 and 10 is a little less generalisable than the material in Chapters 5 to 8. Chapter 9 is concerned with retail real estate research. The content of the chapter is quite specialised and the applied methods are specifically retail focused. Chapter 10 examines the use of option pricing theory in real estate market research and analysis. This is another highly specialised area of real estate market research which is concerned with the evaluation of the cost or value of risk and uncertainty. This is a rapidly evolving area in real estate market research and the chapter is intended to provide a basic background to financial option pricing theory and real estate market economics applications.

Some of the chapters in the book, particularly those focused on the use of econometric methods, are intended to strike a balance between being comprehensive and detailed on the one hand, and useful, relevant and informative on the other. This book cannot provide any more than coverage of the fundamentals of econometric modelling together with a review and demonstration of real estate applications. Readers with a strong interest in econometric modelling are advised to refer to a suitable econometrics text. For example, Greene (1997) is often acknowledged as one of the most comprehensive and detailed texts. Patterson (2000) and Pindyck and Rubinfeld (1997) are also very comprehensive texts.

Chapter 11 introduces aspects of behavioural research and the use of qualitative methods. The chapter is inspired by the argument that the use of complex quantitative methods can never act as a substitute for sound logic and reasoning. This is of particular importance in the context of real estate market research and analysis because many available real estate market datasets suffer from limitations while a significant number of published analyses report results based on heterogeneous primary datasets that differ in terms of a number of aspects including geographical focus, variable definitions and methods used in variable measurement. In Chapter 3 it is argued that quantitative results obtained using sample data can be applied to a population provided that the sample is representative. In practice, there are real difficulties in ensuring that this is the case in quantitative real estate market analyses. This, coupled with conceptual limitations in the assumptions that underpin many quantitative analyses, gives rise to an argument that more valuable analyses and results may be obtained by combining the use of quantitative and qualitative methods. Chapter 11 provides a review of these arguments together with a short overview of some common qualitative methods. Implicit throughout the chapter is the notion that methods of real estate market research and analysis exist as tools to help researchers to construct answers to research questions – this is the antithesis of 'technique led' research and analysis.

REFERENCES

Balchin, P.N. *et al.* (1995) *Urban Land Economics and Public Policy*, 5th edition (Basingstoke: Macmillan).

Ball, M., Lizieri, C. and MacGregor, B.D. (1998) *The Economics of Commercial Property Markets* (London: Routledge).

Brown, G.R. and Matysiak, G.A. (2000) *Real Estate Investment: A Capital Market Approach* (London: Financial Times).

Fraser, W.D. (1993) *Principles of Property Investment and Pricing*, 2nd edition (Basingstoke: Macmillan).

Greene, W.H. (1997) *Econometric Analysis* (New Jersey: Prentice-Hall).

Harvey, J. (2000) *Urban Land Economics*, 5th edition (Basingstoke: Macmillan).

Hoesli, M. and MacGregor, B.D. (2000) *Property Investment: Principles and Practice of Portfolio Management* (Harlow: Pearson Education).

Patterson, K. (2000) *An Introduction to Applied Econometrics: A Time Series Approach* (Basingstoke: Macmillan).

Pindyck, R.S. and Rubinfeld, D.L. (1997) *Econometric Models and Economic Forecasts* (Boston: McGraw-Hill).

Appendix 1: Critical Values for the *t* Distribution

Degrees of freedom	*Significance level*		*Degrees of freedom*	*Significance level*	
	1%	*5%*		*1%*	*5%*
2	9.925	4.303	50	2.678	2.009
3	5.841	3.182	60	2.660	2.000
4	4.604	2.776	70	2.648	1.994
5	4.032	2.571	80	2.639	1.990
6	3.707	2.447	90	2.632	1.987
7	3.499	2.365	100	2.626	1.984
8	3.355	2.306	110	2.621	1.982
9	3.250	2.262	120	2.617	1.980
10	3.169	2.228	130	2.614	1.978
11	3.106	2.201	140	2.611	1.977
12	3.055	2.179	150	2.609	1.976
13	3.012	2.160	160	2.607	1.975
14	2.977	2.145	170	2.605	1.974
15	2.947	2.131	180	2.603	1.973
16	2.921	2.120	190	2.602	1.973
17	2.898	2.110	200	2.601	1.972
18	2.878	2.101			
19	2.861	2.093			
20	2.845	2.086			
21	2.831	2.080			
22	2.819	2.074			
23	2.807	2.069			
24	2.797	2.064			
25	2.787	2.060			
26	2.779	2.056			
27	2.771	2.052			
28	2.763	2.048			
29	2.756	2.045			
30	2.750	2.042			

Appendix 2: Critical Values for the Normal Distribution

z	*Two-tailed*	*One-tailed*	z	*Two-tailed*	*One-tailed*
0.00	1.000	0.500	1.90	0.057	0.029
0.01	0.992	0.496	1.91	0.056	0.028
0.02	0.984	0.492	1.92	0.055	0.027
0.03	0.976	0.488	1.93	0.054	0.027
0.04	0.968	0.484	1.94	0.052	0.026
0.05	0.960	0.480	1.95	0.051	0.026
			1.96	0.050	0.025
			1.97	0.049	0.024
0.10	0.920	0.460	1.98	0.048	0.024
0.20	0.841	0.421	1.99	0.047	0.023
0.30	0.764	0.382			
0.40	0.689	0.345			
0.50	0.617	0.309			
0.60	0.549	0.274			
0.70	0.484	0.242			
0.80	0.424	0.212	2.00	0.046	0.023
0.90	0.368	0.184	2.10	0.036	0.018
1.00	0.317	0.159	2.20	0.028	0.014
1.10	0.271	0.136	2.30	0.021	0.011
1.20	0.230	0.115	2.40	0.016	0.008
1.30	0.194	0.097	2.50	0.012	0.006
1.40	0.162	0.081	2.60	0.009	0.005
1.50	0.134	0.067	2.70	0.007	0.003
1.60	0.110	0.055	2.80	0.005	0.003
1.70	0.089	0.045	2.90	0.004	0.002
1.80	0.072	0.036	3.00	0.003	0.001

Glossary

Absorption The rate at which vacant space is taken up by occupation demand.

Adaptive expectations The hypothesis that the expectations of consumers, households, occupiers or firms are formed by evidence from the recent past. As new information becomes available, these expectations are adapted but new expectations will only partly reflect the new information.

Adjusted *R* square The **coefficient of determination** or proportion of explained to total variance weighted according to sample size (N) and the number of parameters included for estimation (k). This statistic is obtained as part of standard regression output and is a useful measure of goodness of fit.

Agglomeration economies These represent the sum of internal and external economies. For example, a firm may obtain economies of scale by locating in an urban area and increasing output. This is an internal economy. If the firm also benefited from access to a larger, and more highly skilled, workforce then an external economy has also been gained. Agglomeration economies are the sum of these factors.

Aggregation bias Error or bias that occurs when data for small spatial or temporal units are summed or averaged. For example, national data may be obtained by summing regional or urban level data; annual data may be obtained by summing monthly data. Condensing the data results in a loss of information such as variation over space or time. If these variations are important factors in terms of explaining a dependent variable then the loss of information can result in bias in a model designed to explain and predict that variable.

Alternative hypothesis In statistical testing (hypothesis testing), the alternative hypothesis is really the point of interest to the researcher. By convention, an hypothesis cannot be tested directly since the data to hand are likely to be a sample rather than the population. Instead, a direct opposite to the hypothesis is constructed (the null hypothesis) and this is tested. If this is rejected then the alternative hypothesis is not rejected. Often, the alternative hypothesis is that some parameter is not equal to zero.

Anchoring and adjustment A heuristic or short-cut process in which a valuer (in this context) may arrive at an end judgement by making adjustments to an initial view of what the end judgement will be. The literature debates whether this process will lead valuers' end judgements to be biased towards their initial views of what the end judgements will be.

Autoregression A special case of regression analysis in which the independent variables are temporally lagged values of the dependent variable.

Barriers to entry A concept found in microeconomic theory. If new entrants to an industry face set-up costs or must demonstrate compliance with rules and regulations then entry to the industry is not free and costless.

Behavioural research Research in which the research questions and/or hypotheses explicitly acknowledge that individuals, households, firms or agents do not have identical motives and that this may affect outcomes.

Binomial variable A variable that can have only two possible values, normally zero and one.

Call options A contract that grants the owner the right to purchase a good or commodity at some specified point in time at a pre-arranged price. If the exercise date arrives and the contract price is lower than the market price then the call option contract will have a positive value.

Categorical variable A variable that takes on one of a defined set of values (1, 2, 3 or 4, for example). Categorical variables need not be numerical.

Chance variation A numerical difference that is the result of measurement error, random events or small differences in sample composition rather than evidence of a significant and replicable difference. For example, an athlete is unlikely to produce exactly the same lap time every time even when conditions appear identical. Hypothesis testing is concerned with separating chance from real variation.

Coefficient of determination The *R* square statistic or proportion of explained to total variance. This statistic is one of several used to assess goodness of fit.

Coefficients Empirical estimates of model parameters.

Collinearity Linear association between two or more variables.

Composite good A good or product that, as a consequence of its complex nature, is best regarded as a basket containing various amounts of several other, simpler goods.

Contemporaneous Measured within the same time period.

Correlation The statistical association (not inference) that exists between two variables. This is often measured using Pearson's correlation coefficient.

Cross-sectional model A model in which the observations have been made within a single time period. Variation between cases or observations is normally over space rather than time.

Deductive reasoning Theoretical analysis that extends an existing theory or line of argument that is known to be valid.

Degree of freedom A piece of information. As a general rule, quantitative datasets contain one degree of freedom per observation but this does not necessarily follow for the case of non-quantitative data.

Dependent variable A variable hypothesised to be caused, influenced or determined by one or more explanatory or independent variables in a regression model.

Desmoothing A process by which the 'true' volatility of market prices or returns is reintroduced to a temporally smoothed index based on appraisal or valuation data.

Differentiated products A set of highly substitutable, but not completely identical, goods or products.

Dilution A heuristic or short-cut process. In the real estate context, the hypothesis is that valuers may unintentionally down-weight information that is not supportive of a prior notion of value, thus biasing the valuation towards the prior notion of value.

Distance decay A concept in spatial interaction and gravity models in which the attractiveness of a region, urban area or development is assumed to decline with distance. Distance decay functions are not necessarily linear.

Disturbance term A term included in regression equations to denote and measure the random element of variation in the dependent variable.

Econometric Regression analysis.

Empirical Experimental. Empirical research normally involves data collection, testing and model estimation.

Endogenous A variable determined within a system of equations. A variable that is explanatory in one or more equations but dependent in another is said to be endogenous.

Equilibrium The market state in which supply and demand are equal causing the market to clear (see **price mechanism**).

Error correction model A generic term for a set of models in which a series of short-run corrections ensure a long-run equilibrium between a set of variables.

Exogenous A variable determined outside a system of equations. A variable that is explanatory in one or more equations and is not dependent within any others is said to be exogenous.

Gravity models A generic name for a family of models that explain and predict flows of people or revenues to urban areas, facilities or shopping centres.

Hedonic model A special case of regression model in which the price of an individual property is hypothesised as a function of the attributes contained within the property together with the implicit attribute prices. The hypothesis is that an implied market exists for each of the property features and the overall property price is based on the prices of these features.

Heterogeneous Different.

Heteroscedasticity An empirical phenomenon in which the errors or residuals of a regression estimation are not truly random but share a relationship with one or more of the explanatory variables.

Homogeneous Identical.

Homoscedasticity An empirical phenomenon in which the errors or residuals of a regression estimation are random and do not share a relationship with any of the explanatory variables.

Hypothesis A theorised statement of cause and effect. In statistical hypothesis testing the hypothesis is likely to be that some parameter equals, is less than or exceeds some given value rather than a statement of cause and effect.

Hypothesis testing A branch of inferential statistics in which a parameter is conjectured to equal, be less than or exceed some given value. The probable validity of this hypothesis is then tested statistically.

Independent variable An explanatory variable.

Inductive reasoning A process in which theoretical explanations and predictions are developed partly from observed evidence as well as from existing branches of theory.

Institutional economics A paradigm that emphasises the role and importance of groups of firms (institutions) and agents rather than the idea of a large number of independent producers and consumers.

Interaction variable A variable created by multiplying, dividing or adding together two or more other explanatory variables.

χ square test A statistical test useful for testing the difference between observed and expected proportions or for testing for independence between two series.

Least squares The process by which a line of best fit (regression line) is fitted to a set of data points. The best line is the one that minimises the sum of the squared vertical deviations between the line and the data points.

Multicollinearity An empirical phenomenon. If there are linear relationships between several of the explanatory variables in a regression equation then misleading parameter estimates may be obtained.

Multi-equation models Models that do not attempt to capture market dynamics within a single equation but, instead, postulate market dynamics as an interrelated set of equations. Often, the user, investment and development sectors of the market are modelled using separate equations, while exogenous variables in some of these equations appear as endogenous variables in other equations.

Natural vacancy rate The normal or equilibrium proportion of stock that is vacant.

Normal profits A concept contained within microeconomic theory. Normal profits are the profit level required to retain a firm within its current line of production. If actual profits are higher then more firms will join the industry. If actual profits are lower then firms will leave the industry.

Null hypothesis The exact opposite of the alternative hypothesis. Normally, the null hypothesis is the opposite of the hypothesis of interest. In statistical testing the researcher hopes to find grounds statistically to reject the null hypothesis, which then means that the alternative hypothesis should not be rejected.

Occupation demand The demand of firms, or commercial occupiers, to occupy real estate.

Omitted variable bias Systematic error introduced to coefficients, or estimated parameters, because one or more variables that are partial determinants of the dependent variable have been mistakenly omitted from the equation.

Option pricing A branch of financial theory in which the rights and/or obligations contained within options are valued statistically.

Panel data A dataset that contains both spatial and temporal dimensions.

Paradigm Prevailing belief or 'school of thought'.

Perfect competition A microeconomic theory that is often used as a benchmark upon which to compare more realistic or pragmatic analyses of market conditions.

Population The total set of observations for which an hypothesis is conjectured to hold.

Prediction An estimate of the value of the dependent variable using a statistical model which has been estimated using a sample of data that includes the data point now being predicted.

Price mechanism The process of rental or price change that occurs in response to disparity between supply and demand. The pricing mechanism is the process by which prices change to permit equilibrium to occur.

Proxy variable Variables that are used to measure some other source of variation that cannot directly be measured. For example, in real estate rent determination models it is not generally possible to measure the profitability of firms occupying space. Instead, GDP may be used to proxy this source of variation since GDP is likely to be highly correlated to firms' profitability.

Put options A contractual right that gives the owner the ability to sell an asset at a predetermined price on or before an agreed date. If the market price is lower than the exercise price then the put option has a value.

***R* square** The coefficient of determination or ratio of explained to total variation in the dependent variable.

Random sampling A sampling method in which every potential observation in a population has an equal chance of being selected for inclusion in the sample.

Random walk A process in which random events can give rise to seemingly non-random data. A purer statistical definition is a data series in which the autocorrelation coefficient does not rapidly diminish when the lag interval is increased. Most financial and economic series are likely to fulfil the statistical criteria of a random walk. These can be tested using unit root tests.

Rational behaviour A set of assumptions including, for example, the idea that consumers always act in the way that maximises their utility while firms always act in the appropriate way to maximise their profits.

Real options Contractual rights or obligations that concern investment, development or management of physical assets including real estate.

Real variation Differences or variation that are found to be statistically significant.

Recency A heuristic or short-cut process. In the real estate context, the hypothesis is that valuers may unintentionally overrate the most recently acquired, but not necessarily the most recent, information.

Reduced-form equation A single equation that is formed by simultaneously solving structural equations. For example, a rent or price equation can be obtained by solving supply and demand functions.

Rent adjustment model A special case of the rent prediction model in which the determination of rent is not modelled within a single equation but as part of a more complex system of equations that link the user, development and investment sectors of the real estate market.

Representative A sample is representative if it possesses the same properties as its parent population.

Research question The focus or object of interest of a research project. Research questions are formed during a review of literature and previous empirical research. Such an exercise identifies unanswered queries, gaps in the literature or apparently inexplicable empirical phenomenon.

Residuals The errors or unexplained variance in a dependent variable after predicting using an estimated regression equation.

Sample selection bias Systematic error arising from the fact that some observations are more likely to be collected in a sample than others.

Serial correlation Correlation between residuals or error terms when they are sorted with respect to space or time.

Single-equation models These are normally commercial real estate rent prediction models. The dependent variable is specified as a function of a set of variables contained within one regression equation. All explanatory variables are assumed to be exogenous.

Smoothing A form of measurement error that may affect indices of property performance. A smoothed index is one which, as a consequence of the methods used to construct it, does not fully reflect market volatility in each time period but erroneously spreads it out over several time periods.

Spatial aggregation The process of combining, or averaging, data measured at small units of spatial aggregation (such as individual households, streets or neighbourhoods) in order to obtain data points representing larger units of spatial aggregation (such as towns or local market areas).

Spatial interaction The dependence, or partial dependence, of market dynamics in one geographical area on the dynamics of another. The term 'spatial interaction' is very general and encompasses a large range of theoretical concepts and empirical phenomena.

Specification This is a generic term that refers to the dependent and independent variables entered into an equation. When authors discuss 'different specifications', they are referring to variants on an equation in which the variables, or their lag specification, vary.

Stationary/stationarity A property of a data set, normally time series, that exhibits no traces of random walk behaviour.

Stratified random sampling A variation on random sampling in which random sampling methods are undertaken subject to fulfilling a quota of observations or responses in each of a number of predefined groups or clusters.

Structural equations The theoretical equations (often either supply or demand functions) upon which reduced-form equations are based (often price or rent equations).

Submarket A spatial or structural division in the market. Demanders may employ a two-stage locational choice process in which the first stage represents choice of submarket and the second stage involves choice of a specific property.

Supernormal profits A concept found in microeconomic theory. Supernormal profits mean any profit level above the very minimum necessary to retain firms in the industry.

***t* test** A statistical test in which the test statistic is compared with a critical value drawn from the *t* distribution.

Test statistic The output of a statistical test such as a *t* test, *z* test, χ square test, and so on. The test statistic is compared to a critical value obtained from statistical tables in order to allow a formal hypothesis to be tested. See **hypothesis testing**.

Time series model A regression model in which variation is analysed over time rather than across space.

Utility Consumer satisfaction.

Vacancy rate Proportion of unoccupied property stock – often a feature of multi-equation rent determination models of the office occupation market.

Valuation bias The consequence of a process in which systematic error is inadvertently introduced to valuations.

Vector autoregression A special case of regression model in which the value of a dependent variable is hypothesised as a function of its own lagged values together with the lagged values of some other variable(s).

Z score The standardised value of an observation on a variable.

Z test A simple statistical test in which an observed value is expressed in terms of the number of standard deviations removed from a hypothesised value (usually zero). Since Z is Normally distributed, there is a 5% probability that the test statistic is either greater than 1.96 or smaller than −1.96.

Bibliography

Adair, A., Berry, J., McGreal, S., Deddis, B. and Hirst, S. (1999) 'Evaluation of investor behaviour in urban regeneration', *Urban Studies*, vol. 36, no. 12, 2031–45.

Adams, C.D. (1994) *Urban Planning and the Development Process* (London: UCL Press).

Adams, C.D. and May, H.G. (1991) 'Active and passive behaviour in land ownership', *Urban Studies*, vol. 28, no. 5, 687–705.

Alonso, W. (1964) *Location and Land Use: Toward a General Theory of Land Rent* (Cambridge, Mass: Harvard University Press).

Antwi, A. and Henneberry, J. (1995) 'Developers, non-linearity and asymmetry in the development cycle', *Journal of Property Research*, vol. 12, 217–39.

Bailey, M.J., Muth, R.F. and Nourse, H.O. (1963) 'A regression method for real estate price index construction', *Journal of the American Statistical Association*, vol. 58, 933–42.

Balchin, P.N. *et al.* (1995) *Urban Land Economics and Public Policy*, 5th edition (Basingstoke: Macmillan).

Ball, M. (1998) 'Institutions in British property research: a review', *Urban Studies*, vol. 35, 1501–17.

Ball, M. and Kirwan, R. (1977) 'Accessibility and supply constraints in the urban housing market', *Urban Studies*, vol. 14, 11–32.

Ball, M., Lizieri, C. and MacGregor, B.D. (1998) *The Economics of Commercial Property Markets* (London: Routledge).

Barkham, D. and Geltner, D. (1994) 'Unsmoothing British valuation based returns without assuming an efficient market', *Journal of Property Research*, vol. 11, 81–95.

Barras, R. (1983) 'A simple theoretical model of the office development cycle', *Environment and Planning A*, vol. 15, 1381–94.

Black, F. and Scholes, M. (1973) 'The pricing of options and corporate liabilities', *Journal of Political Economy*, vol. 81, 637–59.

Black, R.T. and Diaz, J. III (1996) 'The use of information versus asking price in the real property negotiation process', *Journal of Property Research*, vol. 13, no. 4, 287–97.

Blundell, G. and Ward, C. (1987) 'Property portfolio allocation: a multi-factor model', *Land Development Studies*, vol. 4, no. 2, 145–56.

Boukendour, S. and Bah, R. (2001) 'The guaranteed maximum price contract as call option', *Construction Management and Economics*, vol. 19, 563–7.

Bourassa, S., Hamelink, F., Hoesli, M. and MacGregor, B. (1999) 'Defining housing submarkets', *Journal of Housing Economics*, vol. 8, 160–83.

Brennan, M.J. and Schwartz, E.S. (1985) 'Evaluating natural resource investment', *Journal of Business*, vol. 58, no. 2, 1135–57.

Brookshire, D.S., Thayer, M.A., Schulze, W.D. and D'Arge, R.C. (1982) 'Valuing public goods – a comparison of survey and hedonic approaches', *American Economic Review*, vol. 72, no. 1, 165–77.

Brown, G.R. and Matysiak, G.A. (2000) *Real Estate Investment: A Capital Market Approach* (London: Financial Times).

Case, B. and Shiller, R. (1989) 'The efficiency of the market for single family homes', *American Economic Review*, vol. 79, no. 1, 45–56.

Case, B., Pollakowski, W.O. and Wachter, S.M. (1991) 'On choosing among house price index methodologies', *Journal of the American Real Estate and Urban Economics Association*, vol. 19, 286–307.

Chaplin, R. (1997) 'Unsmoothing valuation based indices using multiple regimes', *Journal of Property Research*, vol. 14, no. 3, 189–210.

Chaplin, R. (1998) 'An *ex post* comparative evaluation of office rent prediction models', *Journal of Property Valuation and Investment*, vol. 16, no. 1, 21–37.

Chaplin, R. (1999) 'The predictability of real office rents', *Journal of Property Research*, vol. 16, no. 1, 21–49.

Chaplin, R. (2000) 'Predicting real estate rents: walking backwards into the future', *Journal of Property Investment and Finance*, vol. 18, no. 3, 352–70.

Christaller, W. (1933) *Central Places in Southern Germany*, translation by C.W. Baskin (1966) (Englewood Cliffs, NJ: Prentice-Hall).

Chun, G.H., Eppli, M.J. and Shilling, J.D. (2001) 'A simulation analysis of the relationship between retail sales and shopping center rents', *Journal of Real Estate Research*, vol. 21, no. 3, 163–86.

Clapp, J. and Myers, D. (2000) 'Graaskamp and the definition of rigorous research', in J.R. Delisle and E. Worzala (eds), *Essays in Honour of James A. Graaskamp: Ten Years After* (New York: Kluwer).

Clapp, J.M. and Giacotto, C. (1992) 'Estimating price indices for residential property: A comparison of repeat sales and assessed value methods', *Journal of the American Statistical Association*, vol. 87, no. 418, 300–6.

Clapp, J.M., Giacotto, C. and Tirtiroglu, D. (1991) 'Housing price indices based on all transactions compared to repeat subsamples', *AREUEA Journal*, vol. 19, no. 3, 270–85.

Clarke, H. and Reed, W. (1988) 'A stochastic analysis of land development timing and property valuation', *Regional Science and Urban Economics*, vol. 18, 367–82.

Crone, T.M. and Voith, R.P. (1992) 'Estimating house price appreciation: a comparison of methods', *Journal of Housing Economics*, vol. 2, 324–38.

Damm, D., Lerman, S.R., Lerner-Lam, E. and Young, J. (1980) 'The response of urban real estate values in anticipation of the Washington Metro', *Journal of Transport Economics and Policy*, September 1980.

D'Arcy, E. and Keogh, G. (2000) 'Graaskamp, institutional economics and the real estate market', in J.R. Delisle and E. Worzala (eds), *Essays in Honour of James A Graaskamp: Ten Years After* (New York: Kluwer).

D'Arcy, E., McGough, T. and Tsolacos, S. (1999) 'An econometric analysis and forecasts of the office rental cycle in the Dublin area', *Journal of Property Research*, vol. 16, no. 4, 309–21.

Diaz, J. III (1990) 'How appraisers do their work: a test of the appraisal process and the development of a descriptive model', *Journal of Real Estate Research*, vol. 5, no. 1, 1–15.

Diaz, J. III (1999) 'The first decade of behavioural research in the discipline of property', *Journal of Property Investment and Finance*, vol. 17, no. 4, 326–32.

Dobson, S. and Goddard, J. (1992) 'The determinants of commercial property prices and rents', *Bulletin of Economic Research*, vol. 44, no. 4, 301–21.

Drewett, R. (1973) 'The developers: decision processes', in P. Hall, H. Gracey, R. Drewett and R. Thomas (eds), *The Containment of Urban England*, Volume 2 (London: Allen & Unwin).

Dunse, N.A. and Jones, C. (1998) 'A hedonic price model of office rents', *Journal of Property Valuation and Investment*, vol. 16, no. 3, 297–312.

Dunse, N.A. and Jones, C. (2002) 'The existence of office submarkets in cities', *Journal of Property Research*, vol. 19, no. 2, 159–82.

Dunse, N., Jones, C., Orr, A. and Tarbert, H. (1998) 'The extent and limitations of local commercial property data', *Journal of Property Valuation and Investment*, vol. 16, no. 5, 455–73.

Dunse, N.A., Leishman, C. and Watkins, C. (2001) 'Classifying office submarkets', *Journal of Property Investment and Finance*, vol. 19, no. 3, 236–50.

Dunse, N.A., Leishman, C. and Watkins, C. (2002) 'Testing the existence of office submarkets: a comparison of evidence from two cities', *Urban Studies*, vol. 39, no. 4, 483–506.

Egan, D.J. and Nield, K. (2000) 'Towards a theory of intraurban hotel location', *Urban Studies*, vol. 37, 611–21.

Eppli, M.J. and Benjamin, J.D. (1994) 'The evolution of shopping center research: a review and analysis', *Journal of Real Estate Research*, vol. 9, no. 1, 5–32.

Evans, A.W. (1995) 'The property market: ninety per cent efficient?', *Urban Studies*, vol. 32, no. 1, 5–29.

Field, B.G. and MacGregor, B.D. (1987) *Forecasting Techniques for Urban and Regional Planning* (London: Hutchinson).

Ford, D.N., Lander, D.M. and Voyer, J.J. (2002) 'A real options approach to valuing strategic flexibility in uncertain construction projects', *Construction Management and Economics*, vol. 20, 343–51.

Fraser, W.D. (1986) 'Supply elasticity and the rental value of investment property', *Journal of Valuation*, vol. 4, no. 4, 354–69.

Fraser, W.D. (1993) *Principles of Property Investment and Pricing*, 2nd edition (Basingstoke: Macmillan).

Gallimore, P. (1994) 'Aspects of information processing in valuation judgement and choice', *Journal of Property Research*, vol. 11, no. 2, 97–110.

Gallimore, P. (1996) 'Confirmation bias in the valuation process: a test for corroborating evidence', *Journal of Property Research*, vol. 13, no. 4, 261–73.

Gardiner, C. and Henneberry, J. (1988) 'The development of a simple regional office rent prediction model', *Journal of Valuation*, vol. 7, 36–52.

Gardiner, C. and Henneberry, J. (1991) 'Predicting regional office rents using habit-persistence theories', *Journal of Property Valuation and Investment*, vol. 9, no. 3, 215–26.

Gatzlaff, D.H. and Haurin, D.R. (1997) 'Sample selection bias and repeat-sales index estimates', *Journal of Real Estate Finance and Economics*, vol. 14, 33–50.

Gatzlaff, D.H. and Ling, D.C. (1994) 'Measuring changes in local house prices: an empirical investigation of alternative methodologies', *Journal of Urban Economics*, vol. 35, 221–44.

Gatzlaff, D.H., Sirmans, G.S. and Diskin, B.A. (1994) 'The effect of anchor tenant loss on shopping center rents', *Journal of Real Estate Research*, vol. 9, no. 1, 99–110.

Geltner, D. (1989) 'Estimating real estate's systematic risk from aggregate level appraisal-based returns', *AREUEA Journal*, vol. 17, no. 4, 463–81.

Ghosh, A. (1986) 'The value of a mall and other insights from a revised central place model', *Journal of Retailing*, vol. 62, 79–97.

Gibson, V. and Lizieri, C. (1998) 'New business practices and the corporate property portfolio: how responsive is the UK property market?', *Journal of Property Research*, vol. 16, 201–18.

Goetzmann, W.N. and Spiegel, M. (1997) 'A spatial model of housing returns and neighbourhood substitutability', *Journal of Real Estate Finance and Economics*, vol. 14, 11–31.

Goodchild, R. and Munton, R. (1985) *Development and the Landowner: An Analysis of the British Experience* (London: Allen & Unwin).

Graves, P., Murdoch, J.C., Thayer, M.A. and Waldman, D. (1988) 'The robustness of hedonic price estimation: urban air quality', *Land Economics*, vol. 64, no. 3, 220–33.

Greene, W.H. (1997) *Econometric Analysis* (New Jersey: Prentice-Hall).

Grenadier, S.R. (1995) 'The valuation of leasing contracts: a real options approach', *Journal of Financial Economics*, vol. 38, no. 3, 297–331.

Grenadier, S.R. (1996) 'The strategic exercise of options: development cascades and overbuilding in real estate markets', *Journal of Finance*, vol. 51, no. 5, 1653–79.

Gruneberg, S.L. (1997) *Construction Economics: An Introduction* (Basingstoke: Macmillan).

Guy, S. and Henneberry, J. (2000) 'Understanding urban development processes: integrating the economic and the social in property research', *Urban Studies*, vol. 37, 2399–416.

Guy, S. and Henneberry, J. (2002) 'Bridging the divide? Complementary perspectives on property', *Urban Studies*, vol. 39, no. 8, 1471–8.

Harvey, J. (2000) *Urban Land Economics*, 5th edition (Basingstoke: Macmillan).

Hekman, J.S. (1985) 'Rental price adjustment and investment in the office market', *AREUEA Journal*, vol. 13, no. 1, 32–47.

Hendershott, P.H. (1996) 'Rental adjustment and valuation in overbuilt markets: evidence from the Sydney office market', *Journal of Urban Economics*, vol. 39, 51–67.

Hendershott, P.H. (1997) 'Uses of equilibrium models in real estate research', *Journal of Property Research*, vol. 14, 1–13.

Hendershott, P., Lizieri, C. and Matysiak, G.A. (1999) 'The workings of the London office market', *Real Estate Economics*, vol. 27, no. 2, 365–87.

Ho, S.P. and Liu, L.Y. (2002) 'An option pricing-based model for evaluating the financial viability of privatized infrastructure projects', *Construction Management and Economics*, vol. 20, 143–56.

Hoesli, M. and MacGregor, B.D. (2000) *Property Investment: Principles and Practice of Portfolio Management* (Harlow: Pearson Education).

Hotelling, H. (1929) 'Stability in competition', *Economic Journal*, vol. 39, 41–57.

Howard, K. and Sharp, J.A. (1996) *The Management of a Student Research Project*, 2nd edition (London: Gower).

Huff, D.L. (1964) 'Defining and estimating a trading area', *Journal of Marketing*, vol. 28, 34–8.

Isard, W. (1998) 'Gravity and spatial interaction models', in W. Isard, I.J. Azis, M.P. Drennan, R.E. Miller, S. Saltzmann and E. Thorbecke (eds), *Methods of Interregional and Regional Analysis* (Aldershot: Ashgate).

Jackson, C. (2002) 'Classifying local retail property markets on the basis of rental growth rates', *Urban Studies*, vol. 39, no. 8, 1417–38.

Jones, C. (1995) 'An economic basis for the analysis and prediction of local office property markets', *Journal of Property Valuation and Investment*, vol. 13, no. 2, 16–30.

Keogh, G. (1994) 'Use and investment markets in British real estate', *Journal of Property Valuation and Investment*, vol. 12, no. 4, 58–72.

Key, T., MacGregor, B., Nanthakumaran, N. and Zarkesh, F. (1994) *Understanding the Property Cycle: Economic Cycles and Property Cycles* (London: Royal Institution of Chartered Surveyors).

Kuhn, T.S. (1970) *The Structure of Scientific Revolutions*, 2nd edition (University of Chicago Press).

Lancaster, K. (1966) 'A new approach to consumer theory', *Journal of Political Economy*, vol. 74, 132–57.

Leishman, C. and Watkins, C. (2002a) 'Estimating local repeat sales house price indices for British cities', *Journal of Property Investment and Finance*, vol. 20, no. 1, 36–58.

Leishman, C. and Watkins, C. (2002b) 'The decision-making behaviour of office occupiers', *Journal of Property Investment and Finance*, forthcoming.

Leishman, C., Jones, C. and Fraser, W. (2000) 'The influence of uncertainty on house builder behaviour and residential land values', *Journal of Property Research*, vol. 17, no. 2, 147–68.

Lucius, D.I. (2001) 'Real options in real estate development', *Journal of Property Investment and Finance*, vol. 19, no. 1, 73–8.

MacGregor, B.D. and Nanthakumaran, N. (1992) 'The allocation to property in the multi-asset portfolio: the evidence reconsidered', *Journal of Property Research*, vol. 9, no. 1, 5–32.

Maclennan, D. (1982) *Housing Economics* (London: Longman).

Maclennan, O., Munro, M. and Wood, G. (1987) 'Housing choice and the structure of urban housing markets', in B. Turner, J. Kennery and L. Lundquist (eds), *Between State and Market Housing: The Post-Industrial Era* (Gothenburg: Almquist & Wicksell International).

Mark, D. and Goldberg, M. (1984) 'Alternative house price indices: an evaluation', *Journal of the American Real Estate and Urban Economics Association*, vol. 12, 30–49.

McGough, T. and Tsolacos, S. (1995) 'Forecasting commercial rental values using ARIMA models', *Journal of Property Valuation and Investment*, vol. 13, no. 5, 6–22.

Meen, G. (1989) 'The ending of mortgage rationing and its effects on the housing market: a simulation study', *Urban Studies*, vol. 26, no. 2, 240–52.

Meen, G. (1990) 'The removal of mortgage market constraints and the implications for econometric modelling of UK house prices', *Oxford Bulletin of Economics and Statistics*, vol. 52, 1–24.

Meen, G. (1996) 'Ten propositions in UK housing macroeconomics: an overview of the 1980s and early 1990s', *Urban Studies*, vol. 33, 425–44.

Meen, G. (1999) 'Regional house prices and the ripple effect: a new interpretation', *Housing Studies*, vol. 14, no. 6, 733–53.

Meen, G. and Andrew, M. (1998) 'On the aggregate housing market implications of labour market change', *Scottish Journal of Political Economy*, vol. 45, no. 4, 393–419.

Meese, R.A. and Wallace, N.E. (1997) 'The construction of residential housing price indices: a comparison of repeat-sales, hedonic regression, and hybrid approaches', *Journal of Real Estate Finance and Economics*, vol. 14, 51–73.

Mieszkowski, P. and Saper, A.M. (1978) 'An estimate of the effects of airport noise on property values', *Journal of Urban Economics*, vol. 5, no. 4, 425–40.

Morck, R., Schwartz, E. and Stangeland, D. (1989) 'The valuation of forestry resources under stochastic prices and inventories', *Journal of Financial and Quantitative Analysis*, vol. 24, no. 4, 473–87.

Morrel, G.D. (1991) 'Property performance analysis and performance indices: a review', *Journal of Property Research*, vol. 8, 29–57.

Morrison, N. (1994) 'The role of planning in the redevelopment process of Glasgow's city centre', *Planning Practice and Research*, vol. 9, no. 1, 31–41.

Muellbauer, J. and Murphy, A. (1997) 'Booms and busts in the UK housing market', *The Economic Journal*, vol. 107, November, 1701–27.

Muth, R.F. (1969) *Cities and Housing* (Chicago University Press).

Northcraft, G.B. and Neale, M.A. (1987) 'Experts, amateurs and real-estate – an anchoring and adjustment perspective on property pricing decisions', *Organizational Behaviour and Human Decision Processes*, vol. 39, no. 1, 84–97.

Ownbey, K.L., Davis, K. and Sundel, H.H. (1994) 'The effect of location variables on the gross rents of neighbourhood shopping centres', *Journal of Real Estate Research*, vol. 9, no. 1, 111–23.

Paddock, J.L., Siegel, D.R. and Smith, J.L. (1988) 'Option valuation of claims on real assets – the case of offshore petroleum leases', *Quarterly Journal of Economics*, vol. 103, no. 3, 479–508.

Pain, N. and Westaway, P. (1996) *Modelling Structural Change in the UK Housing Market: A Comparison of Alternative Approaches to Modelling House Prices in the UK* (London: National Institute of Economic and Social Research).

Patterson, K. (2000) *An Introduction to Applied Econometrics: A Time Series Approach* (Basingstoke: Macmillan).

Philip, L.J. (1998) 'Combining quantitative and qualitative approaches to social research in human geography – an impossible mixture?', *Environment and Planning A*, vol. 30, no. 2, 261–76.

Pindyck, R.S. and Rubinfeld, D.L. (1997) *Econometric Models and Economic Forecasts* (Boston: McGraw-Hill).

Powers, R.T. (1993) 'Office submarket delineation in tenant location behaviour', in J.R. White (ed.), *The Office Building: From Concept to Investment Reality* (Counsellors of Real Estate, Society of Industrial and Office Realtors and Appraisal Institute, Chicago).

Reilly, W.J. (1931) *The Law of Retail Gravitation* (New York: Knickerbocker Press).

Ridker, R. and Henning, J. (1968) 'The determinants of residential property values with special reference to air pollution', *Review of Economics and Statistics*, vol. 46, 246–57.

Robertson, M. and Jones, C. (1999) 'A cross-sectional model of rents in urban retail centres', *Journal of Property Research*, vol. 16, no. 1, 51–66.

Rosen, K.T. (1984) 'Toward a model of the office building sector', *AREUEA Journal*, vol. 12, no. 3, 261–9.

Rosen, S. (1974) 'Hedonic prices and implicit markets: product differentiation in pure competition', *Journal of Political Economy*, vol. 82, 34–55.

Rydin, Y. (1984) 'The struggle for housing land: a case of confused interests', *Policy and Politics*, vol. 12, no. 4, 431–46.

Schnare, A. and Struyk, R. (1976) 'Segmentation in urban housing markets', *Journal of Urban Economics*, vol. 3, 146–66.

Shilling, J.D., Sirmans, C.F. and Corgel, J.B. (1987) 'Price adjustment process for rental office space', *Journal of Urban Economics*, vol. 22, no. 2, 90–100.

Sing, T.F. (2002) 'Time to build options in construction processes', *Construction Management and Economics*, vol. 20, 119–30.

Sirmans, C.F. and Guidry, K.A. (1993) 'The determinants of shopping center rents', *Journal of Real Estate Research*, vol. 8, no. 1, 107–15.

Sloman, J. (2000) *Economics*, 4th edition (Harlow: Pearson Education).

Steele, M. and Goy, R. (1997) 'Short holds, the distribution of first and second sales, and bias in the repeat-sales price index', *Journal of Real Estate Finance and Economics*, vol. 14, 133–54.

Titman, S. (1985) 'Urban land prices under uncertainty', *The American Economic Review*, vol. 75, no. 3, 505–14.

Tsolacos, S., Keogh, G. and McGough, T. (1998) 'Modelling use, investment, and development in the British office market', *Environment and Planning A*, vol. 30, 1408–27.

Uyeno, D., Hamilton, S.W. and Biggs, A.J.G. (1993) 'The density of residential land use and the impact of airport noise', *Journal of Transport Economics and Policy*, Jan. 1993, vol. 27, no. 1.

Ward, C. and French, N. (1997) 'The valuation of upwards-only rent reviews: an option pricing model', *Journal of Property Valuation and Investment*, vol. 15, no. 2, 171–82.

Ward, C., Hendershott, P.H. and French, N. (1998) 'Pricing upwards-only rent review clauses', *Journal of Property Investment and Finance*, vol. 16, no. 5, 447–54.

Wheaton, W. (1987) 'The cyclic behaviour of the national office market', *AREUEA Journal*, vol. 15, no. 4, 281–99.

Wheaton, W.C., Torto, R.G. and Evans, P. (1997) 'The cyclic behaviour of the Greater London office market', *Journal of Real Estate Economics and Finance*, vol. 15, no. 1, 77–92.

Williams, J.T. (1991) 'Real estate development as an option', *Journal of Real Estate Finance and Economics*, vol. 4, 191–208.

Williams, J.T. (1993) 'Equilibrium and options on real assets', *Review of Financial Studies*, vol. 6, no. 4, 825–50.

Index